D0909204

SAMUEL JOHNSON'S

PREFACES & DEDICATIONS

SAMUEL JOHNSON'S

PREFACES &
DEDICATIONS

BY

ALLEN T. HAZEN

KENNIKAT PRESS
Port Washington, N. Y./London

828.6
J69pr

SAMUEL JOHNSON'S PREFACES AND DEDICATIONS

Copyright © 1937 by Yale University Press
Copyright renewed 1965 by A. T. Hazen
Reprinted in 1973 in an unaltered and
unabridged edition with permission by Kennikat Press
Library of Congress Catalog Card No.: 72-86538
ISBN 0-8046-1749-X

Manufactured by Taylor Publishing Company   Dallas, Texas

PREFACE

THIS book represents essentially, despite many minor revisions, a dissertation presented for the degree of Doctor of Philosophy at Yale University. Many years ago Professor C. B. Tinker, recognizing that Johnson's miscellaneous prose ought to be examined, began to collect the books that would be needed in such a study. It was fortunate that he was able to complete such a collection (within practicable limits) just before I was ready to begin this study, it was gracious of him to entrust such a subject and such a valuable library to a tyro, and it was encouraging to me to find that, though his suggestions were always wise, he refused to be alarmed even when my interests led me in unexpected directions. Next to Professor Tinker, I am under greatest obligation to my friend and colleague, Dr. E. L. McAdam, who has been at all times more helpful than he himself has perhaps realized.

For generous permission to make use of Johnsonian manuscripts I am indebted to Dr. A. S. W. Rosenbach of Philadelphia and to Messrs. G. Michelmore & Co. of London. Professors R. S. Crane, F. W. Hilles, F. A. Pottle, and Karl Young read the completed dissertation. For help on specific points it is a pleasure to express my thanks to the following friends: Dr. C. H. Bennett, Dr. R. W. Chapman, Dr. I. L. Churchill, Miss E. H. Hall, Mr. W. S. Lewis, Mr. A. V. McGee, Mr. Stanley Morison, Miss E. J. O'Meara, Dr. L. F. Powell, Mr. C. P. Rollins, Professor W. M. Sale, Professor Miriam Small, Dr. F. B. Williams, and Mr. R. M. Williams. Miss Dorothy Bridgwater and Mr. Monroe Beardsley have helped with the proofs and with the preparation of the index. I have been courteously received and granted every privilege in all the British and American libraries in which I have worked, but the bulk of the work has been done in New Haven. At the time that the dissertation was undertaken, I held the Edward Griffin Selden Fellowship in the Yale Graduate School.

I have compiled the lists of copies of the various books from published catalogues and from libraries that I have consulted. They are not intended as a census of extant copies, although for some of the rarer works they perhaps approach that ideal. They include, in general, three groups: American libraries, British libraries, and private collections. They will, I think, make known the presence of easily available copies, and in a general way will indicate the comparative rarity of the various books. It should be borne in mind, however, that certain books which are common enough in old libraries are almost unpurchasable to-day, and that others, which booksellers call 'rare,' appear frequently.

The date of publication is obtained usually from newspaper advertisements: no one is more keenly aware than I of the dangers of this method, but I have taken every precaution to avoid serious errors. In the case of tri-weekly papers, I have used the latest date of the particular issue, since this was the day on which the paper appeared. From the advertisements I have also taken the price of the book.

The bibliographical descriptions are ordinarily of the copy in the Yale Library or in the collection of Professor Tinker, corrected where necessary by other copies. In transcribing the title-pages I have reduced everything to the lower case, capitalizing only the first significant word of each sentence and all proper nouns. Explanatory notes are added in a few instances. The indication of line divisions is a concession to custom; it is usually unimportant, in this period, and the few books which do have variants require in any case a special note. I have condensed the collation as much as seemed wise, and have employed uneven index numbers without hesitation.[1] A bracketed letter in the collation, e.g., [A], indicates that the letter does not appear in the sheet, but is assumed for convenience. (The Greek letter π, so useful in describing seventeenth-century books, is seldom needed in working with eighteenth-century English printing.) Whenever the signature appears on any leaf of the sheet, the letter is printed without brackets.

In transcribing the Johnsonian text I have intended to preserve the original spelling and capitalization in all cases, although I have not been quite so scrupulous concerning the heading and the complimentary close of the dedications, since these were often added by the authors themselves. I have mentioned the first appearance of each work in the Johnsonian canon, unless this was in the original eleven volumes of the Booksellers' Edition of the *Works* (1787).

I have employed abbreviated references to a few books, as follows:

Boswell, *Life*. James Boswell, *Life of Samuel Johnson*, edited by G. B. Hill and revised by L. F. Powell, in six volumes (Oxford 1934–   ).

Boswell Papers. *The Private Papers of James Boswell*. Prepared for the press by Geoffrey Scott and Frederick A. Pottle, in eighteen volumes (privately printed 1929–34).

---

1. I agree with Dr. Greg (*The Library* xiv[1934]:378) that the printer thought always of even numbers of leaves, save perhaps in the rare 18mo in half-sheets, but common sense forces one to use uneven numbers in collation when the book was so planned for binding.

Boswell Revised. D. Nichol Smith (R. W. Chapman, L. F. Powell), *Johnson and Boswell Revised* (London 1928).

Courtney. W. P. Courtney, *A Bibliography of Samuel Johnson* (Oxford 1915).

Letters. Letters of Samuel Johnson, edited by G. B. Hill (Oxford 1892).

Miscellanies. Johnsonian Miscellanies, edited by G. B. Hill (Oxford 1897).

Works. The Works of Samuel Johnson, edited by Sir John Hawkins, in eleven volumes (London 1787). Also included in the *Works* are: Volumes xii and xiii, 1787; Volume xiv, 1788; and Volume xv, Gleig's edition of the *Voyage to Abyssinia* which included 'various other tracts,' 1789. Later editions of the *Works* are identified by the appropriate date.

A. T. H.

Yale University, April, 1937.

CONTENTS

Introduction   xi

Prefaces and Dedications   1

Appendix   239

Chronological List   251

Index   253

INTRODUCTION

To adjust the minute events of literary history, is tedious and troublesome; it requires indeed no great force of understanding, but often depends upon enquiries which there is no opportunity of making, or is to be fetched from books and pamphlets not always at hand.

Lives of the Poets (Dryden).

To an investigation of the facts of literary history and of bibliographical minutiae such as I have undertaken, every word of Johnson's dictum, with the exception of the epithet 'tedious,' may suitably be applied. That books and pamphlets which are to be consulted only in private collections or in various British and American libraries are 'not always at hand' is readily apparent; that an attempt to ascertain the reason for some bibliographical vagary on the part of printer or binder is often troublesome I can testify by my own experience; that such studies frequently require patience and ingenuity in conjecture rather than 'great force of understanding' I frankly admit; but that this manner of study is tedious is emphatically to be denied. The byways of descriptive bibliography have held for me an unending fascination; and in addition I have been fortunate to possess an assurance of the value of the task, for while broad generalizations are peculiarly the province of mature students, such generalizations must, or should, depend always upon accurate and minute knowledge of pertinent but obscure events. The need for such knowledge of the facts of Johnson's career is a sufficient justification for the work that I have undertaken.

It is perhaps, though not certainly, an unfortunate fact that bibliographical investigation can seldom or never be completed. The full extent of Johnson's published writings will never be known, and of those that are known additional study will regularly produce additional discoveries. An example from my own work will illustrate this: the first edition of Percy's *Reliques* is from a bibliographical point of view an interesting and a difficult book, and I think that I have never consulted a copy without observing some point that had previously been unknown to me. It is also true that such disparate and discursive material as this which I have studied is at times less tractable in the hands of a student, though there are compensatory advantages. The period from 1733 to 1785 saw changes in literary styles and trends, and changes of many sorts in printing-office practice. Most of these changes, however, are of little significance in the published results of bibliographical investigation, although there are occasional snares which may trap the unwary bibliographer. In the belief that 'a long apology is a hideous thing,'[1] I shall merely summarize the principles which have guided me in this work, and then discuss in some detail certain general results which can be derived from it.

I have endeavored to include books, by other people, for which Johnson furnished a Dedication or a Preface. Where he is known to have been concerned in any way with other publications by the same author I have intended to include pertinent information. I have not, however, included books by authors to whom Johnson gave assistance of one sort or another without furnishing a Dedication or Preface. This principle will explain the inclusion of Baretti's *Italian Library,* with one paragraph by Johnson, and the exclusion of books like Davies's *Memoirs of Garrick,* Dalrymple's *Annals of Scotland,* and the various publications of William Shaw. Of such books I have not refused to gather such information as time and opportunity have afforded, but it seemed necessary to keep to a somewhat rigid determination, lest in the maze

1. Letter to Burney, 18 March 1782.

of Johnson's miscellaneous writings this study should grow to an unseemly size, becoming like Burney's *History* 'a Porter's load.'² Also purposely excluded are Johnson's prefaces to his own works: there is for this reason no mention of the *Rambler,* the *Dictionary,* of the editions of *Shakespeare,* or of the Dedication to his translation of Lobo's *Voyage to Abyssinia.* I have decided to omit the Prefaces in the *Gentleman's Magazine,* since Johnson's connection with that work deserves separate study.

It would be impossible to work steadily at such a subject without discovering much that is new: of this new information much is safely tucked into the bibliographical notes which are appended to the descriptions. I have urged, usually with slight evidence, that the following works should be included in any new Johnsonian Bibliography: Baretti's *Guide through the Royal Academy* and his *Proposals* for printing his Italian poems; John Hoole's *Cyrus;* William Payne's *Trigonometry;* Lenglet du Fresnoy's *Chronological Tables;* Cave's edition of *Monarchy Asserted;* and the Preface to the *Universal Chronicle.* I have taken the text of Johnson's Preface to Lauder's *Essay on Milton* from the original *Proposals,* which no one seems to have consulted. I have decided against the Preface to William Payne's *Introduction to the Game of Draughts* and the Dedication of Angell's *Stenography.* Concerning the Dedication of Dr. Arne's *Monthly Melody* I am unwilling to commit myself.³

I

The general principles elucidated by this study are to be divided into two groups, bibliographical and literary.

2. *Letters,* ii:112, to Mrs. Thrale, 21 October 1779. Another reason is of course a gallant determination to complete this work in a reasonable time.

3. There are also three Dedications for Mrs. Lennox, attributed to Johnson in 1935 by Miss Miriam Small. Another Johnsonian item, which has been forgotten since 1785, is James Fordyce's *Sermons to Young Women,* a very rare work.

The evidence is to be found on nearly every page, and cannot be fully summarized, but the following outlines with occasional illustrations may be helpful.

During the last generation much has been added to the stock of knowledge about the bibliography of the eighteenth century. The hypotheses of earlier students have been confirmed (or, in a few points, exploded), and facts which were wholly unknown to them are now common knowledge. A decade hence, doubtless, possible explanations which are now diffidently suggested will be so well known as to require no proof. First of all there is the problem of printer's revisions. When Johnson wrote a preface for a friend, what became of it?

It is now generally known that the author's manuscript was used as printer's copy, and in most cases I think that Johnson's prefaces were similarly treated, without transcription.[4] The spelling and capitalization, however, were always normalized by the printer, so that the text as we have it represents the spelling of the particular printer who did the work, passed by the author in proof.[5] It seems improbable that Johnson read proof for every one of his many prefaces, but that he did so in certain cases is the only inference possible from the revisions in the Dedication of Hoole's *Metastasio*. That the author regularly did much of his revising on the proofs we know from Bos-

4. This is one reason why the manuscripts of only three of Johnson's many prefaces and dedications have survived (although more may be in hiding).

5. Luckombe, in his exceedingly useful book, points out that most authors (Boswell was one of the exceptions) expect the printer to spell, point, and digest their copy, that it may be intelligible and significant to the reader. P. Luckombe, *History of Printing* (London 1770), pp. 377, 390–1. See also p. 379 for a discussion of the change in printing styles. Dr. R. B. McKerrow, in his *Introduction to Bibliography* (Oxford 1927), p. 249 and note 2, suggests that the printer normalized the spelling.

On the authority of Luckombe, p. 380, I have ventured to suggest the use of 'Direction line' instead of the usual term 'Catchword' which is frequently unsatisfactory. Luckombe borrowed these explanations directly from John Smith's *Printer's Grammar* (1755). The word itself is properly the 'Direction,' but it is printed in the 'Direction line' of the page.

well's proof-sheets, and from the proofs of the *Lives of the Poets*. Luckombe also writes that authors revised freely in their proofs—to the inconvenience of the printer.[6] One rather important deduction from these facts is that vagaries in spelling, or capitalization, are ordinarily not reliable tests of authorship; the compositor who set up in the *Gentleman's Magazine* Johnson's Proposals for the *Harleian Catalogue,* for instance, added a 'Saxon k' to Johnson's 'public' in a way that would have brought joy to Boswell, had he known of the change.[7]

The most exciting discovery that a bibliographer can make, in normal circumstances, is the presence of a cancel in a book. Dr. Chapman has made the identification of cancels in eighteenth-century books much easier by the admirable articles which he has collected in his *Cancels*.[8]

Some cancels are routine matters intended to correct an entirely harmless misprint or to make an uninteresting revision in the text. The cancelled leaf in Lindsay's *Evangelical History* is of this type; it is important to collectors, but its intrinsic importance is not much greater than the correction at press of 'gve' to 'give' in the first edition of the *Life.*[9] Much more important are cancels which tell something that would otherwise be hidden concerning the composition, authorship, or revisions of the text in question. One cancel in the *Life,* for instance, is our authority for two Johnsonian Dedications—those to Percy's *Reliques* and to the *Seven Discourses* of Sir Joshua Rey-

6. P. Luckombe, *op. cit.,* p. 399. See also the discussion of Hoole's *Jerusalem Delivered* and *Metastasio,* pp. 63–67.

7. Boswell, *Life,* iv:31, and note 3. Had Boswell investigated he would doubtless have been disturbed to discover that Johnson employed or omitted the 'Saxon k' according to the style that was favoured by the printer concerned. Thus, in the Dedication of Bennet's *Ascham,* the spelling is 'publick,' while in the Preface to Du Fresnoy's *Chronological Tables,* published only a few months later, the reading is 'public.' It is clear that Johnson, like most authors, seldom interfered with the printer's spelling.

8. R. W. Chapman, *Cancels* (London 1930).

9. F. A. Pottle, *Literary Career of James Boswell* (Oxford 1929), p. 151.

nolds. Cancels of this type in the present study are those in Burney's two books and in Kennedy's *Astronomical Chronology*. I do not know that I have enjoyed, in this study, any pleasanter moment than that of the discovery of the important cancel in Kennedy's book, a moment that occurred, as it happens, some months before I ventured to undertake a doctoral dissertation in the field of Johnsonian bibliography.

There are other cancels which are of interest for a very different reason. When a Second Edition is discovered to be nothing but a First Edition with a new title-page, one immediately forms a revised estimate of the success of the work in question, of the profits that were earned by the author and by the bookseller, and (unfortunately) of the honesty of that bookseller. A Second Edition that is merely a reissue of unsold sheets, with a cancel title-page, clearly requires a qualifying note by the bibliographer to distinguish it from a Second Edition that is all reprinted because of steady demand. Rolt's *Dictionary,* Bennet's *Ascham,* and Johnson's edition of Browne's *Christian Morals* are books of this sort.[10] Quite a different problem is that of variant title-pages, as in the case of Baretti's *Dictionary* and James's *Dictionary:* it is difficult to be certain what the significance of these is, but in the case of these two books the altered imprint probably indicates some minor change in publishing arrangements. A book in which the problem is one of reprinting rather than of cancellation is the puzzling second edition of Payne's *Introduction to the Game of Draughts.*

10. The most interesting example known to me is Kearsly's *Beauties of Johnson.* There were six numbered editions within a few months, but these represented only three printings of Part I and only *one,* I think, of Part II. An amusing notice of *The Mystery Revealed . . . in relation to the conduct of the late Ministry,* in the *Monthly Review* for April 1759, indicates that this device of the bookseller did not always escape detection: 'Here *we,* too, have a mystery to reveal; . . . for this pamphlet is itself an errant imposition on the Public, . . . the present publication being no other than a vamp'd-up title-page to an old pamphlet first published in 1757.'

II

In a discussion of the facts of literary history it is more difficult to be precise, principally because I have not stressed that aspect and because records of the publishers are so few and so inaccessible. Without injustice to other publishers, one can say that the most important booksellers in Johnson's career were Cave, Dodsley, Millar, Newbery, John Payne, and Strahan. Johnson's relations with Cave I have intentionally omitted in the belief that it was a problem too complicated to be settled satisfactorily unless it was subjected to intensive and long-continued study. Although every student has his own opinion, no one really knows just what Johnson's status was with Cave during his first years in London; and there are certainly not enough publications in Boswell's list during the early years (1737–1740) to support him.[11]

Many of the books which I have studied are of little importance in this respect, because Johnson's connection with the bookseller concerned was so slight. But I have included in the appropriate places some discussion of the plans for Dodsley's *Preceptor* and *London Chronicle,* Newbery's *World Displayed,* Payne's *Universal Chronicle* and Osborne's Harleian books. (It is of interest in passing to note that at least one of the books, Kennedy's *Chronology,* was printed by Johnson's friend Allen of Bolt Court, later to be Johnson's landlord and his intermediary with the notorious Dr. Dodd.) There is evidence that Johnson's contributions to some of these books were solicited by the bookseller, not by the author. Among these are Bennet's *Ascham,* Rolt's *Dictionary,* and Lindsay's

11. According to Rev. John Hussey, Johnson was *editor* of the *Gentleman's Magazine* from 1738 to 1745, and this may be correct. (Boswell, *Life,* i:532.) See also A. Chalmers, *General Biographical Dictionary,* xix(London 1815):53–56. Chalmers had access to Farmer's notes, and he writes that Johnson was paid one hundred pounds per annum by Cave. After July 1741, Johnson was busy with the Parliamentary Debates, and his work on Osborne's Harleian Library began in the autumn of 1742. (Boswell, *Life,* i:154, 510.)

Evangelical History, three of Newbery's publications. I suspect that Johnson's Preface to Du Fresnoy's *Chronological Tables* was requested, and paid for, by Millar or Newbery, although Flloyd may have approached Johnson directly. In discussing the books, I have pointed out the probability that Johnson's assistance to William Payne was obtained by Thomas Payne, Boswell's 'respectable bookseller.' The Dedication to the *Monthly Melody,* if it is by Johnson, was almost certainly solicited by Kearsly.

These books that I have studied are less interesting to a student of the methods of the booksellers than the great coöperative publishing enterprises with which Johnson was connected, his *Dictionary* and *Lives of the Poets.* Yet the booksellers who participated in those works included the Dodsleys, Millar, the younger Newbery, and Strahan (and Cave was dead): the methods were similar although on a larger scale. It was an age, so far as Johnson was concerned, of booksellers and authors rather than of patrons and authors.

Another considerable group of Johnson's prefaces and dedications consists of those furnished to his friends. Enumeration will suffice: for Baretti he wrote six, for Burney two, for Fordyce one, for Gwynn two, for Hoole three, for Dr. James two, for Mrs. Lennox seven (including the Proposals which have not yet been found), for John Payne three, for Percy two, and for Reynolds two. Of these only a few are mentioned by Boswell, partly because he was asked by the authors concerned to conceal the knowledge of Johnson's assistance.[12] In a somewhat different class are the writings for humbler friends or acquaintances: Bennet's *Ascham,* Kennedy's *Chronology,* Macbean's *Geography,* Maurice's *Poems,* and the help that he

12. I am inclined to believe that Boswell never made any real search for scattered items, but relied on his conversations with Johnson [see *Boswell Papers,* ix:264] and on previous publications: the reader will notice how many of these writings had been included in Vol. xiv of the *Works* and in Davies's *Miscellaneous and Fugitive Pieces.*

extended to Anna Williams and her father. I do not by any means believe that all Johnson's miscellaneous writing has been identified. I have followed certain clues that seemed likely to produce results, chiefly on the theory that where Johnson aided a close friend once or twice the friend very probably came to Johnson on other.occasions; but there is much still to be done.

To these two paragraphs it is wise to add a warning. The publication of Johnson's *Dictionary* did not indicate the end of the system of patronage. Carlyle's emphatic essay has been in this respect unfortunately influential.

At the time of Johnson's appearance on the field, Literature . . . was in the very act of passing from the protection of Patrons into that of the Public; no longer to supply its necessities by laudatory Dedications to the Great, but by judicious Bargains with the Booksellers. . . . At the time of Johnson's appearance, there were still two ways, on which an Author might attempt proceeding. . . . In time, Johnson had opportunity of looking into both methods, and ascertaining what they were; but found, at first trial, that the former would in nowise do for him. Listen, once again, to that far-famed Blast of Doom, proclaiming into the ear of Lord Chesterfield, and, through him, of the listening world, that patronage should be no more![13]

In the case of Johnson, of course, Carlyle was correct: it was an age of booksellers. But that Johnson's letter to Chesterfield proclaimed the blast of doom to the *system* of patronage is amply disproved by the works which I have studied in this thesis. It might well be argued, indeed, that Johnson was a chief propagator of this system. Here are some twenty dedications, written during the period of thirty years that followed the publication of the *Dictionary;* and the last work that Johnson prepared for the press, so far as we know, was the Dedication for Burney's *Commemoration of Handel,* a Dedication that was accurately calculated to prompt the liberality of the King.

13. Review of Croker's *Boswell,* 1831. *Fraser's Magazine,* v(May 1832):396–8.

There are, to be sure, certain books in which the dedication was little more than a gracious act of homage or
acknowledgment. The *Seven Discourses* of Reynolds, for
example, was dedicated to the King as a suitable offering
to him by whose munificence the Royal Academy had
been established; but this work is an exception. Percy's
Reliques, Kennedy's *Chronology,* Bennet's *Ascham,* and
the several works of Mrs. Lennox, to name only a few,
were inscribed to patrons with a lively expectation of reward. We know that Bennet appealed to Shaftesbury on
behalf of a needy family;[14] Mrs. Lennox solicited the interest of the Duchess of Newcastle both for her husband
and for herself. The system of patronage may have been
unfortunate, but it was neither dead nor dying. The art of
dedication and its sister art, the art of publication by subscription,[15] flourished mightily during the Age of Johnson.

III

The statements of Hawkins, Tyers, Mrs. Piozzi, Boswell, and Fanny Burney corroborate the evidence presented in this study that Johnson was preëminent as a
writer of prefaces. His friends, unknown writers, and a
number of booksellers felt free to come to him for a preface or dedication, and they frequently sought his approbation of a projected work and his assistance in its revision. His own attitude towards these requests is important. Dedication to a patron he attempted only in the
Plan of a Dictionary in 1747, and this apparently was

14. See his letter, in Boswell, *Life,* i:551, 'I have a large Family and they
wholly Unprovided for.'

15. Hannah More wrote: 'Hoole has just sent me his preface to his translation of Ariosto, which is coming out; an expensive present; since I can now
do no less than subscribe for the whole work, and a guinea and a half for a
translation of a book from the original is dearish.' *Memoirs of Hannah More,*
edited by W. Roberts (London 1834), i:278. See also Jeremy Bentham's complaint in his *Works* (Edinburgh 1843), x:184.

Bennet, among others, cultivated both arts, and Johnson's *Shakespeare* was
published, in part, by subscription.

written because of Dodsley's importunity. He asserted once that 'the known style of a dedication is flattery,'[16] and he discussed in Number 136 of the *Rambler* the meanness and mischief of indiscriminate dedication. There is evidence that, despite his frequent complaisance, he did not wholly approve his own practice of helping others in such ways. Mrs. Piozzi says that he 'did not like that his friends should bring their manuscripts for him to read, and he liked still less to read them when they were brought,' and Johnson told her that he 'hated to give away literary performances, or even to sell them too cheaply: the next generation shall not accuse me of beating down the price of literature: one hates, besides, ever to give that which one has been accustomed to sell.'[17] In much the same vein he wrote only a few months before he died:

It does not occur to me how I can write a preface to which it can be proper to put my name, and I am not to put my own value without raising at least proportionally that of the book. This is therefore to be considered.[18]

But when Johnson did furnish a preface or dedication he exerted himself to write well, whatever the book might be. The literary ethics of such work doubtless seemed to Johnson analogous to that of the sermons which he wrote for others. He wrote in the person of the author, and did

16. Boswell, *Life*, v:285 (*Hebrides*).

17. *Miscellanies*, i:181, 332.
Nor did he much enjoy the task of literary adviser. See Boswell, *Life*, ii:195. Or, even better, see Boswell's notes of the same conversation, *Boswell Papers*, ix:258.

18. Letter to William Bowles, 5 April 1784, in the Catalogue of the R. B. Adam Library, i:10. This attitude was indeed necessary for self-defense, else the booksellers and various writers would have claimed all his time. Thus Tyers writes that Johnson 'did not choose to have his sentiments generally known; for there was a great eagerness, especially in those who had not the pole-star of judgment to direct them, to be taught what to think or say on literary performances.' (*Miscellanies*, ii:345.)
Hawkins says that the booksellers considered miscellaneous preface writing beneath Johnson's abilities and therefore engaged him to edit Shakespeare. (*Miscellanies*, ii:106.)

not consider that he was expressing his own sentiments. On this point Boswell is explicit.[19] I shall not attempt to determine whether this was a justifiable attitude: to Johnson it was an honest literary venture, whether written to oblige a friend or to earn money that he greatly needed.[20]

Once the preface or dedication was published, Johnson no longer considered it his own. The Hoole manuscripts prove that Johnson wrote and revised carefully before the book was published, but that was always the end of the matter. It is not surprising that Boswell and the other biographers had difficulty in discovering these Johnsonian prefaces. He had written them years before, when his mind was occupied by many cares, and unless a particular reference in later years brought one back to his mind, he perhaps never thought of them again. I have endeavored to discover any possible signs of revisions in Johnson's text, but there are none that are not probably the result of printer's changes.[21] To this assertion there is one exception: the text of the Preface to the *Preceptor* is thoroughly revised in the second edition, which also underwent some revision in the body of the book. In later editions the

19. Boswell, *Life*, ii:2. This is an important fact, indicating that the beliefs expressed in the dedications are not necessarily Johnson's critical opinions and that Johnsonian authorship can hardly be predicated or denied on the evidence of the content of the dedication. The only internal evidence that is valid is the style—unfortunately a dangerous criterion to apply.

It is even a little dangerous, I think, to talk dogmatically of Johnson's earlier or later style: to be sure, he wrote late in life his fine dedications for Dr. Burney and for Pearce's *Commentary*, yet twenty years earlier he had written equally well for Sully's *Memoirs* and for Hoole's *Tasso*.

20. The following complaint I suppose must be aimed at Johnson, Hawkesworth, and others: 'Since Prefaces have been pretty much laid aside, a few authors of the first class, have made Introduction writing a principal part of their study, and very often receive half a crown more for three or four preparatory pages at the head of a performance, than the unfortunate bookmaker for a subsequent three or four hundred.' (Introduction to the *Court Magazine*, 1761, written probably by Hugh Kelly.)

21. There are six verbal changes in the Introduction to the *World Displayed* (besides many changes in spelling and capitalization), but I doubt whether they were made by Johnson. For the discussion of the possibility that Johnson may have revised the Dedication of Lindsay's *Evangelical History*, see that book in the text below, p. 119.

punctuation and spelling (of the Preface) show further revision, but the only textual revision is in the second edition of 1754. These revisions are so extensive and so judicious that one cannot doubt that they are by Johnson. It may be that Johnson was associated with Dodsley in editing the *Preceptor*. With the fact of this revision for Dodsley may be compared the revision of the *Vanity of Human Wishes* for the fourth volume of Dodsley's *Collection of Poems* (1755). That Johnson found time for these revisions and for a final revision of the *Rambler* when he was also completing his work on the *Dictionary* is in some sense a refutation of the belief that Johnson's indolence kept him from accomplishing much that he might otherwise easily have done.[22]

But I have conceived this, after all, not as a study of Johnson's revisions, which were made only in one instance, nor as a study of his publishers, which would require special facilities and special training, nor as a critical appraisal of Johnson's prose style, which is a task reserved for maturity. Perhaps it is best merely to try to atone for Tyers's haste, since he wrote 'There is here neither room nor leisure to ascertain the progress of his publications, though, in the idea of Shenstone, it would exhibit the history of his mind and thoughts.'

22. The fourth edition of the *Rambler*, published in 1756, was printed in 1754. I do not imply that Johnson was not indolent, or that he revised willingly; but that, urged by necessity and by his own conscience, he completed an amount of careful work that might well have overpowered a lesser man.

SAMUEL JOHNSON'S
PREFACES AND DEDICATIONS

GEORGE ADAMS, *TREATISE ON THE GLOBES*

Published: 10 June 1766 (*Public Advertiser*).
References: Boswell, *Life*, ii:44.
    Courtney, p.112.
Johnson's Contribution: Dedication.
Copies: University of Michigan; University of Pennsylvania; Yale; Aberdeen University; Bodleian; British Museum; Cambridge University; Edinburgh University; National Library of Scotland; University of Göttingen; R. B. Adam; Dr. R. W. Chapman.

I DO not think that George Adams was well known to Johnson, so that it is not improbable that he was introduced by some friend when he wished to solicit Johnson's aid. Of the authenticity of the Dedication there can be no doubt. Thomas Tyers wrote 'He composed the Preface . . . to Adams on the Globes.'[1] Hawkins wrote:

For the dedication to his present majesty, of Adams's book on the use of the globes, he was, as himself informed me, gratified with a present of a very curious meteorological instrument, of a new and ingenious construction.[2]

Boswell, although he confused the dates in his proof corrections, wrote:

He furnished Mr. Adams with a Dedication to the King of that ingenious gentleman's *Treatise on the Globes,* conceived and expressed in such a manner as could not fail to be very grateful to a Monarch, distinguished for his love of the sciences.

It was to this Dedication that Boswell intended to apply the

[1]. *Gentleman's Magazine,* lv(1785):87. Concerning the confusion between dedication and preface, see the discussion below under Mrs. Lennox's translation of Sully's *Memoirs.*
[2]. John Hawkins, *Life of Johnson* (London 1787), p. 391. What this instrument was, seems not to be known.

word 'noble' which in the *Life* is applied to the Dedication to Gwynn's *London and Westminster Improved*.[3]

Bibliographical Description

A / Treatise / describing and explaining the / construction and use / of / new celestial and terrestrial / globes. / Designed to illustrate, / in the most easy and natural manner, / the phoenomena of the / earth and heavens, / and to shew the / correspondence of the two spheres. / With a great variety of / astronomical and geographical problems / occasionally interspersed. / [*rule*] / By George Adams, / mathematical instrument-maker to His Majesty. / [*double rule*] / London: / Printed for and sold by the author, at Tycho / Brahe's Head, in Fleet-Street. / [*short rule*] / M.DCC.LXVI.

Facsimile of title-page and dedication in the second volume of the Catalogue of the R. B. Adam Library.
Octavo; 20.2 × 12.5 cm. Price: 5/– bound.

Signatures: [A]⁸; b³; B–Q⁸; R (one leaf); *(in brackets)⁴.

Pagination: [i] title-page; [ii] blank; [iii–vi] Dedication; [vii]–xiv Preface; [xv]–xxii Contents; [1]–242 Text; [1]–8 Catalogue of Instruments made and sold by George Adams, mathematical instrument-maker to the King. (In one copy this Catalogue—a half-sheet—is bound incorrectly after the Contents. The direction line proves that it does not belong there.)

Plate 1, opp. title-page. The new terrestrial globe.
Plate 2, opp. p. 1 of Text. The new celestial globe.
Plate 3, opp. p. 86. Diagrams to illustrate the text.

The collation by signatures which I have given above is I believe the simplest, despite Dr. Greg's dislike of uneven numbers. That b and R were printed as a half sheet, of which the other half contained the Catalogue, is decisively proved by the copy in the Library of Edinburgh University: the sheet was folded and bound, without cutting, after p. xvi. The next eight leaves are *1, b1, b2, *2, *3, b3, R1, *4.

3. Boswell, *Life*, ii:25, 44, 479; *Boswell Revised*, p. 36. Boswell was troubled by the date of this work, and finally entered it under the year 1767, probably because he found it so dated in Volume xiv of the *Works*.

In the *Gentleman's Magazine*, lv(March 1785):188, a correspondent who signs himself 'M. G.' ascribes the Dedication to
Johnson on the authority of Edmund Allen. The attribution is
not new, since Tyers had suggested it twice in the same Magazine (Volume liv[Supplement 1784]:982 and Volume lv[January
1785]:87). The reference to Allen, however, suggests the possibility that he was the printer, and the appearance of the book
makes the suggestion seem very probable.

Editions:
The book was many times reprinted, the later editions being issued by the son, George Adams the Younger. The second edition
was published in June 1769, and advertised as 'greatly enlarged,
with eleven new copper plates.' Third edition 1772; fourth edition 1777; fifth edition 1782. All these early editions are compara-
tively rare. I have noted other editions in 1791 and in 1795, and
the thirtieth edition is dated 1810. The substance of the book was
also included, I think, in the *Astronomical and Geographical Essays* reprinted by the son.

In Capel Lofft's *Eudosia*, 1781, 'the authors which have been
principally used' include *Adams on the Globes.*

Some account of George Adams as an instrument maker may be
found in E. L. Stevenson's *Terrestrial and Celestial Globes* (New
Haven 1921), ii:184–7, 220, 249. See also the notes by Ambrose
Heal in *Notes and Queries,* clxx(June 1936):423.

DEDICATION
TO THE KING.

SIR,
It is the privilege of real greatness not to be afraid of diminution by condescending to the notice of little things; and I therefore can boldly solicite the patronage of Your MAJESTY to the
humble labours by which I have endeavoured to improve the instruments of science, and make the globes on which the earth and
sky are delineated less defective in their construction, and less
difficult in their use.

Geography is in a peculiar manner the science of Princes.
When a private student revolves the terraqueous globe, he be-
holds a succession of countries in which he has no more interest
than in the imaginary regions of Jupiter and Saturn. But Your
MAJESTY must contemplate the scientifick picture with other sentiments, and consider, as oceans and continents are rolling be-

fore You, how large a part of mankind is now waiting on Your determinations, and may receive benefits or suffer evils, as Your influence is extended or withdrawn.

The provinces which Your MAJESTY's arms have added to Your dominions, make no inconsiderable part of the orb allotted to human beings. Your power is acknowledged by nations whose names we know not yet how to write, and whose boundaries we cannot yet describe. But Your MAJESTY's lenity and beneficence give us reason to expect the time when science shall be advanced by the diffusion of happiness; when the desarts of America shall become pervious and safe, when those who are now restrained by fear shall be attracted by reverence; and multitudes who now range the woods for prey, and live at the mercy of winds and seasons, shall by the paternal care of Your MAJESTY enjoy the plenty of cultivated lands, the pleasures of society, the security of law, and the light of Revelation.

I am, SIR, Your MAJESTY's most humble, most obedient, and most dutiful, Subject and Servant,

GEORGE ADAMS.

JOHNSON AND BARETTI

IT is difficult to generalize satisfactorily about the literary career of Joseph Baretti. Yet to one who attained eminence in two languages in the fields of philology and literary criticism it would be manifestly unjust to deny the possession of very exceptional abilities, however much he may have been hindered by unfortunate limitations. Of more immediate interest in this study, however, is the fact of his long-continued and close literary friendship with Dr. Johnson. I do not doubt that Johnson gained much from Baretti; the evidence of Baretti's indebtedness to Johnson is contained in book after book that he published in English, and it has recently been traced in Baretti's Italian criticism.[1]

In addition to the books which will be discussed in turn below, I mention a few: Johnson (and Burney) gave assistance to Baretti in his arrangement of the *Carmen Seculare*, and

1. Albertina Devalle, *Giuseppe Baretti* (Milan 1932). One chapter is devoted to the influence of Johnson.

both the 'Epilogus' and its translation are attributed to Johnson.[2] Johnson assisted Baretti in his French translation of
Rasselas (a version that is still extant, but unpublished) by
dictating to him a translation of the first paragraph. The Italian translation of Zachariah Williams's *Longitude* (1755) is
by Baretti: Johnson's English essay and Baretti's Italian translation are printed on opposite pages. In the Advertisement to
his *Dictionary of Spanish and English,* Baretti gratefully acknowledges the help he has received from Johnson's *Dictionary* and concludes with this graceful compliment:

> To conclude in Johnson's words, 'of such a work as this, it is not
> necessary to say more; and it is presumed, it will not be found that
> truth required the editor to say less.'

The Preface to *A Grammar of the Italian Language* (1760,
and later editions) acknowledges the use of a 'Praxis of sentences, collected from the works of my friend and instructor
Mr. Samuel Johnson,' which, under the title of 'Thoughts
on various subjects,' occupies more than one hundred pages
of the book. In the Preface to *A Journey from London to
Genoa,* Baretti writes that Johnson suggested the plan of publication to him. Two chapters from *Rasselas* are included in
Baretti's *Introduction to the most useful European Languages* (1772).

I shall now discuss in alphabetical order the works that
contain Prefaces, or introductory paragraphs, or Dedications,
by Johnson. There is external evidence for only one, *Easy
Phraseology;* the rest are attributed because of internal evidence confirmed by known facts of Johnson's interests and his
acquaintance with Baretti. There are in all six works.

2. *Works,* Vol. xiv. See also Boswell, *Life,* iii:373, and *Letters,* ii:80.

DICTIONARY OF THE ENGLISH AND ITALIAN LANGUAGES

Published: 24 April 1760 (*London Chronicle*).
References: Boswell, *Life*, i:353.
              Courtney, p. 98.
Johnson's Contribution: Dedication.
Copies: Boston Public Library; Harvard; Huntington Library; Library Company of Philadelphia; Yale; Aberdeen University; Bodleian; British Museum; Edinburgh University; Bibliothèque Nationale; R. B. Adam; Dr. R. W. Chapman; A. T. Hazen; Dr. L. F. Powell; Boswell's copy is owned by Col. R. H. Isham.

BOSWELL ascribed the Dedication to Johnson on internal evidence, and it had earlier been included with other Dedications in Volume xiv of the *Works*. Years later a contributor to *Notes and Queries*,[1] unaware of the earlier attributions, pointed out that the style was Johnsonian. Among Johnson's many dedications, this one is perhaps chiefly remarkable for the extraordinary length of the sentences.

In 1757 Baretti agreed with eight booksellers to revise Altieri's *Dictionary*, for two hundred guineas. The book was a great success, and was frequently reprinted, with minor revisions, for upwards of a hundred years, although the Dedication was reprinted only in the second edition. The booksellers, wrote Baretti, 'soon agreed unanimously to give me a good additional present, as they were convinced that I had done something more to the Dictionary than another man would have done.'[2]

Bibliographical Description

A / Dictionary / of the / English and Italian / languages. / By Joseph Baretti. / Improved and augmented with above ten thousand words, / omitted in the last edition of Altieri. / To which is added, / an Italian and English grammar. / Vol-

---

1. Second Series, xi:207.
2. Lacy Collison-Morley, *Giuseppe Baretti* (London 1909), pp. 101, 107.

ume I. / [*parallel rule*] / London: / Printed for J. Richardson, in Pater-noster-row. / MDCCLX.

The second volume has the title-page in Italian, but the imprint is in English. In many copies, the imprint of both volumes is: London: Printed for C. Hitch and L. Hawes, R. Baldwin, W. Johnston, W. Owen, J. Richardson, G. Keith, T. Longman, S. Crowder and Co. P. Davey and B. Law, and H. Woodgate and S. Brookes, and the advertisement in the *London Chronicle* has this list.
Two volumes, quarto; 26 × 20 cm. Price: two pounds bound.

Signatures: Vol. I: one leaf; A,a–d4; e(one leaf); B–4T4; 4U(one leaf).
Vol. II: one leaf; half-sheet; a–e,A–4P4; 4Q2.

Pagination: Vol. I: [i] title-page; [ii] blank; [iii–v] Dedication; [vi] blank; [vii–ix] Preface; [x] blank; [i]–xxxiv English Grammar (in Italian); unpaged text of Italian-English Dictionary.
Vol. II: [i] title-page; [ii] blank; [iii–vi] Preface in Italian; [i]–xxxix Italian Grammar (in English); [xl] blank; unpaged text of English-Italian Dictionary, with 4Q2 verso blank.

In one copy which I have examined (Edinburgh University), the Italian Preface is incorrectly bound in Volume I immediately after the English Preface.
Johnson's copy is listed in lot 439 in the *Catalogue* of his Library (1785).
Two new editions of the *Dictionary* appeared before Baretti died, and in the nineteenth century many editions were based on Baretti's work.

DEDICATION

To His Excellency Don Felix, Marquis of Abreu and Bertodano, Ambassador Extraordinary and Plenipotentiary from his Catholick Majesty to the King of Great Britain.

My Lord,
That acuteness of penetration into characters and designs, and that nice discernment of human passions and practices which have raised you to your present height of station and dignity of employment, have long shown you that Dedicatory Addresses are written for the sake of the Author more frequently than of the

Patron; and though they profess only reverence and zeal, are commonly dictated by interest or vanity.

I shall therefore not endeavour to conceal my motives, but confess that the Italian Dictionary is dedicated to your Excellency, that I might gratify my vanity, by making it known, that, in a country where I am a stranger, I have been able, without any external recommendation, to obtain the notice and countenance of a Nobleman so eminent for knowledge and ability that in his twenty third year he was sent as Plenipotentiary to superintend at Aix-la-Chappelle the interests of a Nation remarkable above all others for gravity and prudence; and who now at an age, when very few are admitted to publick trust, transacts the most important affairs between two of the greatest Monarchs of the World.

If I could attribute to my own merits, the favours which your Excellency every day confers upon me, I know not how much my pride might be inflamed; but when I observe the extensive benevolence and boundless liberality by which all who have the honour to approach you are dismissed more happy than they came, I am afraid of raising my own value, since I dare not ascribe it so much to my power of pleasing as your willingness to be pleased.

Yet as every man is inclined to flatter himself, I am desirous to hope that I am not admitted to greater intimacy than others without some qualifications for so advantageous a distinction, and shall think it my duty to justify by constant respect and sincerity the favours which you have been pleased to show me.

I am, My Lord, Your Excellency's Most humble And most obedient Servant,

J. BARETTI.

London, January the
    12th, 1760.

EASY PHRASEOLOGY

Published: 5 October 1775 (*Public Advertiser*).
References: Boswell, *Life,* ii:290, 509.
        Courtney, p. 127.
Johnson's Contribution: Preface.
Copies: Harvard; Yale; Bodleian; British Museum; Bibliothèque
    Nationale; Cambridge University.

BOSWELL ascribes the Preface of this book to Johnson on internal evidence only, but Fanny Burney asserts, in an important passage, that Johnson acknowledged his authorship to her. She says that she has promised to make a list of Johnson's miscellaneous works, 'Though, indeed, it will be very difficult, as I daresay he hardly knows himself what he has written; for he has made numerous prefaces, dedications, odd chapters, and I know not what, for other authors, that he has never owned, and probably never will own. But I was sure, when I read it, that the preface to Baretti's *Dialogues* was his; and that I made him confess.'[1] Mrs. Piozzi writes that the English translation of the verses at the end of the book, 'Long may live my lovely Hetty,' was also by Johnson.[2] They were addressed to 'Queeney' Thrale.

Bibliographical Description

Easy phraseology, / for the use of / young ladies, / who intend to learn / the colloquial part / of the / Italian language. / By / Joseph Baretti, / secretary for foreign correspondence to the Royal / Academy of Painting, Sculpture, / and Architecture. / London, / Printed for G. Robinson, in Pater-noster Row; and / T. Cadell, in the Strand. / MDCCLXXV.

Octavo in fours; 21.7 × 13.6 cm.; 6/– bound.

Signatures: 5 preliminary leaves; a,B–Hhh[4].

Pagination: [i] title-page; [ii] blank; [iii]–iv Preface; [iii] Erratum; [iv]–xv Dedication to Miss Hetty (Italian and English on opposite pages); [xvi] blank; [1]–424 Text.

The five preliminary leaves are somewhat puzzling; but Johnson's Preface is the extra leaf, and the others were printed together as a half-sheet, and I have therefore called the Erratum page iii. The Preface may appear after the Dedication.

Dialogue 43 (pp. 253–267) deals with Ossian and the Italian translations. On this point Dr. Campbell recorded in his *Diary*

---

1. *Diary of Madame D'Arblay,* edited by Austin Dobson (London 1904), ii:206.
2. *Miscellanies,* i:194. Baretti also translated the whole book into Spanish, for Queeney, and the manuscript is extant; see Marquis of Lansdowne, *Johnson and Queeney* (1932), pp. xiv–xv.

for 25 March 1775 an amusing anecdote of Baretti: 'Baretti was very humorous about his new publication, which he expects to put out next month. He there introduces a dialogue about Ossian, wherein he ridicules the idea of the double translation into Italian, in hopes, he said, of having it abused by the Scots, which would give it an imprimatur for a second edition, and he had stipulated for twenty-five guineas additional if the first should sell in a given time.'[3]

Contrary to Baretti's optimistic expectations, the book was not published until October, and it was attacked in a brief review in the *London Magazine* for November, but not in such a manner as to make a second edition necessary.

The work was reprinted in Italy long afterwards, and issued at Leghorn in 1836.

Johnson's copy is listed in lot 189 in the *Catalogue* of his Library (1785).

PREFACE.

Of every learned and elegant people the language is divided into two parts: the one lax and cursory, used on slight occasions with extemporary negligence; the other rigorous and solemn, the effect of deliberate choice and grammatical accuracy. When books are multiplied and style is cultivated, the colloquial and written diction separate by degrees, till there is one language of the tongue, and another of the pen.

No language can be said to have been learned till both these parts are understood: but to reach the colloquial without the opportunities of familiar conversation, is very difficult. By reading great Authors it cannot be obtained, as books speak but the language of books; and those, who in England intend to learn Italian, are seldom within the reach of Italian conversation.

This deficience I have, by a bold experiment, endeavoured to supply, in the following Dialogues, in which I have undertaken to comprize not the gross and barbarous, but the careless and airy diction of casual talkers. Let no supercilious contemner of trifles look upon these productions with too much elevation, or indulge himself in merciless censures on the humble author, who knows already, with full conviction, the levity of his subjects, and the unimportance of his personages. His design is not to refine the

---

3. L. Collison-Morley, *Baretti* (London 1909), p. 280. Baretti received only fifty pounds for the book. See the statement in Boswell, *Life*, ii:509, from Mr. Adam's *Catalogue*, iii:15.

language of the senate or the school: it is only to teach Italian; to teach those words and phrases, which are appropriated to trifles; but of which, as life is made of trifles, there is a frequent use. In other books, words are sought for the illustration of images and enforcement of reason; but in this, images and reason, such as they are, have been chosen merely as they afford an opportunity of words. I have only contrived a chain to hold those words together; and as it was to bear no great weight, it needed not the strength of that, by which the earth is suspended from the throne of Jupiter.

These are, however, not the first pages that have been compiled only for the sake of teaching words; but, as I cannot boast of having invented the method that I have taken, I will not, by voluntary degradation, place myself below other nomenclators. Let my Dialogues be compared for copiousness of language, variety of topics, and power of entertainment, with other collections of words and phrases; and of the place, which honest criticism may give me, I shall have no reason to be much ashamed.

GUIDE THROUGH THE ROYAL ACADEMY

Published: May 1781.[1]
Johnson's Contribution: Opening sentences attributed to Johnson on internal evidence.
Copies: Harvard; Yale; Bodleian; British Museum (3 copies); A. T. Hazen.

WHEN I first looked at this little pamphlet, it occurred to me that the vigor of the opening sentences might indicate that by 1780 Baretti had at length learned the balance of Johnson's style and that for a short passage he might be able to equal his master. It is more probable however that Dr. Chapman was right when he wrote 'Baretti was incapable of a successful imitation of Johnson's manner,' and I do not believe that anyone but Johnson wrote these sentences.

1. Announced in *London Magazine*, April–June 1781, and in *Critical Review,* June 1781. But Walpole wrote to Mason on the sixth of May: 'When I was talking of the Academy, I should have told you that Baretti has printed a catalogue of its ornaments and plaster casts.' The Royal Academy Exhibition, the second in the new building, had opened on the thirtieth of April, and Baretti's *Guide* was probably printed in time for the opening.

The pamphlet is a slight one, but it is worthy of remark that none of the descriptions of the decorations and statuary could ever be mistaken for Johnsonian prose.

Bibliographical Description

A / Guide / through the / Royal Academy, / by / Joseph Baretti / secretary for foreign correspondence / to the Royal Academy. / [*rule*] / London: / Printed by T. Cadell, / Printer to the Royal Academy. / [Price One Shilling.]

Quarto, with vertical chain-lines; 25.5 × 20 cm.

Signatures: A–D⁴.

Pagination: [1] title-page; [2] blank; [3]–32 Text.

INTRODUCTION

To those, whom either vagrant curiosity, or desire of instruction, brings into the Apartments of the Royal Academy, not to know the design, the history, and the names of the various Models that stand before them, is a great abatement of pleasure, and hindrance of improvement. He who enters, not knowing what to expect, gazes a while about him, a stranger among strangers, and goes out, not knowing what he has seen.

INTRODUCTION TO THE ITALIAN LANGUAGE

Published: 19 July 1755 (*Public Advertiser*).
References: Boswell, *Life,* i:542.
          Courtney, p. 73.
Johnson's Contribution: Preface (in part).
Copies: Library of Congress; New York Public Library; Yale; Bodleian; British Museum; Cambridge University; Dr. R. W. Chapman; A. T. Hazen.

JAMES CROSSLEY first attributed this Preface to Johnson in 1852, and he also assigned to Johnson footnotes on pp. 48 and 198.[1] The last two paragraphs of the Preface are hardly by

1. *Notes & Queries,* First Series, v(1852):101. Dr. Chapman also discusses the book in the *Colophon,* Part Sixteen.

Johnson, although much of the rest probably is, despite the curious harshness of the phrase in the third paragraph, 'unknown to nobody that knows books.' It seems to me not improbable that Johnson looked through the manuscript of this book as he did those of so many others, added a note or two, and revised the Preface extensively.

If only as an apology for this study, Crossley's remarks on the need of a new and complete edition of Johnson's *Works* may be of interest. 'His prefaces and dedications to the works of other writers are all models in their way, and not one of them ought to be lost.'

Bibliographical Description

An / Introduction / to the / Italian language. / Containing / specimens both of prose and verse: / selected from / [*list of authors*] / with / a literal translation and grammatical notes, / for the use of those who being already acquainted / with grammar, attempt to learn it without a master. / [*rule*] / [*motto*] / [*rule*] / By Giuseppe Baretti. / [*parallel rule*] / London: / Printed for A. Millar, in the Strand. / [*short rule*] / MDCCLV.

Octavo; 20.2 × 12.5 cm.; 6/– bound.

Signatures: A⁶; B–Gg⁸; Hh².

Pagination: [i] half-title; [ii] blank; [iii] title-page; [iv] blank; v–xi Preface, with English and Italian in parallel columns; [xii] blank; [1]–467 Text, with English and Italian on opposite pp.; [468] blank.

In the first sheet, I believe that the two middle leaves, A4 and A5 have been removed. It is probable that Sig. Hh was printed on this quarter-sheet.

The PREFACE.

Unjust objections commonly proceed from unreasonable expectations, and writers are often censured for omitting what they never intended to perform.

To obviate such criticism I think it necessary to declare, that I intend this Collection as nothing more than an initiatory Volume, an easy Introduction to the Italian Tongue; and am confident that he who peruses it diligently, having first learned the grammatical Elements of our speech, will find no other help wanting to a competent knowledge of our best writers.

I have brought into these sheets as large a quantity of our language as it was possible; and the Authors, from whom I have selected specimens, are by the general consent of my countrymen numbered among the best that Italy has produced. The names of Redi, Galileo, Caro, Navagero, Fracastoro, Poliziano, Ariosto, Tasso, Petrarca, &c. are unknown to nobody that knows books. Their works are of long standing, therefore they are good, because mankind never unanimously join to praise a bad book and preserve it from oblivion. I do not give here an account of them, because I did not make my collection to gratify curiosity, but to assist instruction and facilitate study. Scholars know who those Authors are; and the unlearned, who study our language for other purposes, will not value such information which at best would be very imperfect, unless my preface took up more room than I can spare.

I will make no apology for my translation, which I have made as literal as possible, the difference between the two languages considered. A free translation was not intended, because it would not have served my end, which is to teach Italian, not English. Yet the Prose does not lose quite so much by it as the Poetry. By keeping so close to the originals as I was to do here, it was impossible to preserve any of their beauties; and whoever knows two languages will be aware of this impossibility. He will see that what is simple and easy will become uncouth and vulgar, and what is energetick and sublime will seem whimsical and tumorous: that embarassment and obscurity will often appear in the place of method and perspicuousness; that wit and humour will sink into coldness and puerility; that the spirit will evaporate, the graces will be destroyed; and that propriety of words, choice of phrases, justness of allusions, concatenation of thoughts, sweetness of numbers, and musick of rhimes; every thing will be transformed into weakness, harshness, dissonance and confusion.

Let therefore my book be considered only as a simple vocabulary, as indeed it is nothing else; and then my translation will not be useless for want of elegance.

The student will often wonder at finding both in my text and notes that the Italians spell and pronounce the same word different ways; that they say with equal propriety, *esempio* and *esem-*

plo; novo and *nuovo; femina* and *femmina; giungere* and *giu-gnere; republica* or *reppubblica; rinuncia* and *rinunzia; rimaso* and *rimasto; nascoso* and *nascosto; altrimenti* and *altramente; Francese Franzese Francesco* and *Francioso:* He will be astonished at the endless variety of terminations in some of our tenses; as for instance, the third person plural of the preterimperfect of the conjunctive mood of the verb *avere,* which is written by different writers ten different ways: *avrèbbero, arèbbero, avrèbbono, arèb-bono, avrèbbeno, arèbbeno, avrìano, arìano, avrièno,* and *arièno.* The reason of this is, that our Language at first was written by many persons of different parts of Italy, and particularly by many members of the several little commonwealths and sovereignties, into which Italy was at that time divided. Every one writ in his own dialect. Even among the Tuscans, one used a Florentine word or termination, another a Lucchese, another a Sienese, another an Aretine, a Pisan, a Pistojese, a Pratese, and so forth. When the language began to be polished and grew important, the Florentine dialect prevailed, and every one subscribed to the authority of Dante, Petrarca, and Boccaccio. Yet contemporary and successive writers, especially the Poets, found so much convenience in using one word rather than another, that a kind of general adoption or naturalization ensued; and the Accademicians della Crusca were obliged to admit in their Catalogue of pure Writers many of their Neighbours, and consider them as Citizens of Florence.

Many of these differences and variations I have pointed out in my notes; though not always, because the notes would have filled too great a part of my book, and bewildered perhaps rather than helped my readers. But let none of them be frightened away from studying Italian by this, in appearance, unconquerable difficulty. A little practice will soon clear such obstructions, and make the path easy before them, to the most harmonious of all living Languages.

THE ITALIAN LIBRARY

Published: 14 February 1757 (*Public Advertiser*).
Reference: Boswell, *Life,* i:542.
Johnson's Contribution: One paragraph.
Copies: Not rare.

THAT Johnson furnished the first paragraph for Baretti's Preface in this book was first pointed out by Dr. Chapman.

The ascription rests only upon internal evidence, but that is quite sufficient in this case.[1]

The book contains, so far as I have observed, no bibliographical pitfalls, and I have never had occasion to test the accuracy or completeness of Baretti's compilation. To many students, Johnson's contribution may be the chief item of interest in the volume.

Bibliographical Description

The / Italian library. / Containing / an account of the lives and works / of the / most valuable authors of Italy. / With a preface, / exhibiting / the changes of the Tuscan language, from / the barbarous ages to the present time. / [*rule*] / By Giuseppe Baretti. / [*rule*] / [*ornament*] / London: / Printed for A. Millar, in the Strand. / [*short rule*] / MDCCLVII.

Octavo; 20.5 × 12.3 cm. Price 6/– bound.

Signatures: one leaf; a–f⁸; B–Aa⁸; one leaf.

Pagination: title-page with verso blank; i–xciv History of the Italian Tongue; [xcv] Errata; [xcvi] blank; [1]–343 Text; [344] blank; [345–369] Index; [370] blank.

TEXT

The beginning of every language is necessarily obscure; all speech is oral before it is written, and rude before it is polished. Words not committed to writing are lost with the breath that formed them; and the first rude essays are despised and neglected when a style nearer to perfection is once attained. It is therefore impossible to fix the time at which one language ceased and another begun, or to mark exactly the gradations by which the change proceeded: it is at least impossible to a native of Italy to say when the present language had its first formation, amidst the confusion of war, and the incursions of barbarians, who for a time suspended all attention to literature, and left behind them no other memorials but mischief and desolation.

1. Dr. Chapman has included this book in his discussion of Johnsonian Bibliography in Part Sixteen of the *Colophon*.

BARETTI'S *PROPOSALS*

A WORK which I believe to be by Johnson, and one about which I know very little, is *Proposals for Printing by Subscription, Le Poesie di Giuseppe Baretti*. A copy has recently been presented to the Yale Library, and a second copy is in the Bodleian. It is a half-sheet, in quarto, of which the first page contains the Proposals for printing and pp. 2–4 contain, as a specimen, *Amor di Gloria, Oda*. The poems were to be printed in a quarto volume containing about twelve thousand lines, priced at one guinea. I do not think that the volume was ever published.

These Proposals must have been issued at some time between 1751 and 1760, the time of Baretti's first visit to England. At the Bodleian the Proposals are bound with a letter from Baretti that is dated 1757, but the letter is concerned with other matters, so that this is no indication at all of the date of the Proposals. The Proposals state the conditions, and add that subscriptions are taken in by Messrs. Dodsley, Mr. Vaillant, and the Author, in Poland-Street, five doors from the King's Arms. I do not know whether Baretti's places of abode in London can be identified: only his residences after 1765 are known to me. The name of Dodsley does offer a clue, however, since Millar was Baretti's publisher in 1755 and 1757.[1] Therefore I think that these Proposals should be dated before 1755, but not many years before, because Baretti is not known to have met Johnson until 1752 or 1753. This period seems also to agree with normal probability, since he would be likely to attempt to publish Italian poems, which he had already composed, as soon as he was at all acquainted in London, rather than after he had published several books in English. But it is quite clear that Baretti knew

1. Dodsley was the publisher of Baretti's *Dissertation on Italian Poetry*, 1753, and I should suppose that Baretti might have proposed an edition of his own poems at about the same time. Johnson's remark in the life of Milton, however, is worth quoting: 'Why a writer changed his bookseller a hundred years ago, I am far from hoping to discover.'

very little English when he came to England; Johnson was
the man to whom he would most naturally turn, more especially since he was introduced to Johnson by Charlotte Lennox, for whom Johnson had just performed similar services.[2]
The text of the Proposals, I think, will bear out this point of
view. The somewhat unusual verb 'embolden' appears again
in the Dedication to Payne's *Trigonometry*.

TEXT

Italian Poetry has been the business of one part of my life, and
the amusement of the other. As different occasions have risen, as
I have been influenced by different examples, and as I have varied
my temper or my connections, I have, from time to time, tried all
the colours of style, and almost all the modes of composition.
Those pieces which I have found most approved by my friends I
have selected and polished, and now offer them to the Favourers
of the Italian Language. I shall surely be pardoned the vanity of
hoping that a nation which cultivates and encourages every kind
of literature, will not make me the first instance of rejection or
neglect; yet I should not have dared to solicit a subscription even
from English liberality, had I not been emboldened by the patronage of a Nobleman conspicuous alike for his learning and his
virtue, to whom, if these poems should find reception and applause, I shall be indebted for my advantages, and the publick for
its pleasure.

2. The only absolute posterior limit to the date is 1764, when by the death
of Robert Dodsley the firm of the Messrs. Dodsley became J. Dodsley, but I
think that 1760 (the date of Baretti's return to Italy for a visit) is a safe practical limit. The watermark (lily, Strasburg Arms, LVG) is interesting: it is similar to W. A. Churchill's No. 434 (*Watermarks in Paper*, Amsterdam, 1935), but
the bars on the Strasburg Arms slope in the opposite direction. Furthermore,
Churchill has seen it only with the initials of Gerrevink and Villedary (LVG
and IV). But I find a watermark that seems to be identical with that of Baretti's *Proposals* in two books: John Dalton's *Descriptive Poem, addressed to
two Ladies* (London 1755), a slender quarto printed (probably by Richardson)
in December 1754 for the Rivingtons and Dodsleys; and Hampton's *Polybius*,
quarto 1756, printed for the Dodsleys by J. Hughs. In these, the countermark
is JW (Whatman). Whether this means that the paper was produced at Maid-
stone or at Gerrevink's Dutch Mill at Egmond, I do not know; but in any case
it seems necessary to postulate that paper from Whatman's mill was available
somewhat earlier than 1760, the accepted date. Perhaps all that can be said, at
present, is that the watermark fits a suggested date of 1754.

BENNET'S *ASCHAM*

Published: 7 January 1762 (*London Chronicle*).
References: Boswell, *Life,* i:464, 550–2.
  Courtney, p. 100.
Johnson's Contribution: Dedication; Life of Ascham; Notes.
Copies: Boston Athenaeum; Bowdoin; Columbia; Library of Congress; Massachusetts Historical Society; New York Society Library; Yale; Bodleian (Douce); British Museum (2 copies); Cambridge University; Edinburgh University; Glasgow University; National Library of Scotland; John Rylands Library; R. B. Adam; Dr. R. W. Chapman.

PROPOSALS for printing by Subscription the English Works of Ascham were advertised late in January, 1758. To these Proposals was annexed an Advertisement of two paragraphs which is clearly by Johnson and has been accepted as his since 1789, although Boswell neglected to mention it.[1] To the published book Johnson contributed the Dedication to the Earl of Shaftesbury and the Life of Ascham.[2] In addition, Tom Davies wrote that Johnson was really the editor of the work and that he undertook it to assist Bennet, a poor schoolmaster with a large family. Dr. Hill believed that Davies had exaggerated the importance of Johnson's contribution, but Dr. Powell has reëxamined the matter and concluded that Bennet's part in the book was probably confined to reading the proofs.

There seems little doubt that most of the notes are Johnson's. That they are few, particularly in the latter part of the book, may indicate that his editorial task was undertaken without interest and that its execution was perfunctory.[3] In editing the *Schoolmaster* Johnson reprinted all the notes in

---

1. First assigned to Johnson by a contributor to the *European Magazine,* xvi(July 1789):4. Dr. Powell has reprinted the Advertisement from a copy of the Proposals in the British Museum. See his discussion, to which I am largely indebted in the following paragraphs, in Boswell, *Life,* i:550–2.

2. They are marked *acknowl.* in Boswell's list, although in the text he used daggers, his symbols for ascriptions based on internal evidence.

3. The book was severely censured in the *Critical Review,* xvi(July 1763):25–30.

the edition of James Upton. To these he added a few explanations of obsolete words which, to distinguish them from Upton's notes, are signed by two asterisks.[4]

John Newbery, the publisher, was perhaps the man who
planned the edition, with the intention of benefiting both
Bennet and Johnson. The testimony of Newbery's son, Francis, though it is confused, seems to agree sufficiently well with
the facts as they are known to be accepted as reliable:

> In the year 1754 he (Francis Newbery) was removed to Mr. Bennet's
> school at Hoddesdon, for no other reason probably than that his father
> being engaged at this time to publish for him (Mr. Bennet) an edition
> of the works of Roger Ascham, which was a scarce book, and for which
> Dr. Johnson, at the desire of John Newbery, wrote the life and dedica-
> tion. The publication was by subscription, and was intended as an aid to
> Mr. Bennet, who was under some pecuniary embarrassments. Mr. Ben-
> net had no pretensions to scholarship. . . .[5]

If Francis Newbery's date is correct, it may mean that Bennet
had been preparing the text for four years before Johnson
drew up the Proposals. Thereafter Bennet's chief duties were
perhaps the solicitation of a patron and the correction of
proof. The receipt of additional letters also delayed the work
to some extent; with their preparation Dr. Birch assisted.[6]
For the delay an apology was inserted in the *London
Chronicle*.[7]

The facts in the Life of Ascham Johnson obtained principally from Edward Grant's *Oratio de vita et obitu Rogeri
Aschami,* which was first published in 1576; a few points were
drawn from allusions in Ascham's *Works* and from the mem-

4. The second edition of Upton's work was published in 1743. One of Upton's notes was omitted, perhaps by inadvertence. No notes are added beyond
the first twenty pages of the *Schoolmaster.* On p. 199 there is an identifying
note for Whittington, which is added, but on p. 288 Upton's note concerning
Whittington is copied notwithstanding. In the case of two glosses on p. 192
the double asterisk is not appended.

5. From the Autobiography of Francis Newbery the Younger, printed by
Charles Welsh in his *Bookseller of the last Century* (London and New York
1885), pp. 119–120. I am unable to assign the blame for the lapse in grammar.

6. Boswell, *Life,* i:552.

7. 22 October 1761.

oir in the *Biographia Britannica*.[8] One long passage (pp. vi, vii) is quoted from William Windham's *Plan of Discipline composed for the militia of the County of Norfolk* (1759), a very learned work. On the whole, the censure by the *Critical Review* was perhaps not undeserved, for Johnson neglected to make a careful study of the Letters which could have given him new materials.

Johnson's copy is in lot 276 in the *Catalogue* of his Library (1785).

Bibliographical Description

The / English works / of / Roger Ascham, / preceptor to Queen Elizabeth: / containing, / I. A report of the affairs of Germany, and the Em- / peror Charles's court. / II. Toxophilus or the school of shooting. / III. The Schoolmaster, or perfect way of bringing up youth, / illustrated by the late learned Mr. Upton. / IV. Letters to Queen Elizabeth and others, now first / published from the manuscripts. / With notes and observations, and the author's life. / [*rule*] / By James Bennet, / master of the boarding-school at Hoddesdon in Hertfordshire. / [*parallel rule*] / London: / Printed for R. and J. Dodsley, in Pall-Mall, and J. Newbery, in St. Paul's Church-Yard. / [*short rule*] / M,DCC,LXI.

Facsimile of Dedication in the second volume of the Catalogue of the R. B. Adam Library.

Quarto; 26.6 × 20.7 cm.; Subscription: one guinea (it was offered in 1763 for 10/6, and in 1767, with a new title-page, for 12/0).

Signatures: A4; one leaf; b,c,B–3D4; 3E (half-sheet).

---

8. The editor returned the compliment, in the second edition of the *Biographia Britannica*, by the inclusion of selections from Johnson's Life of Ascham.

The Life was included by Davies in the first volume of his *Miscellaneous and Fugitive Pieces*.

The Dedication and an omitted paragraph from the Life were reprinted in Vol. xiv of the *Works* (1788). There the book is dated 'about 1770,' clear proof that the compiler of Volume xiv had seen only the second issue with its undated title-page.

Pagination: [1] title-page; [2] blank; [3]–4 Dedication; [5–8] Subscribers; [9] Additional subscribers; [10] blank; [i]–xvi Life of Ascham; [1]–395 Text; [396] blank.

Editions:

Despite repeated advertisements in 1763, Dodsley and Newbery seem not to have been able to dispose of all copies of the edition. After the death of Robert Dodsley (1764), therefore, another attempt was made to dispose of the unsold sheets in 1767.⁹ The title-page was cancelled, and a new half-sheet containing half-title and title-page inserted. The original issue never has a half-title. The leaf of Additional Subscribers is always omitted in the second issue.

The new title-page, which was of course wholly reset, reads 'the Emperor Charles the Fifth's court,' and the imprint reads 'Printed for T. Davies, in Russell-Street, Covent-Garden, and J. Dodsley, in Pall-Mall.' There is no date. In this form the book occurs about as often as in the original form.

There have been two later editions, in 1815 and in 1904.

DEDICATION

To the Right Honourable Anthony Ashley Cooper, Earl of Shaftesbury, Baron Ashley, Lord Lieutenant and Custos Rotulorum of Dorsetshire, F. R. S.

My LORD,

Having endeavoured, by an elegant and useful edition, to recover the esteem of the publick to an authour undeservedly neglected, the only care which I now owe to his memory, is that of inscribing his works to a patron whose acknowledged eminence of character may awaken attention, and attract regard.

I have not suffered the zeal of an editor so far to take possession

9. Courtney assumed that this second edition was issued in 1762. In the *Review of English Studies,* v(1929):69, Dr. Chapman pointed out that the new issue did not appear until 1767, and that it was merely Dodsley's unsold stock. Davies advertised the book in his Catalogue for 1767. The *Monthly Review* did not recognize that it was a reissue, for it was noticed briefly in Volume xxxviii(February 1768):147. See also the old *Catalogue* of the British Museum. Dr. Chapman has again discussed the book in *The Colophon,* Part Sixteen (1934).

It is somewhat interesting to note that Johnson undertook two perfunctory tasks of editing after he was a well-known literary man, Browne's *Christian Morals* and Ascham's *English Works,* and that in each case the publishers had recourse to a new cancel title-page after some years in order to sell the edition.

of my mind, as that I should obtrude upon your Lordship any productions unsuitable to the dignity of your rank or of your sentiments. *Ascham* was not only the chief ornament of a celebrated college, but visited foreign countries, frequented courts, and lived in familiarity with statesmen and princes; not only instructed scholars in literature, but formed *Elizabeth* to empire.

To propagate the works of such a writer will be not unworthy of your Lordship's patriotism: for I know not what greater benefit you can confer on your country, than that of preserving worthy names from oblivion, by joining them with your own.

I am, My LORD, Your Lordship's Most obliged, Most obedient, and Most humble servant,

JAMES BENNET.

DR. JOHNSON AND DR. BURNEY

DR. BURNEY's *History of Music* found a place in Courtney only because of Johnson's translation of a few lines from the *Medea* of Euripides. The style of the Dedication, however, is unmistakable, and it has been long known to be by Johnson; the omission of this work from the bibliographies illustrates the curious and rapid obsolescence that overtakes many details of literary history. But now a recently discovered letter from Johnson to Burney furnishes proof that Johnson wrote Dedications both for the *History of Music* and for Burney's *Account of the Commemoration of Handel*. Fanny Burney, in her *Diary* and in the *Memoirs* of her father which she edited, although she discusses in detail the composition of both books, makes no mention of the assistance that Johnson rendered her father.[1] Whether these omissions were inadvert-

1. According to the *Early Diary* (edited by A. R. Ellis, 1889), all the Journal and letters for 1776, being on family matters, were destroyed. Yet Miss Burney does discuss the making of the *History*, much of which she herself transcribed, in the *Diary* for 1775. There are even some details about the Dedication. It is barely possible that the Dedication by Johnson was substituted, without Miss Burney's knowledge, for one of Dr. Burney's own composition. (See *Early Diary*, ii:34, 44, 85–88; *Memoirs of Dr. Burney*, 1832, ii:71–77, 100. Her dates are unreliable.) Part of the Dedication to the *Commemoration of Handel* is quoted in the *Memoirs of Dr. Burney*, ii:386.

It is possible that a letter to an unnamed correspondent, dated 29 November

ent or calculated, whether they were occasioned by honest ignorance or by an unwillingness to have it known that her father (like Reynolds in a similar case) had received the help of Johnson, will perhaps be always obscure, but it can now make little difference.

The letters that contain the proof of Johnson's assistance are of considerable interest.[2] In a part of a letter omitted by Boswell, Johnson wrote to Burney:

> The Post at this devious town goes out so soon after it comes in that I make haste to tell you, what I hope you did not doubt, that you shall have what my thoughts will supply, in recommendation of your new book. Let me know when it will be wanted.[3]

This letter, written in August of 1784, can refer only to the *Commemoration of Handel,* upon which Burney was engaged throughout the summer. The conclusive proof that Johnson wrote both the Dedication to the Queen for the *History of Music* and the Dedication to the King for the *Commemoration of Handel* is in a letter written 23 August:

> When I came to think on this, I had quite forgot what we had said to the Queen, and as it was natural to say the same again on the same subject, I was forced to look out for some remote track of thought, which I believe, you will think I have found; but it has given me some trouble, and perhaps may not please at last so well. But necessity must be obeyed.[4]

[no year], was written to Burney in 1775 in connection with the Dedication to the *History of Music:* 'I have seen your proof as I told you, and saw, I think, only one word that I wished to alter. Be pleased to make my compliments to the ladies at your house.' *Letters,* ii:433; resold at Sotheby's in April, 1921.

2. The following references may be consulted for additional proofs. The Dedication to the *History of Music* was known to Dr. Parr; see H. B. Wheatley, *The Dedication of Books* (London 1887), p. 176. It was also recorded by Mrs. Thrale in her *Thraliana;* see the note by Miss Balderston, *PMLA* xlix (Sept. 1934):966–8. Miss Balderston's deduction that Johnson's attitude toward music had changed seems doubtful to me, since we have Boswell's explicit warning that Johnson in writing dedications never considered himself to be expressing his own sentiments. The newly discovered letters are discussed by R. W. Chapman in *Review of English Studies,* x(July 1934):329–331, and by L. F. Powell in Boswell, *Life,* iv:544–7.

3. *Letters,* 2 August 1784, No. 984. This first part of the letter will be included by Dr. Chapman in his revised edition of the *Letters.*

4. *Catalogue* 254 (1926) of Myers and Co. Offered again in their *Catalogue* 274 (1930).

This letter indicates clearly that, although Johnson composed rapidly, he thought carefully and wrote accurately when he furnished a Dedication for a book. This is one of the reasons for the lack of revision in later editions; the other reason, of course, is the fact that he dismissed the Dedication from his mind after it was written and paid no attention to later editions.

Having furnished the Dedication to the *History of Music* in 1776, Johnson also seems to have assisted Dr. Burney to a very considerable extent in the preparation of the second volume. It has long been known that he wrote letters of introduction for Dr. Burney to his friends at Oxford, and the translation of the lines from the *Medea* was by Johnson.[5] I suspect that Johnson read in proof a large part of the volume. On 21 October 1779, Johnson wrote to Mrs. Thrale:

> Dr. Burney has passed one Evening with me. He has made great discoveries in a library at Cambridge, and he finds so many precious materials, that his Book must be a Porter's load. He has sent me another sheet.[6]

It would be very natural for Burney, full of enthusiasm about his new discoveries, to call on Dr. Johnson and talk about them. But that Johnson had time to correct many of the sheets of the *History,* while he himself was busied with his *Lives of the Poets,* is renewed proof that his industry when spurred by friendship was able to overcome his indolence. I think that when Johnson writes 'another sheet' he expects Mrs. Thrale to remember that he has already corrected several. During the next two and a half years Burney was busied with his work, and it is very probable that Johnson continued to help. In any case, he wrote to Burney, 18 March 1782:

5. Boswell, *Life,* iii:366–7; the letters are dated 2 November 1778. Courtney, p. 154.

6. *Letters,* ii:112. The name is left blank, and Dr. Hill suspected that this should be filled with the name of Dr. Burney. The original, now in the Library of R. B. Adam, confirms Hill's conjecture. See also *Letters,* ii:118, 'I have seen some more sheets.'

It is perhaps likely that Johnson referred to 'sheets' of manuscript, rather than to proof.

I have taken great liberties by shortening your paper, but have, I hope, omitted nothing important. A long apology is a hideous thing.[7]

The volume was published on the first of June, and the last two pages contain Burney's apology for the long delay in publication, with the explanation that the materials had been much more abundant than he had expected to find them. It is sufficiently brief and dignified to render quite certain the belief that the text was shortened and edited by Dr. Johnson.

Some further details concerning the composition of both books will be most conveniently studied when the cancels in each book are discussed in turn. Dr. Johnson's copy of the *History* is listed in lot 332 in the *Catalogue* of his Library (1785).

HISTORY OF MUSIC

A / General history / of / music, / from the / earliest ages to the present period. / To which is prefixed, / a dissertation / on the / music of the ancients. / By / Charles Burney, Mus.D. F.R.S. / Volume the first. / London, / Printed for the author: and sold by T. Becket, Strand; J. Robson, / New Bond-Street; and G. Robinson, Paternoster-Row. / MDCC-LXXVI.

Quarto; 26.5 × 21 cm.

Published: 31 January 1776 (*London Chronicle*); one guinea to subscribers, or £1/11/6 to nonsubscribers.
Johnson's Contributions: Dedication; proof-reading of second volume; lines from the *Medea*.
Copies: Not rare, but in many sets the first volume is of the second edition.

Signatures: [A],a–c,B–Ee,*Ee,*Ff,Ff–Uuu⁴; Xxx (half-sheet).

Pagination: [i] title-page; [ii] blank; [iii]–v Dedication; [vi] blank; [vii]–xx Preface; [xxi–xxxii] Contents and List of Subscribers

---

7. Chicago Book and Art Auctions, 15 December 1931. This letter was not known to Hill. I have utilized this letter to support my view of the authorship of the Preface to the third volume of the *Harleian Catalogue*, 1744.

(see Notes); [1]–80, *81–*86, 81–194 Dissertation on the Music of the Ancients; [195]–216, *217–*232, 217–495 History of Music; [496] blank; [497]–516 Additional Notes, etc.; [517]–522 List and Description of plates; [523] Errata, etc.; [524] blank.

Cancels: E4 and F1 are both cancels; they were perhaps printed in the same half-sheet, but they were cut and then pasted separately. Sheet L is puzzling: I think that the last two leaves (L3 & L4) were cancelled, and a new sheet was inserted, signed L3 & L4 on the first two leaves and unsigned on the last two leaves; then a single leaf, signed *L, was pasted to the stub (of the original L3 or L4) in some manner so that L1 & L2 were both held firmly. As a result there are seven leaves: signed L, L2, L3, L4, –, –, *L. The extra pages with asterisks (81–86) which are used for the last three leaves are thus easily understood if one does not forget that the pages with asterisks do not correspond exactly to the total number of cancels. Sheets *Ee and *Ff are insertions which were necessitated by the new information which was furnished by James Bruce the famous traveller.[1]

In some copies, leaf c4, containing the Contents, was cut and inserted in front of the List of Subscribers. The collation in such a copy is thus made to read: b, b2, c4, b3, b4, c1–c3. The catchwords (or direction lines) in sheet c seem to be wrong in all copies: what caused the trouble is not immediately apparent. Perhaps it was caused by some shift in the list of names which caused overrunning, analogous to the case described by Mr. I. A. Williams.[2]

Proposals: These are dated 20 April 1773. I have not seen the original *Proposals,* but they are reprinted, at the beginning of the second volume, in the *Present State of Music in Germany* (1773).

The chapter on Hebrew music (p. 217ff.) also exists as a separate pamphlet. (See *Catalogue* 89 [1930] of Harold Reeves.)

1. See Fanny Burney's *Memoirs of Dr. Burney* (1832), i:308. Plates VII–IX were of course added after the text had been planned. See also the note to the Binder, following the Errata: 'There are twenty-six *double pages,* marked with asterisms. These were occasioned by the late arrival of Mr. Bruce's communications, and by other additions to the text, occurring after the Press was broken up.'

2. See his article, in the seventh number of the *Book-Collector's Quarterly,* ii(1932):53–59. It is reprinted in his *Points in Eighteenth Century Verse* (1934).

The plates in this volume are almost as fine as those in the
Commemoration of Handel:

I (frontispiece)	Apollo and the Nine Muses; Cipriani, engraved by Bartolozzi.
VII (pp. 204–205)	Drawing of an Egyptian musical instrument.
VIII (pp. *222–*223)	Theban Harp; engraved by Grignion.
IX (pp. 252–253)	Folded page of music.
II (pp. 274–275)	Mercury and Apollo; Cipriani, engraved by Bartolozzi.
III (pp. 326–327)	Orpheus and Eurydice; Cipriani, engraved by Bartolozzi.

(Plates I–III were first used as concert tickets.)

IV (pp. 522–523)	Antique masques; by Grignion.
V–VI (pp. 522–523)	Various instruments; by Maleuvre.

(In some copies the Errata leaf precedes plates IV–VI.)

VOLUME II.

Published: 1 June 1782 (*St. James's Chronicle*); one guinea to
subscribers, one guinea and a half to others.

Signatures: [A] (half-sheet); B–Yyy4; Zzz (half-sheet). Inserted
leaves, which are included in the pagination, thus:
1 after F2; 2 after Ppp3; 1 after Rrr2; 2 after Rrr3; 2 after
Sss2; 2 after Sss4; 1 after Ttt3; 2 after Ttt4; 5 after Uuu1; 4
after Uuu4; 2 after Yyy3; 6 after Zzz1.

Pagination: [i] title-page; [ii] blank; [iii–iv] Contents; [1]–597
Text; [598] blank; [599] Corrections and Additions; [600]
blank.

In the imprint, Becket's name is omitted. The title-page is considerably altered.

The six inserted leaves after Zzz1 follow Zzz2 in some copies.

Johnson's translation of the lines from the *Medea* is on p. 340.
The Apology is on pp. 585–6 (see pp. 25–26 above).

There are two plates in this volume:

I (frontispiece)	Designed by Cipriani, and engraved by Bartolozzi.
II (opposite p. 264)	By Dr. Burney's son.

The second edition of the first volume was printed in 1789.
The Preface was considerably altered, and the frontispiece is a

portrait of Dr. Burney which was engraved in 1784. The Dedication is a line-for-line reprint: the only changes in the text are two typographical errors which are introduced by the printer.

Mr. Frank Mercer (in his edition of Burney's *History*, 1935, ii:1050) mentions a copy of the second volume with an index.

The second volume was all reprinted (except for the last few leaves of engraved music), with the original date in the imprint, about thirty years later. This reprint can be identified quickly by the following features: it uses the modern *s* throughout instead of the long *f*, and it is carelessly printed on wove paper watermarked '1809.' One copy is in the New York Public Library, and Mr. Frank Mercer has a copy. As a literary curiosity, this may be classed with the strange reprint of William Payne's *Draughts*.

DEDICATION

TO THE QUEEN.

MADAM,

The condescension with which your Majesty has been pleased to permit your name to stand before the following History, may justly reconcile the author to his favourite study, and convince him, that whatever may be said by the professors of severer wisdom, the hours which he has bestowed upon Music have been neither dishonourably, nor unprofitably spent.

The science of musical sounds, though it may have been depreciated, as appealing only to the ear, and affording nothing more than a momentary and fugitive delight, may be with justice considered as the art that unites corporal with intellectual pleasure, by a species of enjoyment which gratifies sense, without weakening reason; and which, therefore, the Great may cultivate without debasement, and the Good enjoy without depravation.

Those who have most diligently contemplated the state of man, have found it beset with vexations, which can neither be repelled by splendor, nor eluded by obscurity; to the necessity of combating these intrusions of discontent, the ministers of pleasure were indebted for that kind reception, which they have perhaps too indiscriminately obtained. Pleasure and innocence ought never to be separated; yet we seldom find them otherwise than at variance, except when Music brings them together.

To those who know that Music is among your Majesty's recreations, it is not necessary to display its purity, or assert its dignity. May it long amuse your leisure, not as a relief from evil, but as an augmentation of good; not as a diversion from care, but as a variation of felicity. Such, Madam, is my sincerest wish, in which I can however boast no peculiarity of reverence or zeal; for the virtues of your Majesty are universally confessed; and however the inhabitants of the British empire may differ in their opinions upon other questions, they all behold your excellencies with the same eye, and celebrate them with the same voice; and to that name which one nation is echoing to another, nothing can be added by the respectful admiration, and humble gratitude of,

MADAM, your Majesty's most obedient and most devoted Servant,

CHARLES BURNEY.

COMMEMORATION OF HANDEL

An / Account / of the / musical performances / in / Westminster-Abbey, / and the / Pantheon, / May 26th, 27th, 29th; and June the 3d, and 5th, 1784. / In / commemoration / of / Handel. / By Charles Burney, Mus.D. F.R.S. / [*motto*] / [*parallel rule*] / London, / Printed for the benefit of the musical fund; and sold by T. Payne and / Son, at the Meuse-Gate; and G. Robinson, Pater-noster-Row. / MDCCLXXXV.

Quarto; 27.2 × 21.5 cm.; large paper copy 29.2 × 22.5 cm.

Published: 1 February 1785 (*St. James's Chronicle*); one guinea in boards.
Johnson's Contribution: Dedication.
Copies: Not rare.

Signatures: A,a,b,B,*B,C4; D(with cancels)7; E4; F3; G,H4; I(one leaf); B–S4; T(half-sheet); one leaf.

Pagination: [i] title-page; [ii] blank; [iii–vi] Dedication; vii–[viii] Contents and list of plates; [i]–xvi Preface; [1]–8, *1–*8, 9–20, *19–*24, 21–38 Life of Handel; 39–56 Character of Handel, Chronological List, and Addenda; [1]–125 Commemoration; [126] blank; [127]–139 Appendix; [140] Advertisement of *History of Music;* one leaf (with verso blank) containing Errata and Directions to the Binder.

Cancels:
The extra leaf, which is lacking in some copies, contains a

list of cancels to help the binder; it is also a great aid to the bibliographer. Sheet *B is of course an addition. D2 & D3 were cancelled, and replaced by a whole sheet (signed D2) plus one leaf (signed *D). Therefore the seven leaves are: D, D2, D3, –, –, *D, original D4 unsigned. F4 was cancelled before Sheet G had been printed, so that there is no break in the pagination.

These cancels were necessitated by new information concerning Handel's life. A letter from Burney explains the matter: 'When Handel died, I knew so much more of his works than any poet or biographer could tell me, that I read nothing then on the subject, except Mr. Mainwaring's life of the great musician, which is very deficient and inaccurate concerning Handel's early life, which I did not know till it was too late: for trusting to him before I had received better documents from Germany, I was obliged to cancel my account of Handel previous to his arrival in England and write it over again.'[1]

E4 and F1 were cancelled, and replaced by a half-sheet signed *E and F. The faulty direction line, corrected by Errata, on the verso of F4 seems to indicate revision of the first sentence on G1 recto after sheet F had been printed.

In the *Memoirs,* Fanny writes that her father cancelled two sheets in order to incorporate the suggestions made by the King in two notes which he communicated to Dr. Burney after he had seen the book in sheets.[2] On internal evidence it is clear that these sheets were L and P, since the King's suggestions deal with the fugue, 'He trusted in God,' and with Mr. Fischer's solo in the Fourth Hautbois Concerto. It is interesting to find that Burney utilized, to a large extent, the King's own words.

Plates:
The book contains some very handsome plates, worthy in themselves to attract collectors.

I (opposite title-page) Handel Medal.

II (facing first page of Life) Handel's Monument in West-

---

1. Quaritch's *Catalogue* 471(1933), p. 100. The letter, dated 2 February 1801, is addressed to J. C. Walker. This delay is probably the explanation of Johnson's remark: 'That your book has been delayed I am glad, since you have gained an opportunity of being more exact.' (Boswell, *Life*, iv:361, 1 November 1784.) Fanny Burney attributes the delay to the engravers, justifiably, for two of the plates are dated 14 January 1785. The changes which Dr. Burney felt obliged to make in response to the suggestions of the King furnish a third explanation of the five months' delay after the Dedication had been written.

2. *Memoirs of Dr. Burney* (1832), ii:384ff.

minster Abbey, with the plaque recording the commemoration.

III (facing p. 23) Sarcophagus and medallion.

IV (facing p. 43) Handel composing, the Genius of Harmony,
and a seraph. (In a second state, the seraph's ribbon is
darkened and the neckcloth is altered.)

V (facing p. 71) Britannia, a Genius, pyramid, Westminster
Abbey in the background.

VI (facing p. 91) View of gallery.

VII (facing p. 109) View of orchestra.

Plates III–V were designed originally as tickets of admission
to the performances. The position of the plates may vary by a
page or two in different copies. There are four other inserted
leaves: 2 between p. 24 & p. 25; 1 facing p. 45; 1 facing p. 91.

The plates are to be found frequently without titles, doubtless the result of haste. Various artists, including E. F. Burney,
were employed to design and engrave them.

Editions:

There is a copy of the large paper edition in the Lowell Mason
Collection at Yale; it is not only taller, but the paper is of a much
finer quality. This copy is inscribed on the fly-leaf: 'From the
Royal Society of Musicians.' It has also the name: 'Lowell Mason Savannah, Geo. 1825.'

An edition was printed at Dublin in 1785, in octavo. Since 1785
the book has been reprinted only once, I believe, in 1834.

DEDICATION

(Probably the last work that Johnson prepared for press.)

TO THE KING.

Greatness of mind is never more willingly acknowledged, nor
more sincerely reverenced, than when it descends into the regions
of general life, and by countenancing common pursuits, or partak-
ing common amusements, shews that it borrows nothing from distance or formality.

By the notice which Your Majesty has been pleased to bestow
upon the celebration of HANDEL'S memory, You have condescended to add Your voice to public praise, and give Your sanction to musical emulation.

The delight which Music affords seems to be one of the first attainments of rational nature; wherever there is humanity, there is
modulated sound. The mind set free from the resistless tyranny

of painful want, employs its first leisure upon some savage melody. Thus in those lands of unprovided wretchedness, which Your Majesty's encouragement of naval investigation has brought lately to the knowledge of the polished world, though all things else were wanted, every nation had its Music; an art of which the rudiments accompany the commencements, and the refinements adorn the completion of civility, in which the inhabitants of the earth seek their first refuge from evil, and, perhaps, may find at last the most elegant of their pleasures.

But that this pleasure may be truly elegant, science and nature must assist each other; a quick sensibility of Melody and Harmony, is not always originally bestowed, and those who are born with this susceptibility of modulated sounds, are often ignorant of its principles, and must therefore be in a great degree delighted by chance; but when Your Majesty is pleased to be present at Musical performances, the artists may congratulate themselves upon the attention of a judge in whom all requisites concur, who hears them not merely with instinctive emotion, but with rational approbation, and whose praise of HANDEL is not the effusion of credulity, but the emanation of Science.

How near, or how distant, the time may be, when the art of combining sounds shall be brought to its highest perfection by the natives of Great Britain, this is not the place to enquire; but the efforts produced in other parts of knowledge by Your Majesty's favour, give hopes that Music may make quick advances now it is recommended by the attention, and dignified by the patronage of our Sovereign.

I am, With the most profound Humility, Your MAJESTY's most dutiful And devoted Subject and Servant,

CHARLES BURNEY.

FORDYCE, *SERMONS TO YOUNG WOMEN*

Published: 5 June 1766 (*Public Advertiser*).
Johnson's Contribution: Preface.
Copy: Harvard.

BOSWELL refers briefly in two places to Johnson's Presbyterian friend, the Reverend Dr. James Fordyce, but he tells little about him. In the *Memoirs of Johnson* attributed to William Shaw, however, there is an unequivocal assertion that Johnson gave some assistance to Fordyce:

An acquaintance commenced between Johnson and the Reverend Dr. James Fordyce, so well known for his popular talents in the pulpit, and his Sermons to young women. These were shown to Johnson and published by his advice. He even interested himself so far in the work as to write the title and the advertisement.[1]

Now Shaw was a controversialist but he was not a liar, and I see no reason why his definite statement should not be accepted as an accurate one, and there is every reason to suppose that he might have known about this matter from Johnson, from Dr. Fordyce, or from Elphinston.

The word 'title' can refer only to the title of the book, *Sermons to Young Women.* The word 'advertisement,' I think, can be applied to a newspaper notice in the modern sense, but it was also applied regularly in the eighteenth century to the Preface. It is quite possible, therefore, that Shaw referred to the following notice which appeared in the newspapers:

This day are published, . . . *Sermons to Young Women:* Being a series of free but affectionate addresses, in which their instruction is attempted, as well in the accomplishments that will adorn their sex, as in the virtues that will promote their happiness.

But, while I must admit that this is a possibility, I am inclined on the whole to ascribe the Preface to Johnson on the authority of Shaw's statement, even though there are sentences in it that hardly sound Johnsonian.

It may seem strange at first that this work should have been completely overlooked for a century and a half: I believe that the obscurity of Shaw's book, the anonymity of Fordyce's first edition, and the extreme scarcity of the original publication, are sufficient explanations.

The work proved to be exceedingly popular, despite Fordyce's initial diffidence about it which caused him to conceal his name until the second edition. Three editions were published in 1766 (though I have never seen the second edition), and there were many later editions. The latest numbered edi-

1. W. Shaw, *Memoirs of Johnson* (1785), p. 143.

tion in the British Museum is the Fourteenth (1814). There was an edition at Edinburgh in 1793–4, and doubtless others as well. Editions were published at Philadelphia in 1787 and 1809. In the later editions the second paragraph of the Preface was considerably revised, in order to express the author's satisfaction at the popularity of his discourses.[2] In the Sixth Edition, however, the text is approximately that of the original Preface, and there is a Dedication to the Lady Arabella Denny.[3]

The book is celebrated in some very bad but very laudatory verses which were contributed by 'a young lady of the Author's acquaintance' to G. P. Tousey's *Flights to Helicon* (1768). Miss Talbot wrote to Mrs. Carter: 'I have just been reading a book, lately published, which I entreat you to like, as I do, exceedingly. . . . It is in two volumes, Sermons to Young Women. *You* are in, and handsomely in, but not so handsomely as you would have been, had the author known you better.'[4]

Goldsmith writes, in the preface to his *Collection of Poems for Young Ladies* (1766), that Fordyce's *Sermons for Young Women* 'in some measure gave rise to the following compilation.'

2. It is possible that this revision of the middle paragraph is an indication that it was originally written by Fordyce, and that Johnson's contribution was limited to the first and third paragraphs. There are slight changes in the other paragraphs in later editions.

Concerning the editions, see also *Scots Magazine*, xxviii(November 1766): 591n.

3. This edition is dated 1766, but could hardly have been published before 1767 or 1768. The *Dictionary of National Biography* and Watt's *Bibliotheca Britannica* both date the first edition 1765. Whether this is a misprint or an assumption based on the fact that the third edition is dated 1766, I do not know. There are no newspaper or magazine notices of it until June 1766.

4. Letter of 23 August 1766. (*A Series of letters between Mrs. Elizabeth Carter and Miss Catherine Talbot*, edited by M. Pennington [London 1809]iii: 141). Mrs. Carter had not seen this work when she wrote to Mrs. Montagu, 5 September 1766. (*Letters from Mrs. Carter to Mrs. Montagu*, edited by M. Pennington, 1817, i:319.)

Boswell did not like them. He read them aloud to his wife in 1779. 'I was quite disgusted with the affected, theatrical style. I left out many superfluous words in many sentences. Yet they were still florid.' (See *Boswell Papers*, xiv: 10).

Bibliographical Description

Sermons / to / young women: / in two volumes. / Volume I. / London: / Printed for A. Millar and T. Cadell / in the Strand, J. Dodsley in / Pall-Mall, and J. Payne in / Paternoster Row. / MDCCLXVI.

Two volumes, small octavo; 15 × 9.4 cm.; 6/– sewed.

Signatures: Vol. I: B–R⁸; S³.
Vol. II: A⁴; one leaf; B–Y⁸; Z⁵.

Pagination: Vol. I: [1]–262 Text of Sermons I–VI.
Vol. II: [i] title-page to Vol. I; [ii] blank; [iii]–vi Preface; [vii]–viii Contents of Volume I; one leaf containing Contents of Volume II; [1]–346 Text of Sermons VII–XII and Conclusion.

This is the collation of the copy at Harvard, but it is clear at once that it is not a correct general collation. The preliminary leaves of the first volume have been bound in the second volume by mistake. The title-page of the second volume is lacking, and the last few sentences of the Conclusion are lacking. Therefore, though it can be only a guess, I am quite certain that the collation of a perfect copy would be:

Vol. I: A⁴; B–R⁸; S⁴ (S4 blank, and may have been used for a cancel).
Vol. II: Two preliminary leaves containing title-page and Contents; B–Y⁸; Z⁶.

The copy at Harvard, bound in contemporary calf, was presented to the college library by Dodsley.

Cancels:
Vol. I: M7, N5, O2, R1.
Vol. II: D3, F8, L8, O3, O8, P2, P8.

It seems to be an extraordinary number of cancels for such small volumes. I should think that Dr. Fordyce might have tried the patience of his printer.

PREFACE.

The corruption of the age is a complaint with many men who contribute to increase it. In like manner, the inattention of the people is a complaint with many preachers who are themselves to blame. A dull discourse naturally produces a listless audience; there being few hearers who will attend to that by which their hearts are not engaged, or their imaginations entertained. To entertain the imagination chiefly, is a poor, and indeed a vicious aim in a preacher. To engage the heart, with a view to mend it, should be his grand ambition. Any farther than as it may prove some way or other subservient to that, entertainment should never be admitted into a Sermon. There, to say the truth, we seldom meet with too much of the latter. Would to God we often met there with more of the former!

The author of the following Discourses was prompted to publish them, from an unfeigned regard for the Female Sex; from a fervent zeal for the best interests of society, on which he believes their dispositions and deportment will ever have a mighty influence; and, lastly, from a secret desire long felt of trying whether that style of preaching, which to him appears, upon the whole, adapted to an auditory above the vulgar rank, might succeed on a subject of this nature; nothing in the kind, that he knows of, having been endeavoured before, in any language. If he should be found to fail in an attempt as difficult as it is new, and of which that very difficulty is probably the reason why it has been hitherto declined; the public, on whose candour he relies, will make every proper allowance. It will do so particularly for some singularities in the manner, on which he would not have ventured, but for the uncommonness of the occasion. If on the other hand he should be approved, it will afford him pleasure. But indeed it will afford him much more, if, by the blessing of heaven, which he humbly implores, any thing here suggested shall contribute to the improvement of the most agreeable part of the creation, and by consequence both to their own felicity, and that of millions with whom they are now, or may be hereafter connected. In this case too, it will add to his happiness to reflect, that he has rendered the voice of Truth acceptable amongst those who are daily addressed in the language of Flattery.

The preacher is willing to hope, that women of most conditions, and at all ages, may meet with some useful counsel, or some salutary hint, should curiosity incite them to look into these Sermons. Should any of those young persons in genteel life, to whom they are principally addressed, deem the reprehensions they contain too severe, or too indiscriminate; he can only say, that as all were dictated by friendship no less than by conviction, so he wishes it to be understood, that many were occasioned by a particular observation of those characters and manners which are esteemed fashionable amongst the Young and the Gay of this metropolis. In the Country (a denomination which, as matters are commonly conducted, he can by no means allow to the neighbourhood of London) the contagion of vice and folly, it may be presumed, is not so epidemical. In short, he is persuaded, that women of worth and sense are to be found every where, but most frequently in the calm of retreat, and amidst the coolness of recollection.

GWYNN'S *LONDON AND WESTMINSTER IMPROVED*

Published: 14 June 1766 (*London Chronicle*).
References: Boswell, *Life*, ii:25, 479.
          Courtney, p. 111.
Johnson's Contribution: Dedication.
Copies: Columbia; Harvard; Peabody Institute; Aberdeen University; Bodleian; British Museum; Edinburgh University; Glasgow University; London Library; National Library of Scotland; John Rylands; R. B. Adam; Dr. R. W. Chapman; Professor F. W. Hilles; Professor C. B. Tinker.

In 1925 Elkin Mathews offered Garrick's copy for sale.

JOHN GWYNN was a charter member of the Royal Academy, representing Architecture, and his early *Essay on Design* helped to form the sentiment which led to the founding of the Academy. He was not primarily a literary man,[1] and he was no doubt glad to accept the assistance of his friend Dr. Johnson when he undertook to dedicate his most ambitious literary work to the King. That the Dedication is not felicitous is perhaps the fault neither of Johnson nor of Gwynn.

In Boswell's text this Dedication is marked with an asterisk, Boswell's symbol for 'acknowledged,' although the work is not included in the Chronological List of Johnson's prose. Since the inclusion of the work in the text was due to a last-

---

1. It has been suggested that his friend Samuel Wale, the designer, also an original member of the Royal Academy, helped Gwynn in some of his literary work. See DNB 'Wale'.

minute revision, one presumes that its omission from the List was merely an oversight, in 1793. Boswell describes it as 'the noble dedication to the King,' of which Hill remarks in a note that it is difficult 'to discover anything noble or even felicitous in this dedication.'[2] The discovery of Boswell's revises has vindicated both Boswell and Dr. Hill, since in the proof the words 'Gwyn's *London and Westminster Improved*' are a correction of the original which reads 'Adam's *Treatise on the Globes*.' The word 'noble' is also blotted in the proof, so that Boswell may have intended to omit it, although there is no marginal direction to the corrector. Thus Dr. Hill's judgment is correct; the adjective doesn't belong here, but applies to Gwynn's book only by chance or by error. That Boswell's original description of the Dedication to Adams's *Globes* was justified, a perusal of that Dedication will make evident.[3]

Johnson wrote also three letters in support of Gwynn's design for Blackfriars Bridge, and to Gwynn's *Thoughts on the Coronation* he 'lent his friendly assistance.'[4]

Johnson's copy of this work is listed in lot 647 in the *Catalogue* of his Library (1785).

Bibliographical Description

London and Westminster / improved, / illustrated by plans. / To which is prefixed, / a discourse on publick magnificence; / with / observations on the state of arts and artists

2. Boswell, *Life*, ii:25. Possibly when Boswell substituted Gwynn's book, he ought to have altered the asterisk in his text to a dagger ('internal evidence'), since he seems to use the dagger for writings that he includes only on the authority of Volume xiv. But he marks *Thoughts on the Coronation* with an asterisk.

3. This discussion is drawn almost unchanged from *Boswell Revised*, p. 36.

4. See Courtney, pp. 98, 100; and Dr. Chapman's article in the *Colophon* (New York 1934), Part Sixteen.

Some account of Gwynn's trip to Oxford with Johnson is preserved, and may be consulted in the *Oxford Historical Publications* (1901), Number 41, pp. 342–3; also in Boswell, *Life*, v:454.

The Dedication was reprinted in Vol. xiv of the *Works*, as was *Thoughts on the Coronation*.

in this / kingdom, wherein the study of the polite arts / is recommended as necessary to a liberal education: / concluded by / some proposals relative to places not laid down in the plans. / By John Gwynn. / [*quotation from the* Rambler] / London: / Printed for the author. / Sold by Mr. Dodsley, and at Mr. Dalton's Print-Warehouse in Pall- / Mall, Mr. Bathoe in the Strand, Mr. Davies in Russel-Street, Covent- / Garden, and by Mr. Longman in Pater-noster-Row. / MDCCLXVI.

Quarto; an uncut copy measures approximately 28 × 22 cm. Price: 10/6 bound; 9/– in boards.

Facsimile of title-page in the second volume of the Catalogue of the R. B. Adam Library.

Signatures: a,a,B–R⁴; S²; four folded plates.

Pagination: [i] title-page; [ii] blank; [iii–iv] Dedication; v–xi Preface; xii Contents; xiii–xv Introduction; [xvi] Errata; 1–132 Text; plates.

The plates I think are usually coloured, although in Dr. Chapman's copy they are plain.

Copies are still advertised in the *London Chronicle*, 1 June 1771.

TO THE KING.

SIR,

The patronage of works which have a tendency towards advancing the happiness of mankind, naturally belongs to great Princes; and publick good, in which publick elegance is comprised, has ever been the object of your Majesty's regard.

In the following pages your Majesty, I flatter myself, will find, that I have endeavoured at extensive and general usefulness. Knowing, therefore, your Majesty's early attention to the polite arts, and more particular affection for the study of architecture, I was encouraged to hope that the work which I now presume to lay before your Majesty, might be thought not unworthy your Royal Favour; and that the protection which your Majesty always affords to those who mean well, may be extended to,

SIR, Your Majesty's most dutiful subject, and most obedient and most humble servant,

JOHN GWYNN.

GWYNN'S *THOUGHTS ON THE CORONATION*

Published: 8 August 1761 (*London Chronicle*).[1]
References: Boswell, *Life*, i:361.
　　　　　Courtney, p. 100.
Johnson's Contribution: Introductory paragraphs.
Copies: British Museum (2 copies); Dr. R. W. Chapman.

CONCERNING this scarce pamphlet Boswell remarks merely that Johnson 'lent his friendly assistance to correct and improve' it.[2] It had been included in Volume xiv of the *Works*, whence perhaps Boswell derived his knowledge of the book.

There is little more that can be said about it. After the first four paragraphs there is nothing that sounds to me like Johnson. I believe that Johnson wrote the first four paragraphs as they stand, and that this book is one of the many in which Johnson furnished an Introduction which was not set apart from the text.

Bibliographical Description

Thoughts / on the / coronation / of his present Majesty / King George the Third. / Or, / reasons offered against confining the procession to / the usual track, and pointing out others more / commodious and proper. / . . . London: / Printed for the proprietor, and sold by F. Noble, opposite Gray's-Inn / Gate, Holbourn; J. Noble, in St. Martin's Court, near Leicester-Square; / W. Bathoe, near Exeter-Change, in the Strand; and H. Yates, / at the Royal-Exchange. / [*short rule*] / M DCC LXI. / [Price one shilling and six-pence.]

1. This is advertised as the Second Edition, a fact which puzzles me. The Coronation took place on September 22, and this book would have had no interest until plans for the Coronation had been announced. The book was noticed by the *Critical* and *Monthly Reviews* for August; the *Gentleman's Magazine* did not list it until October. Nor do I know of the existence of any Second Edition. Therefore I assume, though with misgivings, that the 'Second Edition' of the advertisement is an error. It is of course quite possible that two almost identical issues appeared within a few weeks.

2. Boswell, *Life*, i:361. It is discussed by Dr. Chapman in Part Sixteen of the *Colophon* (New York 1934).

Small folio; British Museum copy is 28 × 17 cm.

Signatures: [A],B².

Pagination: [1] title-page; [2] Advertisement; [3]–8 Text.

There is a folded plan in front of the title-page.

The first five paragraphs were reprinted in the *London Spy*, 8 August 1761, and the whole pamphlet was included in Volume xiv of the *Works* (1788).

TEXT

All Pomp is instituted for the sake of the Public. A Shew without Spectators can no longer be a Shew. Magnificence in Obscurity is equally vain with *a Sun-dial in the Grave*.

As the Wisdom of our Ancestors has appointed a very splendid and ceremonious Inauguration of our Kings, their Intention was that they should receive their Crown with such awful Rites, as might for ever impress upon them a due Sense of the Duties which they were to take, when the Happiness of Nations is put into their Hands; and that the People, as many as can possibly be Witnesses to any single Act, should openly acknowledge their Sovereign by universal Homage.

By the late Method of conducting the Coronation, all these Purposes have been defeated. Our Kings, with their Train, have crept to the Temple through obscure Passages; and the Crown has been worn out of Sight of the People. Of the Multitudes, whom Loyalty or Curiosity brought together, the greater Part has returned without a single Glimpse of their Prince's Grandeur, and the Day that opened with Festivity ended in Discontent.

This Evil has proceeded from the narrowness and shortness of the Way through which the Procession has lately passed. As it is narrow, it admits of very few Spectators; as it is short, it is soon passed. The first Part of the Train reaches the Abbey before the whole has left the Palace; and the Nobility of *England,* in their Robes of State, display their Riches only to themselves.

HARLEIAN CATALOGUE

Published: Volumes I & II, 12 March 1743 (*General Evening Post*).

Volumes III & IV, 4 January 1744 (*Daily Post*).

Volume V, 8 April 1745 (*Westminster Journal*).

References: Boswell, *Life,* i:154, 158.

Courtney, p. 13.

Johnson's Contributions: Proposals, which were reprinted as the Preface to the first volume; revision of Preface to the third volume; editing and some notes in the earlier volumes.

Copies: Boston Public Library; Columbia; Library Company of Philadelphia; Library of Congress; Princeton; University of Iowa; Yale; Bodleian; British Museum; Glasgow University (2 copies); London Library; National Library of Scotland; Signet Library; R. B. Adam; Col. R. H. Isham; Johnson Birthplace at Lichfield and Johnson House at Gough Square.

Not a rare work.

JOHNSON's *Proposals* for printing 'the two first volumes of *Bibliotheca Harleiana*' are dated November 1, 1742. This was the first publication of his *Account of the Harleian Library,* a work that is still of considerable interest for its pronouncements on the importance of Catalogues to those engaged in literary and historical research, on the shortcomings of the great Bodleian collection, and on the scope of the collector's interest.[1]

Osborne had bought the Harleian Collection from the daughter of the Earl of Oxford as a speculative investment, and it is to his credit that he determined to preserve a record of it by preparing a careful catalogue, even though his primary purpose was to improve the salability of his stock. The general plan of the *Catalogue* was drawn up by Michael Maittaire, author of *Annales typographici,* who also wrote the Latin dedication to Lord Carteret. It is generally supposed

---

1. This was reprinted in the *Gentleman's Magazine,* xii(December 1742): 636–9, in the first volume of the *Harleian Catalogue,* in Davies's *Miscellaneous and Fugitive Pieces* (1773), and in the *Works.* A collotype facsimile of the original *Proposals* was printed for Dr. Chapman at the Clarendon Press in 1926, and is readily accessible.

that William Oldys, the compiler of the *Harleian Miscellany*, described most of the English books in the *Catalogue,* and that Johnson worked principally with the Latin books, but it' is difficult to distinguish between them, as Sir John Hawkins observed. When Johnson wrote in the *Proposals* 'Men of letters are engaged, who cannot even be supplied with amanuenses, but at an expence above that of a common catalogue,' he may have meant that he and Oldys were to supervise, revise, and annotate the entries which were made by subordinates. The fifth volume is not nearly so carefully prepared, and it is difficult to be sure that some entries are not repeated from the earlier volumes: Hawkins called the fifth volume 'nothing more than a catalogue of Osborne's old stock.'[2] One very valuable feature of the work to Johnson was that over a period of two years he was assured of a small but steady income from this source.[3]

Boswell does not mention the Preface to the third volume as a Johnsonian work, but it is included in the *Works* (Oxford 1825) and is usually accepted as Johnson's. It is not a very distinguished piece of writing, although there are characteristic Johnsonian touches. It is assuredly unnecessarily long, for it is chiefly an apology for the methods that Osborne has followed. I dislike to think that Johnson himself would have elaborated such a dull subject to such great length, more particularly since he wrote (forty years later) to Burney, 'A long apology is a hideous thing.'[4] I think, with Mr. Wheatley,[5]

2. Concerning the editing, see J. Hawkins, *Life of Johnson* (1787), pp. 133–143; and an article by Mr. Arundell Esdaile in the *Contemporary Review*, 126 (1924):200–210.

3. Johnson probably began work on the Collection in the autumn of 1742, and continued at least until the end of 1743. Note that Osborne was the publisher of Dr. James's *Medicinal Dictionary* in parts, 1742–5. I find no evidence that Johnson actually assisted in compiling the *Harleian Miscellany*, 1744–6, though he may have done so. During this period he seems to have had some regular income also from Cave. (See Introduction, p. xvii.)

4. Chicago Book and Art Auctions, 15 December 1931. The letter is dated 18 March 1782.

5. In *Transactions of the Bibliographical Society*, viii(1907):48.

that Johnson rewrote or revised Osborne's draught of the Preface.

Boswell suggests that the Advertisement in the *Gentleman's Magazine* for October 1743 is Johnson's, but this is an extremely doubtful attribution: the grammar is peculiar and the construction does not seem at all in Johnson's manner. There is another long Advertisement in the *Daily Post*,[6] but this is hardly by Johnson although it is rather better than the earlier one. I do not find it difficult to believe that some one else could write them, and I think it would have been impossible for Johnson to write two such advertisements without betraying his authorship.

Bibliographical Description

Catalogus / Bibliothecae Harleianae, / in locos communes distributus cum indice auctorum. / [*rule*] / [*mottoes*] / [*rule*] / Vol. I. / [*parallel rule*] / [*ornament*] / [*parallel rule*] / Londini: / Apud Thomam Osborne. / MDCCXLIII.

In Vols. II, III, and IV the first rule is removed, and there is only a single rule below the volume number. Vols. III & IV are dated 1744. The fifth volume has a long and crowded title-page in English, and is dated 1745.

Five volumes, octavo in half-sheets. Fifth volume on cheaper paper. The first two volumes were issued in parts, five sheets in

---

6. Issue for 16 March 1744. One of the better sentences is: 'As the price of books was no obstacle to the late noble collector, nothing was more frequent, than to have in this library, not only a great variety of editions of the same writer, but many copies of the same edition, and sometimes of such editions as are not to be found in those collections which have been formed with the greatest diligence; have been long transmitted from one hand to another, and improved by the successive labours of many proprietors.' But this does not seem Johnsonian.

Croker seems to imply that Boswell referred to the Advertisement of the Proposals for the *Harleian Miscellany* at the end of the volume. R. Anderson in his *Life of Johnson* (1815), p. 98, likewise considers it a reference to the Proposals. Boswell's ambiguity is perhaps changed to a real error by Hill. Unless one is willing to accept the suggestion of Anderson and Croker, and to agree that Boswell has carelessly written *Catalogue* instead of *Miscellany,* one must believe that Boswell overlooked completely the unmistakable Proposals for the *Miscellany*. See p. 52 below.

each part, at one shilling. (See *Proposals* and Advertisement in *Gentleman's Magazine,* November 1742.)

Copy at Yale measures 21 × 12.5 cm.

Facsimile of title-page in second volume of the Catalogue of the R. B. Adam Library.

Copies were priced at 10/– for two volumes, and the purchaser later could return the volumes and apply the purchase price to any book that he wished to buy.

Signatures: Vol. I: a,A–Qqq⁴.
    Vol. II: [a],b⁴; c²; B–Mmmm⁴.
    Vol. III: 4 leaves; a,B–Fff⁴.
    Vol. IV: 3 leaves; Ggg–5Q⁴; 5R(one leaf).
    Vol. V: 2 leaves; A–3K⁴.

Pagination: Vol. I: [i] title-page; [ii] blank; [iii–vi] Dedication; [vii–viii] Advertisements of books; [1]–8 An Account of the Harleian Library (Johnson's Proposals); 1–488 Catalogue.

  Vol. II: [i] blank; [ii] Advertisement; [iii] title-page; [iv] Correction; v–xx Index titulorum; 489–1034 Catalogue; 1–37 Prints and Drawings; [38–40] Advertisements of books.

  Vol. III: [i] title-page; [ii] Advertisement; [iii–viii] Proposals for *Harleian Miscellany* (Johnson); [ix–xii] Preface (see text below); [xiii]–xvi Index capitum; [1]–408 Catalogue.

  Vol. IV: [i] title-page; [ii] Advertisement; [iii–vi] Proposals for Salmon's History; 409–858 Catalogue.

  Vol. V: [i] title-page; [ii] blank; [iii–iv] Index capitum; 1–448 Catalogue.

The second volume lacks Sigs. Yy, Zz, & Bbbb-Gggg; the pagination skips from 831 to 842. The irregularities are probably caused by errors in calculation and by carelessness.

The notes in the third volume are infrequent after the first five sheets, and in the fourth volume there are no notes except in special cases. For an explanation see the apology in the fifth paragraph of the Preface below.

The preliminary leaves of the third volume are puzzling. The first leaf, the title-page, is unsigned. The second leaf, the title-page of the *Proposals,* is likewise unsigned. The third leaf is signed A2. It may be that the title-page of the volume was imposed as A4.

The last leaf of Vol. IV was probably printed as the first leaf of the preliminary sheet.

It is immediately apparent that the fifth volume was an after-thought. It is carelessly prepared and printed on a cheaper paper. The books are not classified, so that it is merely an alphabetical list of miscellaneous books.

PREFACE
(In third volume, rewritten by Johnson)

Having prefixed to the former Volumes of my Catalogue an Account of the prodigious Collection accumulated in the *Harleian* Library, there would have been no Necessity of any Introduction to the subsequent Volumes, had not some Censures, which this great Undertaking has drawn upon me, made it proper to offer to the Public an Apology for my Conduct.

The Price, which I have set upon my Catalogue, has been represented, by the Booksellers, as an avaricious Innovation; and, in a Paper published in the *Champion*, they, or their Mercenary, have reasoned so justly, as to allege, that, if I could afford a very large Price for the Library, I might therefore afford to give away the Catalogue.

I should have imagined, that Accusations, concerted by such Heads as these, would have vanished of themselves, without any Answer; but, since I have the Mortification to find that they have been in some Degree regarded by Men of more Knowledge than themselves, I shall explain the Motives of my Procedure.

My original Design was, as I have already explained, to publish a methodical and exact Catalogue of this Library, upon the Plan which has been laid down, as I am informed, by several Men of the first Rank among the Learned. It was intended by those who undertook the Work, to make a very exact Disposition of all the Subjects, and to give an Account of the remarkable Differences of the Editions, and other Peculiarities, which make any Book eminently valuable; and it was imagined, that some Improvements might, by pursuing this Scheme, be made in Literary History.

With this View was the Catalogue begun, when the Price was fixed upon it in the public Advertisements; and it cannot be denied, that such a Catalogue would have been willingly purchased by those who understood its Use. But, when a few Sheets had been printed, it was discovered, that the Scheme was impracticable, without more Hands than could be procured, or more Time than the Necessity of a speedy Sale would allow, the Catalogue was therefore continued without Notes, at least in the greatest Part; and, though it was still performed better than those which are daily offered to the Public, fell much below the original Design.

It was then no longer proper to insist upon a Price; and therefore, though Money was demanded upon Delivery of the Catalogue, it was only taken as a Pledge, that the Catalogue was not, as is very frequent, wantonly called for, by those who never intended to peruse it, and I therefore promised that it should be taken again in Exchange for any Book rated at the same Value.

It may be still said, that other Booksellers give away their Catalogues without any such Precaution, and that I ought not to make any new or extraordinary Demands. But, I hope, it will be considered, at how much greater Expence my Catalogue was drawn up; and be remembered, that when other Booksellers give their Catalogues, they give only what will be of no Use when their Books are sold, and what, if it remained in their Hands, they must throw away; whereas, I hope, that this Catalogue will retain its Use, and, consequently, its Value, and be sold with the Catalogues of the *Barberinian* and *Marckian* Libraries.

However, to comply with the utmost Expectations of the World, I have now published the second Part of my Catalogue, upon Conditions still more commodious for the Purchaser, as I intend, that all those, who are pleased to receive them at the same Price of five Shillings a Volume, shall be allowed at any Time, within three Months after the Day of Sale, either to return them in Exchange for Books, or to send them back, and receive their Money.

Since, therefore, I have absolutely debarred myself from receiving any Advantage from the Sale of the Catalogue, it will be reasonable to impute it rather to Necessity than Choice, that I shall continue it to two Volumes more, which the Number of the single Tracts, which have been discovered, make indispensably requisite. I need not tell those who are acquainted with Affairs of this Kind, how much Pamphlets swell a Catalogue, since the Title of the least Book may be as long as that of the greatest.

Pamphlets have been for many Years, in this Nation, the Canals of Controversy, Politics, and Secret History, and therefore will, doubtless, furnish Occasion to a very great Number of curious Remarks. And I take this Opportunity of proposing to those who are particularly delighted with this Kind of Study, that, if they will encourage me, by a reasonable Subscription, to employ Men qualified to make the Observations, for which this Part of the Catalogue will furnish Occasion, I will procure the whole fifth and sixth Volumes, to be executed in the same Manner with the most laboured Part of this, and interspersed with Notes of the same Kind.

If any excuse were necessary for the Addition of these Volumes, I have already urged, in my Defence, the strongest Plea, no less than absolute Necessity, it being impossible to comprise in four Volumes, however large, or however closely printed, the Titles which yet remain to be mentioned.

But, I suppose, none will blame the Multiplication of Volumes, to whatever Number they may be continued, which every one may use, without buying them, and which are therefore published at no Expence but my own.

There is one Accusation still remaining, by which I am more sensibly affected, and which I am therefore desirous to obviate, before it has too long prevailed. I hear that I am accused of rating my Books at too high a Price, at a Price which no other Person would demand. To answer this Accusation, it is necessary to enquire what those, who urge it, mean by a high Price. The Price of Things valuable for their Rarity is intirely arbitrary, and depends upon the variable Taste of Mankind, and the casual Fluctuation of the Fashion, and can never be ascertained, like that of Things only estimable according to their Use.

If, therefore, I have set a high Value upon Books; if I have vainly imagined Literature to be more fashionable than it really is, or idly hoped to revive a Taste well nigh extinguished, I know not why I should be persecuted with Clamour and Invective, since I only shall suffer by my Mistake, and be obliged to keep those Books, which I was in Hopes of selling.

If those, who charge me with asking an *high Price*, will explain their Meaning, it may be possible to give them an Answer less general. If they measure the Price at which the Books are now offered, by that at which they were bought by the late Possessor, they will find it diminished at least Three Parts in Four: If they would compare it with the Demands of other Booksellers, they must first find the same Books in their Hands, and they will be, perhaps, at last reduced to confess, that they mean, by a high Price, only a Price higher than they are inclined to give.

I have, at least, a Right to hope, that no Gentleman will receive an Account of the Price from the Booksellers, of whom it may easily be imagined that they will be willing, since they cannot depreciate the Books, to exaggerate the Price; and I will boldly promise those who have been influenced by malevolent Reports, that, if they will be pleased, at the Day of Sale, to ex-⋅ amine the Prices with their own Eyes, they will find them lower than they have been represented.

HARLEIAN MISCELLANY

First number published: 24 March 1744 *(Daily Post)*.
References: Boswell, *Life,* i:175.
        Courtney, p. 15.
Johnson's Contribution: Proposals; Introduction.
Copies: Amherst (2 vols.); Harvard; Library of Congress; Yale; Bodleian; British Museum; Edinburgh University; Glasgow University; National Library of Scotland; Signet Library; R. B. Adam; Col. R. H. Isham.

THE separate folio printing of Johnson's *Proposals* for the *Harleian Miscellany* has only recently been discovered, and it is a rarity. Proposals were issued at the beginning of January 1744, and reprinted in the third volume of the *Harleian Catalogue* and at the end of the *Gentleman's Magazine* for 1743.[1] There are no important changes in the text, except the amusing addition of the 'Saxon k' in the word 'public' by the printer of the *Gentleman's Magazine*.[2] The text is reproduced from a copy of the folio *Proposals* now owned by Professor Tinker:

An ACCOUNT of this UNDERTAKING.

It has been for a long Time, a very just Complaint, among the Learned, that a Multitude of valuable Productions, published in small Pamphlets, or in single Sheets, are in a short Time, too often by Accidents, or Negligence, destroyed, and intirely lost; and that those Authors, whose Reverence for the Public has hindered them from swelling their Works with Repetitions, or encumbering them with Superfluities, and who, therefore, deserve the Praise and Gratitude of Posterity, are

1. I have found the *Proposals* advertised all through the month of January in the *Daily Post*. It is possible that they were first announced in December. Professor Tinker's copy, like the copy formerly owned by Mr. Jerome Kern, was printed in April or May, 1744. The copy in the R. B. Adam Library seems to be of the same issue.

2. Similarly, in reprinting Johnson's Life of Sydenham, the *Gentleman's Magazine* adds the 'Saxon k' to the words 'rustic' and 'physic.'

forgotten, for the very Reason for which they might expect to be remembered. It has been long lamented, that the Duration of the Monuments of Genius and Study, as well as of Wealth and Power, depends in no small Measure on their Bulk; and that Volumes, considerable only for their Size, are handed down from one Age to another, when compendious Treatises, of far greater Importance, are suffered to perish, as the compactest Bodies sink into the Water, while those, of which the Extension bears a greater Proportion to the Weight, float upon the Surface.

This Observation hath been so often confirmed by Experience, that, in the Neighbouring Nation, the common Appellation of small Performances is derived from this unfortunate Circumstance; a *flying Sheet,* or a *fugitive Piece,* are the Terms by which they are distinguished, and distinguished with too great Propriety, as they are subject, after having amused Mankind for a While, to take their Flight, and disappear for ever.

What are the Losses which the Learned have already sustained, by having Neglected to fix those Fugitives in some certain Residence, it is not easy to say; but there is no Doubt that many valuable Observations have been repeated, because they were not preserved; and that, therefore, the Progress of Knowledge has been retarded, by the Necessity of doing what had been already done, but was done for those who forgot their Benefactor.

The obvious Method of preventing these Losses, of preserving to every Man the Reputation he has merited by long Assiduity, is to unite these scattered Pieces into Volumes, that those, which are too small to preserve themselves, may be secured by their Combination with others; to consolidate these Atoms of Learning into Systems, to collect these disunited Rays, that their Light and their Fire may become perceptible.

Of encouraging this useful Design, the Studious and Inquisitive have now an Opportunity, which, perhaps, was never offered them before, and which, if it should now be lost, there is not any Probability that they will ever recover. They may now conceive themselves in Possession of the Lake into which all those Rivulets of Science have for many Years been flowing; but which, unless its Waters are turned into proper Channels, will soon burst its Banks, or be dispersed in imperceptible Exhalations.

In the *Harleian* Library, which I have purchased, are treasured a greater Number of Pamphlets and small Treatises, than were, perhaps, ever yet seen in one Place; Productions of the Writers of all Parties, and of every Age, from the Reformation; collected with an unbounded and unwearied Curiosity, without Exclusion of any Subject.

So great is the Variety, that it has been no small Labour to peruse the Titles, in order to reduce them to a rude Division, and range their Heaps under General Heads; of which the Numbers, though not yet encreased by the Subdivision, which an accurate Survey will necessarily produce, cannot but excite the Curiosity of all the Studious, as there is scarcely any Part of Knowledge, which some of these Articles do not comprehend.

This is the extent of Johnson's essay in the folio issue. In the *Gentleman's Magazine* and in the *Harleian Catalogue* there are two additional paragraphs:

The Heads under which they lie ranged at present, but ranged without any nice Distinction, or regular Method, are those of,

[long list]

As many of these Tracts must be obscure by Length of Time, or defective for Want of those Discoveries which have been made since they were written, there will be sometimes added Historical, Explanatory, or Supplemental Notes, in which the Occasion of the Treatise will be shewn, or an Account given of the Author, Allusions to forgotten Facts will be illustrated, or the Subject farther elucidated from other Writers.

Although Boswell overlooked this pamphlet, Hawkins assigned it to Johnson.[3] It is a pleasantly written essay: my personal preference is greatest for the fourth paragraph, in which the allusion to Atoms of Learning and disunited Rays recalls long searches for learned monographs which, in our time, are scattered and lost in the bulky volumes of miscellaneous periodical publications.

Professor Walter Raleigh wrote that Osborne employed Johnson and William Oldys as fellow-labourers in the compilation of the *Harleian Miscellany*.[4] This assertion, while I think it very likely, I cannot prove. Short notices are printed by way of preface to many of the pamphlets which are included in the *Miscellany,* and it may be that a thorough search would reveal Johnson's style in some of them.

Bibliographical Description

The / Harleian miscellany: / or, a / collection / of / scarce, curious, and entertaining / pamphlets and tracts, / as well in manuscript as in print, / found in the late / Earl of Oxford's

---

3. Sir John Hawkins, *Life of Johnson* (1787), p. 146. See note, p. 45.
4. *Six Essays on Johnson* (Oxford 1910), p. 119. He may have intended to write *Harleian Catalogue.*

library. / Interspersed / with historical, political, and critical notes. / With / a table of the contents, and an alphabetical index. / [*rule*] / Vol. I. / [*parallel rule*] / London: / Printed for T. Osborne, in Gray's-Inn. MDCCXLIV.

Eight volumes, in quarto; 26.7 × 20.8 cm. uncut. Issued in weekly parts, one shilling each, and usually thirteen parts to a volume. Volumes iii–vi are dated 1745; volumes vii and viii are dated 1746. I collate only the first volume.

Signatures: [A],a,b,B–4H⁴.

Pagination: [i] title-page; [ii] blank; [iii] Dedication; [iv] blank; v–xii Subscribers and list of booksellers; xviii(*i.e.* xiii)–xvi Contents; i–viii Introduction by Johnson; [1]–600 Text; 601–608 Index.

Each volume in turn is inscribed to a dedicatee.

The set in the Harvard College Library was the gift of Thomas Hollis. (See below, *Proceedings of the Committee for French Prisoners.*)

The Proposals were reprinted more than once with the advertisements of the parts. One advertisement (*Westminster Journal,* 29 December 1744) announces that the first volume has been reprinted to satisfy the demand. If this statement is reliable, a systematic search may discover two early editions before that of 1753 and, presumably, two editions of Johnson's Preface. (I have not yet attempted a thorough search.)

Editions:

There were two independent reprints of the *Harleian Miscellany* which were undertaken simultaneously in 1808. One or the other of these is in most libraries. Johnson's Introduction, under its better known title, 'Essay on the Origin and Importance of Small Tracts and Fugitive Pieces,' was included in Ernest Rhys, *Literary Pamphlets* (London 1897), i:41–54, and in the Oxford *World's Classics,* No. 304. It was first included in Johnson's Works by Davies in his *Miscellaneous and Fugitive Pieces* (1773).

In 1753 the first volume only of the *Harleian Miscellany* was reprinted: the effects on Johnson's Introduction offer a good example of the degeneration of texts. None of the typographical mistakes of the first edition have been corrected, and several new errors have been introduced by the compositor. (For the possibility of a variant first edition, see the preceding note.)

THE INTRODUCTION.

Though the Scheme of the following *Miscellany* is so obvious, that the Title alone is sufficient to explain it; and though several Collections have been formerly attempted upon Plans, as to the Method, very little, but, as to the Capacity and Execution, very different from Ours; we, being possessed of the greatest Variety for such a Work, hope for a more general Reception than those confined Schemes had the Fortune to meet with; and, therefore, think it not wholly unnecessary to explain our Intentions, to display the Treasure of Materials, out of which this *Miscellany* is to be compiled, and to exhibit a general Idea of the Pieces which we intend to insert in it.

There is, perhaps, no Nation, in which it is so necessary, as in our own, to assemble, from Time to Time, the *small* Tracts and *fugitive* Pieces, which are occasionally published: For, besides the general Subjects of Enquiry, which are cultivated by us, in common with every other learned Nation, our Constitution in Church and State naturally gives Birth to a Multitude of Performances, which would either not have been written, or could not have been made publick in any other Place.

The *Form* of our *Government,* which gives every Man, that has Leisure, or Curiosity, or Vanity, the Right of enquiring into the Propriety of publick Measures; and, by Consequence, obliges those, who are intrusted with the Administration of *National* Affairs, to give an Account of their Conduct, to almost every Man, who demands it, may be reasonably imagined to have occasioned *innumerable* Pamphlets, which would never have appeared under *arbitrary* Governments, where every Man lulls himself in Indolence under Calamities, of which he cannot promote the Redress, or thinks it prudent to conceal the Uneasiness of which he cannot complain without Danger.

The Multiplicity of *Religious Sects* tolerated among us, of which every one has found Opponents and Vindicators, is another Source of unexhaustible Publication, almost peculiar to ourselves; for, *Controversies* cannot be long continued, nor frequently revived, where an *Inquisitor* has a Right to shut up the Disputants in Dungeons, or where Silence can be imposed on either Party, by the Refusal of a *License*.

Not that it should be inferred from hence, that *Political* or *Religious* Controversies are the *only* Products of the *Liberty* of the *British Press;* the Mind once let loose to Enquiry, and suffered to operate without Restraint, necessarily deviates into peculiar Opinions, and wanders in new Tracks, where she is indeed sometimes lost in a Labyrinth, from which, tho' she cannot return, and scarce knows how to proceed; yet, sometimes, makes useful Discoveries, or finds out nearer Paths to Knowledge.

The boundless Liberty, with which every Man may write his own Thoughts, and the Opportunity of conveighing new Sentiments to the Publick, without Danger of suffering either Ridicule or Censure, which every Man may enjoy, whose Vanity does not incite him too hastily to own his Performances, naturally invites those, who employ themselves in Speculation, to try how their Notions will be received by a Nation, which exempts Caution from Fear, and Modesty from Shame; and it is no Wonder, that where Reputation may be gained, but needs not be lost, Multitudes are willing to try their Fortune, and thrust their Opinions into the Light, sometimes with unsuccessful Haste, and sometimes with happy Temerity.

It is observed, that, among the Natives of *England,* is to be found a greater Variety of Humour, than in any other Country; and, doubtless, where every Man has a full Liberty to propagate his Conceptions, Variety of Humour must produce Variety of Writers; and, where the Number of Authors is so great, there cannot but be some worthy of Distinction.

All these and many other Causes, too tedious to be enumerated, have contributed to make *Pamphlets* and *small Tracts* a very *important* Part of an *English* Library; nor are there any Pieces, upon which those, who aspire to the Reputation of *judicious* Collectors of Books, bestow more Attention, or greater Expence; because many Advantages may be expected from the Perusal of these small Productions, which are scarcely to be found in that of larger Works.

If we regard *History,* it is well known, that most *Political* Treatises have for a long Time appeared in this Form, and that the first Relations of Transactions, while they are yet the Subject of Conversation, divide the Opinions, and employ the Conjectures of Mankind, are delivered by these *petty* Writers, who have Opportunities of collecting the different Sentiments of Disputants, of enquiring the Truth from living Witnesses, and of copying their Representations from the Life; and, therefore, they preserve a Multitude of particular Incidents, which are forgotten in a short Time, or omitted in formal Relations, and which are yet to be considered as Sparks of Truth, which, when united, may afford

Light in some of the darkest Scenes of State, as, we doubt not, will be sufficiently proved in the Course of this *Miscellany;* and which it is, therefore, the *Interest* of the Publick to preserve unextinguished.

The same Observation may be extended to Subjects of yet more Importance. In Controversies that relate to the Truths of Religion, the first Essays of Reformation are generally timorous; and those, who have Opinions to offer, which they expect to be opposed, produce their Sentiments, by Degrees; and for the most Part in *small Tracts:* By Degrees, that they may not shock their Readers with too many Novelties at once; and in *small Tracts,* that they may be easily dispersed, or privately printed; almost every Controversy, therefore, has been, for a Time, carried on in Pamphlets, nor has swelled into larger Volumes, till the first Ardor of the Disputants has subsided, and they have recollected their Notions with Coolness enough to digest them into Order, consolidate them into Systems, and fortify them with Authorities.

From *Pamphlets,* consequently, are to be learned the *Progress* of every Debate; the various State, to which the Questions have been changed; the Artifices and Fallacies, which have been used; and the Subterfuges, by which Reason has been eluded: In such Writings may be seen how the Mind has been opened by Degrees, how one Truth has led to another, how Error has been disentangled, and Hints improved to Demonstration. Which Pleasure, and many others are lost by him, that only reads the *larger Writers,* by whom these scattered Sentiments are collected, who will see none of the Changes of Fortune, which every Opinion has passed through, will have no Opportunity of remarking the transient Advantages, which Error may sometimes obtain, by the Artifices of its Patron, or the successful Rallies, by which Truth regains the Day, after a Repulse; but will be to him, who traces the Dispute through, into particular Gradations, as he that hears of a Victory, to him that sees the Battle.

Since the Advantages of preserving these *small Tracts* are so numerous; our Attempt to unite them in Volumes cannot be thought either *useless* or *unseasonable;* for there is *no other* Method of securing them from Accidents; and they have already been so long neglected, that this Design cannot be delayed, without hazarding the Loss of many Pieces, which deserve to be transmitted to another Age.

The Practice of publishing Pamphlets, on the most important Subjects, has now prevailed more than *two Centuries* among us;

and, therefore, it cannot be doubted, but that, as no large Collections have been yet made, many curious Tracts must have perished; but it is too late to lament that Loss; nor ought we to reflect upon it, with any other View, than that of quickening our Endeavours, for the Preservation of those that yet remain, of which we have now a *greater Number,* than was, perhaps, ever amassed by any *one* Person.

The first Appearance of Pamphlets among us is generally thought to be at the new Opposition raised against the Errors and Corruptions of the Church of *Rome.* Those, who were first convinced of the Reasonableness of the *New Learning,* as it was *then* called, propagated their Opinions in small Pieces, which were cheaply printed; and, what was then of great Importance, easily concealed. These Treatises were generally printed in foreign Countries, and are not, therefore, not⁵ always very correct. There was not then that Opportunity of Printing in *private,* for, the Number of Printers were small, and the Presses were easily overlooked by the Clergy, who spared no Labour or Vigilance for the Suppression of *Heresy.* There is, however, Reason to suspect, that some Attempts were made to carry on the Propagation of Truth by a *secret* Press; for one of the first Treatises, in Favour of the Reformation, is said, at the End, to be printed *at Greenwich, by the Permission of the Lord of Hosts.*

In the Time of King *Edward the Sixth,* the Presses were employed in Favour of the *Reformed* Religion, and *small Tracts* were dispersed over the Nation, to reconcile them to the new Forms of Worship. In this Reign, likewise, *Political* Pamphlets may be said to have been begun, by the Address of the Rebels of *Devonshire;* all which Means of propagating the Sentiments of the People so disturbed the Court, that no sooner was Queen *Mary* resolved to reduce her Subjects to the *Romish* Superstition; but she artfully, by a *Charter* granted to certain Freemen of *London,* in whose Fidelity, no doubt, she confided, intirely prohibited *all* Presses, but what should be licensed by them; which Charter is that by which the Corporation of *Stationers,* in *London,* is at this Time incorporated.

Under the Reign of Queen *Elizabeth,* when Liberty again began to flourish, the Practice of writing Pamphlets became more general; Presses were multiplied, and Books more dispersed; and, I believe, it may properly be said, that the *Trade of Writing* be-

5. Not even this glaring error was corrected in the second edition.

gan at this Time, and that it has ever since gradually increased in the Number, though, perhaps, not in the Stile of those that followed it.

In this Reign, was erected the first *secret* Press against the Church as now Established, of which I have found any certain Account. It was employed by the *Puritans,* and conveighed from one Part of the Nation to another, by them, as they found themselves in Danger of Discovery. From this Press issued most of the Pamphlets against *Whitgift,* and his Associates, in the Ecclesiastical Government; and, when it was at last seized at *Manchester,* it was employed upon a Pamphlet, called, *MORE WORK FOR A COOPER.*

In the peaceable Reign of King *James,* those Minds, which might, perhaps, with less Disturbance of the World, have been engrossed by War, were employed in Controversy; and Writings of all Kinds were multiplied among us. The Press, however, was not wholly engaged in Polemical Performances, for more innocent Subjects were sometimes treated; and it deserves to be remarked, because it is not generally known, that the Treatises of *Husbandry* and *Agriculture,* which were published about that Time, are so numerous, that it can scarcely be imagined by whom they were written, or to whom they were sold.

The next Reign is too well known to have been a Time of Confusion, and Disturbance, and Disputes of every Kind; and the Writings, which were produced, bear a natural Proportion to the Number of the Questions that were discussed at that Time; each Party had its Authors, and its Presses, and no Endeavours were omitted to gain Proselytes to every Opinion. I know not whether this may not properly be called, *The Age of Pamphlets;* for, though they, perhaps, may not arise to such Multitudes as Mr. *Rawlinson* imagined, they were, undoubtedly, more numerous than can be conceived by any who have not had an Opportunity of examining them.

After the Restoration, the same Differences, in Religious Opinions, are well known to have subsisted, and the same Political Struggles to have been frequently renewed; and, therefore, a great Number of Pens were employed, on different Occasions, till, at length, all other Disputes were absorbed in the *Popish* Controversy.

From the Pamphlets which these different Periods of Time produced, it is proposed, that this *Miscellany* shall be compiled; for which it cannot be supposed that Materials will be wanting, and, therefore, the only Difficulty will be in what Manner to dispose them.

Those who have gone before us, in Undertakings of this Kind, have ranged the Pamphlets, which Chance threw into their Hands, without any Regard either to the Subject on which they treated, or the Time in which they were written; a Practice, in no wise, to be imitated by us, who want for no Materials; of which we shall chuse those we think best for the *particular* Circumstances of *Times* and *Things,* and most instructing and entertaining to the Reader.

Of the different Methods which present themselves, upon the first View of the great Heaps of Pamphlets, which the *Harleian Library* exhibits, the two which merit most Attention, are to distribute the Treatises according to their *Subjects* or their *Dates;* but neither of these Ways can be conveniently followed. By ranging our Collection in *Order of Time,* we must necessarily publish those Pieces first, which least engage the Curiosity of the Bulk of Mankind, and our Design must fall to the Ground for want of Encouragement, before it can be so far advanced as to obtain general Regard: By confining ourselves for any long Time to any *single Subject,* we shall reduce our Readers to one Class, and, as we shall lose all the Grace of Variety, shall disgust all those who read chiefly to be diverted. There is likewise one Objection of equal Force, against both these Methods, that we shall preclude ourselves from the Advantage of any future Discoveries, and we cannot hope to assemble at once all the Pamphlets which have been written in any Age or on any Subject.[6]

It may be added, in Vindication of our intended Practice, that it is the same with that of *Photius,* whose Collections are no less Miscellaneous than ours, and who declares, that he leaves it to his Reader, to reduce his Extracts under their proper Heads.

Most of the Pieces, which shall be offered in this Collection to the Publick, will be introduced by short Prefaces, in which will be given some Account of the Reasons for which they are inserted; Notes will be sometimes adjoined for the Explanation of obscure Passages, or obsolete Expressions; and Care will be taken to mingle Use and Pleasure through the whole Collection. Notwithstanding *every Subject* may not be relished by *every Reader;* yet the Buyer may be assured that each Number will repay his generous Subscription.

6. The reader will observe that the problem of arrangement which Johnson discusses in this paragraph is precisely the problem that confronted Percy in the preparation of the *Reliques* twenty years later.

DR. JOHNSON AND JOHN HOOLE

ALMOST the only personal anecdote recorded about John Hoole is that he three times had the misfortune to fracture the patella of his leg. He was a quiet, unobtrusive man who spent a great part of his life as a clerk in the India Office. To most of his contemporaries he was known merely as John Hoole, the translator, or, from his most successful translation, 'Tasso' Hoole. Yet he was one of Johnson's most intimate friends over a long period of years, they frequently dined together, and Johnson took some part in almost every one of Hoole's publications. To Hoole and to his son, the Reverend Samuel Hoole, Johnson bequeathed 'each a book at their election.'[1]

Johnson read the manuscripts and advised the presentation of *Cyrus* and *Cleonice,* he wrote Dedications certainly for *Jerusalem Delivered* and for *Metastasio* and probably for *Cyrus,* and he at least assisted in the distribution of the Proposals for *Ariosto.*[2]

CYRUS: A TRAGEDY

Published: 20 December 1768 (*London Chronicle*).
Johnson's Contribution: Dedication.
Copies: Boston Public Library; Columbia (2 copies); Harvard; Library Company of Philadelphia; New York Public Library (2 copies); Texas (2 copies); Yale (2 copies); Bodleian (3 copies);

1. They chose *Lucretius* (1725) and *Terence* (1726). The volumes are now in the Johnson Birthplace at Lichfield. Several lots were bought by Hoole at the sale of Johnson's Library, according to the annotated copy of the *Catalogue* which is now in the Yale Library.
2. Three of these books will be discussed below. For *Cleonice* see Boswell, *Life,* ii:289. The Manuscripts of the Dedications to *Jerusalem Delivered* and *Metastasio* were sold at Sotheby's, 17–19 February 1930. For the Proposals for *Ariosto* (of which I have not yet seen a copy), see Johnson's letter of January, 1781 (Boswell, *Life,* iv:70). I think that Johnson may have helped in the composition of the Preface to Hoole's pamphlet, the *Present State of the English East-India Company's Affairs.*
   According to the memoir in the *Monthly Mirror,* xvi(August 1803):121ff., Hoole was introduced to Johnson by Hawkesworth in 1761.

British Museum (2 copies); Bibliothèque Nationale; Cambridge University.

Cyrus was adapted from Metastasio's *Ciro Riconosciuto,* and it was acted successfully on 3 December 1768, but it has never been a good play to read. A contributor to the *European Magazine* in 1792 wrote that Hoole, encouraged perhaps by Oldmixon, his chief in the India Office, retired to the country to write the tragedy, and that he then communicated it to Anna Williams. She encouraged him to read it to Johnson, who told Hoole 'he might send his play to the stage.'[1] An Epilogue was furnished by Hawkesworth. The Dedication to the book speaks of the favorable reception which the play met with from the public, and must therefore have been composed later than the third of December. It is very brief, yet it seems to me to be characteristic of Johnson's manner, not only from the use of his favorite phrase 'goodness and condescension' but also because of the balance of the last clause of the second paragraph. When Hoole dedicated his *Cleonice* in 1775 he did not attempt a dedicatory essay, so that it is impossible to contrast his style with that of Johnson in such a composition.

Bibliographical Description

Cyrus: / a / tragedy. / As it is performed at the / Theatre Royal / in / Covent-Garden. / By / John Hoole. / London: / Printed for T. Davies, in Russel-Street, Covent-Garden. / M.DCC.LXVIII.

Octavo in half-sheets; Price: 1/6.

Signatures: [A],B–L⁴.

Pagination: [i] half-title; [ii] blank; [iii] title-page; [iv] blank; [v–vi] Dedication; [vii] Prologue; [viii] Dramatis Personae; [1]–79 Text; [80] Epilogue.

The only bibliographical peculiarity is the lack of a second edition, probably through a mistake in numbering. There is a third

1. A. Sägesser, *John Hoole* (Berne 1917), p. 20.

edition dated 1769, and also a third edition dated 1772. They are distinct editions. There was also an edition printed at Dublin in 1769, and the play was included in Bell's *British Theatre* in 1795.

DEDICATION

TO THE DUCHESS OF NORTHUMBERLAND, &c.

MADAM,

Permit me to assure YOUR GRACE of the deep sense I retain of Your great Goodness and Condescension in the Protection which You have been pleased to extend to my first Effort in the Drama.

Were I to listen to those suggestions that naturally arise in the mind of a Writer, on the first dawnings of success, the favourable reception which this Tragedy has met with from the Public would lead me to hope that it might not be found wholly unworthy of YOUR GRACE's Patronage: but when I reflect how many circumstances contribute to please on the Stage, where every Thought or Expression is enforced with the graces of action and utterance, I cannot but be anxious lest the Reader should withhold that approbation in the closet which the Spectator testified in the representation.

It is with the utmost Deference I submit the following Scenes to YOUR GRACE's Perusal; and am, MADAM, with the greatest respect, YOUR GRACE's most obliged most obedient and most devoted servant,

JOHN HOOLE.

Clement's Inn,
14 Dec. 1768.

JERUSALEM DELIVERED

Published: 1 June 1763 (*London Chronicle*).
References: Boswell, *Life,* i:383.
          Courtney, p. 101.
Johnson's Contribution: Dedication.
Copies: Yale; British Museum; R. B. Adam; Dr. R. W. Chapman.

PROPOSALS for Hoole's translation were advertised 10 April 1761.[1] No copies are known to me to have survived, but I

1. This is the date given by C. Welsh, *A Bookseller of the last Age.* The Proposals were advertised in the *London Chronicle* for 21 May 1761. It was with Johnson's approbation that Hoole undertook this translation. See Hoole's

doubt whether Johnson assisted with the Proposals. The Dedication, one of Johnson's best, was printed by Boswell in his second edition. The manuscript of this Dedication, in Johnson's hand, is now owned by Dr. A. S. W. Rosenbach; by his kindness I have been enabled to study the very interesting revisions in the text. Unlike the Dedication to *Metastasio,* there is in this case no certain proof that Johnson read the proofs of the Dedication. It does offer, however, convincing evidence of two facts: that Johnson revised carefully when he composed, and that the printer corrected the spelling and punctuation.

In the first line of the third paragraph, Johnson substituted 'observe' for 'consider,' and in the next line he altered 'honour' to 'happiness.' 'Countenance,' in the fourth line of the same paragraph, was inserted to replace a word which may have been 'sanction.' More interesting is the revision of the third line of the second paragraph. Johnson first wrote: 'and if he could return again to his former state would rejoice to put(?) the.' Then the last two words were deleted to alter the tense of the infinitive, when he wrote: 'to have been reserved to.' He seems finally to have decided that the sentence was not likely to attain a felicitous conclusion, for he deleted the whole clause, and wrote above the line: 'and in reviewing his life it is not easy to forbear to wish that he had lived in a happier time.' (The published text reads 'forbear a wish.') This surely is proof, if any were needed, that the exactness of Johnson's diction was due not to accident but to study.

The printer followed his usual custom when he capitalized certain important nouns which Johnson had begun with small letters. The printer also corrected (perhaps silently) Johnson's spelling of the words 'Authours' and 'Descendents.'

Preface, p. xiv. In the *Gentleman's Magazine,* xxxi(September 1761):422, a specimen is printed, with the statement that the first book has been printed and presented to the friends of the translator.

Both Hoole and Johnson seem to have been unaware that a translation of the *Jerusalem Delivered* into blank verse, by Philip Doyne, was published at Dublin in 1761.

In the first line of the last paragraph, the printer inserted 'been' which Johnson had carelessly omitted. In the fourth line of the third paragraph Johnson wrote, I think, 'secured.' The word 'procured' may be the compositor's mistake; if so, it was overlooked in proof or else allowed to stand as an equally suitable word. Johnson's manuscript concludes with the words 'Madam Your Majesty's,' so that in this case the last words were added by Hoole or by the printer. Such are the most interesting alterations in the text.

Hoole's translation is little read now, but it was reprinted many times, well into the nineteenth century. Johnson was of course in the list of subscribers to the first edition. His copy is listed in lot 128 in the *Catalogue* of his Library (1785).

Bibliographical Description

Jerusalem Delivered; / an heroick poem: / translated from the Italian / of / Torquato Tasso, / by John Hoole. / Vol. I. [II] / [*engraving, a different scene in each volume*] / London, / Printed for the author: / and sold by R. and J. Dodsley, in Pall-mall; P. Vaillant, / in the Strand; T. Davies, in Russell Street, Covent Garden; / J. Newbery, in St. Paul's Church Yard; Z. Stuart, in / Pater-noster-Row; J. Brotherton, at the Royal Exchange; / D. Prince, at Oxford; and W. Thurlbourn and J. / Woodyer, at Cambridge. MDCCLXIII.

Two volumes; octavo; 21 × 13 cm.
Price: 10/6 sewed; 12/– bound.

Signatures: Vol. I: one leaf; a²; a(in brackets)⁷; a–c⁸; e(one leaf); B–Y⁸.
  Vol. II: one leaf; B–Aa⁸.

Pagination: Vol. I: [i] title-page; [ii] blank; [iii]–v Dedication; [vi] blank; [i–xiii] Subscribers; [xiv] Errata; i–xv Preface; [xvi] blank; xvii–xlviii Life of Tasso; one leaf, containing title of poem with verso blank; [1]–336 Text.
  Vol. II: title-page with verso blank; [1]–326 Text; 327–367 Index; [368] blank.
I have seen one copy in which the Dedication by the binder's error was bound after the list of subscribers.

The sheet containing the list of subscribers was probably intentionally missigned, and then the first leaf was cut away. There are some printer's errors in the signatures.

The engravings on the title-pages were by A. Walker.

The second edition, in duodecimo, was published in February, 1764. Thereafter I have recorded, from various sources, the following editions: Third, 1767; Fourth, 1772; Fifth, 1783; Seventh (Dublin), 1788; Seventh, 1792; 1797; Eighth, 1802; Eighth, 1803; 1807; 1810 (Chalmers' Poets); 1810 (First American edition, Newburyport); Tenth, 1811; 1816; 1818; 1819; 1821 (one volume, 24 mo).

DEDICATION

TO THE QUEEN.

MADAM,

To approach the High and the Illustrious has been, in all ages, the privilege of Poets; and though Translators cannot justly claim the same honour, yet they naturally follow their Authors as Attendants; and I hope that, in return for having enabled TASSO to diffuse his fame through the British Dominions, I may be introduced by him to the presence of YOUR MAJESTY.

TASSO has a peculiar claim to YOUR MAJESTY's favour, as a Follower and Panegyrist of the House of ESTE, which has one common Ancestor with the House of HANOVER; and in reviewing his life, it is not easy to forbear a wish that he had lived in a happier time, when he might, among the Descendants of that Illustrious Family, have found a more liberal and potent patronage.

I cannot but observe, MADAM, how unequally Reward is proportioned to Merit, when I reflect that the Happiness, which was with-held from TASSO, is reserved for me; and that the Poem, which once hardly procured to its Author the countenance of the Princes[2] of FERRARA, has attracted to its Translator the favourable notice of a BRITISH QUEEN.

2. In the manuscript, Johnson wrote 'Princess,' and this would be a natural word to use, for the sake of balance, with 'Queen.' In the manuscript, however, part of the double 's' (long and short) has been blotted, and a single letter which is probably intended for 's' has been inserted above the 'e' of 'Princess.' The printer clearly understood this as a correction, to 'Princes.' Compare Boswell, *Life*, i:383, where Dr. Powell has collated the text. It has 'Princes,' like the original, in the second edition, but 'Princess' in the third edition. Historically, either word is suitable, and I do not see how any final determination between the two is possible, except on the authority of the manuscript. In the third edition of the *Life*, Boswell (or Malone) appears to have thought that 'Princess' was more Johnsonian, and the manuscript indicates that this was Johnson's intention when he first constructed the sentence.

Had this been the fate of TASSO, he would have been able to
have celebrated the Condescension of YOUR MAJESTY in nobler
language, but could not have felt it with more ardent gratitude,
than,

MADAM, YOUR MAJESTY's most faithful, and devoted Servant,

John Hoole.

THE WORKS OF METASTASIO

Published: 20 June 1767 (*London Chronicle*).
Reference: Boswell, *Life,* iv:360, note 1.
Johnson's Contribution: Dedication.
Copies: Boston Public Library; Harvard; Library Company of
  Philadelphia; Bodleian; British Museum; Dr. R. W. Chapman;
  Professor C. B. Tinker.

THIS Dedication was first recognized as Johnson's when his
manuscript was offered for sale at Sotheby's in 1930. In the
Catalogue[1] a short passage was quoted inaccurately. The
original manuscript is now owned by the London firm of
G. Michelmore and Company, who very kindly permitted me
to examine it. The numerous alterations in Johnson's hand
disprove any suggestion that Johnson's dedications were written without very careful thought and frequent revision as he
wrote.[2] There are also certain differences of importance between the final reading of the manuscript and the printed
text: in the first line the manuscript reads, 'surveys that work
which he has'; the third paragraph begins, 'The writer'; the
fourth paragraph begins, 'Of the Wisdom'; at the end of the
same sentence the manuscript has 'every good mind' instead
of 'breast'; and the third line from the end reads in the manuscript, 'what to me appeared worthy to engage the greatest
mind.' (The manuscript ends with 'My Lord.') Every change
is slight, to be sure, but every one is felicitous, an improvement over the reading of the manuscript. These changes
establish conclusively, in my opinion, unless there was an-

1. Sotheby and Co., 17–19 February 1930, lot 184.
2. On this point, see also Johnson's revisions in the Dedication for Hoole's
Jerusalem Delivered and in his introductory paragraphs for Percy's review of
Grainger's *Sugar-Cane.*

other copy of the manuscript, that Johnson himself corrected the proofs, for Hoole would hardly have made such changes himself.

This book was never so successful as the *Jerusalem Delivered*. I think, on the evidence of a single play in the Yale Library, that the book was cut up in an attempt to dispose of the unsold copies as single plays. An enlarged edition, in three volumes, was published by Hoole in 1800.

Bibliographical Description

The / Works / of / Metastasio; / translated from the / Italian, / by / John Hoole. / Vol. I. [II] / London: / Printed for T. Davies, / in Russel Street Covent Garden. / MDCC-LXVII.

Two volumes, small octavo; 18 × 11 cm. Price: 6/–.

Signatures: Vol. I: plate; a⁶; B–X⁸; Y⁴; Z².
            Vol. II: plate; B–Z⁸.

Pagination: Vol. I: engraved title-page; [i]–iv Dedication; [v]–xi Preface; [xii] blank; [1]–332 Text, including *Artaxerxes, The Olympiad,* and *Hypsipile.*
        Vol. II: engraved title-page; [1]–350 Text, including *Titus, Demetrius,* and *Demophoon;* one blank leaf.

The title-pages are very beautifully designed, with a handsome border, by Isaac Taylor, who also engraved a headpiece for each drama. The headpiece for the Dedication is by Hall.

Signatures are frequently omitted on the second, third, and fourth leaves.

The first sheet in Volume I (Sig. a) was probably imposed so that the first and eighth leaves could be cut off. The blank leaf at the end of Volume II is sometimes wanting.

There was also, I think, a large-paper edition. Johnson's copy is listed in lot 189 in the *Catalogue* of his Library (1785).

DEDICATION

TO THE DUKE OF NORTHUMBERLAND, &c.

MY LORD,

The fondness with which every man surveys the work that he

has performed with labour, naturally disposes him to hope that it may please them, whose approbation is most to be desired.

By presenting this translation to YOUR GRACE, I may incur the charge of having indulged too far the passions of a writer; nor should I easily refute the accusation, were not my vanity supported by greater merit than my own.

The poet, whose works I have endeavoured to interpret, has a natural right to the notice of the Great. He is distinguished sometimes by graceful familiarity, and sometimes by easy magnificence; his mien is soft, though his sentiments are sublime. He mingles the wisdom of the politician with the passion of his dialogues, and the precepts of the moralist with the levity of his songs.

Of the justness of his civil reflections YOUR GRACE's own experience in great affairs will easily decide; and the purity of his moral maxims will in every good breast raise him a patron. His power of poetry is such, if it be not diminished by the inability of his translator, as gives novelty to that truth which is already known, and charms to that virtue which is already loved.

Such are the Dramas for which I take the liberty of soliciting YOUR GRACE's protection; and such is my veneration for YOUR GRACE's character, that nothing but what appeàred worthy to engage the most exalted mind, should have been presented to YOU by, MY LORD, YOUR GRACE's most obliged, most obedient, and most devoted servant,

JOHN HOOLE.

DR. JAMES, *MEDICINAL DICTIONARY*

First number published: 4 February 1742 (*Daily Post*).
References: Boswell, *Life,* i:18, 159; iii:22, 473.
   Courtney, p. 13.
Johnson's Contributions: Proposals; Dedication; some articles.
Copies: Boston Medical Library; Boston Public Library; Library Company of Philadelphia; Library of Congress; Surgeon-General's Library; University of Pennsylvania; Yale; Aberdeen University; Bodleian; British Museum (3 copies); Edinburgh University; Glasgow University; Signet Library; Col. R. H. Isham (vol. I).

THE name of Dr. Robert James, I find, is now hardly known to members of his own profession, although the Fever Powders, to which he owed his wealth and much of his fame, are still manufactured and sold. He was for many years one of Johnson's friends, though in later life not a very intimate one; perhaps his closest friend was bustling John Newbery who advertised and sold his Fever Powders so successfully. Johnson went to school with James at Lichfield, but it was in 1741 that Johnson first helped him with his publications.

Boswell ascribes to Johnson on internal evidence the Dedication of the *Medicinal Dictionary,* asserts that Johnson wrote, or assisted in writing, the Proposals, and adds that Johnson furnished some of the articles, although he himself is unable to identify any. Mrs. Piozzi says that the Dedication was acknowledged to her, and Mr. Hussey says, 'For this dedication Johnson received five Guineas of Dr. James.'[1] Of the authenticity of the Dedication there is therefore no doubt.

The Proposals have been properly catalogued under the name of Dr. James for many years in the British Museum, but no one seems to have looked at them until Dr. Powell called attention to them. They are dated 24 June 1741, four pages in folio. A study of the text makes it quite clear that Johnson was largely if not wholly the author. Four paragraphs at least are worth quoting:

As those to whom the foregoing Proposals shall be offered, may justly require an Account of the Design which they are requested to encourage, it seems necessary to subjoin a distinct View of our Undertaking, by which its Extent may be comprehended, and its Usefulness estimated.

It is doubtless of Importance to the Happiness of Mankind, that whatever is generally useful should be generally known; and he therefore that *diffuses* Science, may with Justice claim, among the Benefactors to the Public, the next Rank to him that *improves* it.[2]

Many MEDICINAL DICTIONARIES have been already written, some by Men whose only Praise was Assiduity and Labour; others, by such as added Learning to their Industry; and some, perhaps, by those, to whom an impartial Critic would have allowed neither the Wages of

1. Boswell, *Life,* i:18, 159.
2. Note that Johnson expressed much the same thought in his Advertisement subjoined to the Proposals for Bennet's *Ascham,* 1758 (reprinted in Boswell, *Life,* i:550).

Labour, nor the Laurels of Science, who have transcribed Truth and Error without Distinction, have been too ignorant to lop off the Superfluities of their Predecessors, and too lazy to supply their Defects.

The Art of *Chymistry* will only fall under our Consideration as a Branch of *Pharmacy,* for we are writing not a Philosophical, but a *Medicinal Dictionary;* and we shall think our Labour usefully bestowed, if we shall, by a familiar Explanation of its Terms and Processes, clear it from that Obscurity that has been thrown upon it, generally by the Folly of the Ignorant, but perhaps sometimes by the Envy of the Learned.

There is one other paragraph, near the end, which I shall reproduce because it seems to me to indicate more particularly Johnson's contributions to the *Dictionary:*

As an Inquiry after those who have contributed to our Advantage, is not only the Consequence of a natural Curiosity, but of a laudable Gratitude, the *History of Physicians,* being an Account of the Lives, Writings, and Characters of the principal Authors in Physic, will be inserted in the Work, as their Names occur in the Alphabet.

In other words, the most likely contributions of Johnson to the work would seem to be the Lives of the physicians. I have printed elsewhere[3] my reasons for accepting the following biographical entries as Johnsonian: Actuarius, Aegineta, Aesculapius, Alexander, Archagathus, Aretaeus, Boerhaave (in an enlarged form), and the historical and biographical part of the article 'Botany,' including the Life of Tournefort.

One later literary venture of Dr. James deserves brief notice. He published *A Dissertation on Fevers and Inflamma-*

3. (The Johns Hopkins University) *Bulletin of the Institute of the History of Medicine,* iv(June 1936):455–65. In 1773, in the second volume of his *Miscellaneous and Fugitive Pieces,* T. Davies printed the *Life of Boerhaave* from the *Medicinal Dictionary,* but in the *Works* and in the *Miscellaneous Pieces* published at Sheffield in 1804, the original version from the *Gentleman's Magazine* is reprinted.

A large section of Boerhaave's lectures on *Air* from his *Chemistry,* is inserted in the *Dictionary* under the article 'Aer.' This and other uses of Boerhaave's writings may have led to the expansion of the *Life of Boerhaave,* in order to include a brief criticism of his works.

The accounts of Hippocrates in the *Dictionary* suggest that Johnson and Dr. James worked independently. There are accounts, with cross-references, in the Preface, under 'Asclepiades,' and under 'Hippocrates.' But under 'Botany' (and hence, as I believe, by Johnson) is a brief account, entirely independent and noticeably different, without cross-references to the other passages.

tory Distempers. After the death of Goldsmith, the Fever Powders were violently attacked, and Dr. James prepared a *Vindication of the Fever Powder,* but he died before it was published. Dr. Johnson wrote the concluding paragraph to the Advertisement of this *Vindication;*[4] it has not been generally known that this was printed (a Johnsonian first edition) in the *London Chronicle,* 20 February 1777.

Of the value of the *Dictionary* itself, which has been called 'a mass of ignorance and conservatism,' I have no professional qualifications to judge. Fifty years later, Bartholomew Parr, in the Preface to his *London Medical Dictionary,* discussed it in a brief review of earlier Medical Dictionaries. His opinion seems to me fair and of some interest:

> About the middle of the century, Dr. James offered a vast work to the public, in three ponderous folios. The erudition which he displays is extensive, and his explanations are often satisfactory. He has collected all the learning of his predecessors, preserved their controversies, and added whatever a diligent attention to the works of the ancient physicians could contribute to the former stock. In the more strictly practical part of his dictionary, he has collected, with the same care, and has copied, not always with sufficient discrimination, the opinions of different practical authors. The diffuseness of his language contributes, however, to lessen the advantages which such a work ought to possess, as a ready resource in cases of difficulty; nor, in the mass of contending opinions, is it always easy to collect those comprehensive views, which will at once lead to a decisive and discriminated practice.

Bibliographical Description

A / Medicinal / dictionary; / including / [physic, surgery, anatomy, chymistry, and botany,] / in all their branches relative to medicine. / Together with a / history of drugs; / an account of their various / preparations, combinations, and uses; / and an / introductory preface, / tracing the progress

4. C. Welsh, *A Bookseller of the last Century* (1885), pp. 138–140. The *Vindication* was published with the eighth edition of the *Dissertation on Fevers* in 1778. See also Boswell, *Life,* iii:4, 389, 533.

Much interesting, but not very important, correspondence concerning the Powders was published in *The Times,* 24 December 1929 to 15 February 1930. Much of the same information was printed in *Notes and Queries* for 1925, *passim.*

of physic, and explaining the theories which / have princi-pally prevail'd in all ages of the world. / [*rule*] / With copper plates. / [*rule*] / By R. James, M.D. / [*rule*] / Vol. I. / [*rule*] / [*mottoes*] / [*parallel rule*] / London: / Printed for T. Os-borne, in Gray's-Inn; / and sold by J. Roberts, at the Oxford-Arms in Warwick-Lane. / [*short rule*] / M.DCC.XLIII.

The title-pages of the second and third volumes, both dated 1745, are all reset, although the page makes a similar appearance.

Folio; 40.5 × 25.5 cm.; three volumes. The first four numbers were published fortnightly; weekly thereafter. Each number con-tained five sheets and was sold for 1/–. I collate the first volume.

Signatures: [A],a–bb,B–11N².

Pagination: [i] title-page; [ii] blank; iii–iv Dedication; [i]–xcix Preface; [c] blank; Unpaged text (Sigs. B–11K): A– to Calculus; on Sigs. 11L–11N are eleven pp. of Explications of Plates, with one blank page.

(One plate is bound after Sig. T, one after Sig. Ii, and one after Sig. Kk. 19 plates are bound after Sig. 11K or, in some copies, after Sig. 11N.)

In the first volume, there is frequently a different title-page, which reads: . . . and / an introductory preface, tracing the progress of physic, and explaining / the theories which have prin-cipally prevail'd in all ages of the world. / . . . London, / Printed; and sold by T. Osborne, in Grays-Inn. Since the imprints of the second and third volumes, to the best of my knowledge, al-ways have the name of Roberts, it seems likely that this imprint, containing Osborne's name only, is an earlier form, or that alter-nate title-pages were prepared simultaneously.

The name of James Crokatt of the Society of Booksellers for Promoting Learning never appeared on the title-pages; he was associated with Osborne, however, in the advertisements of the Proposals and of the early numbers of the *Dictionary*. Concerning him, see the discussion of the *Publisher* below, pp. 193–4.

The third volume has a strange mixture of signatures, utilizing letters in brackets, Black Letter type, and asterisks, daggers, and asterisms; even then there is some repetition. It is probable that these various parts of the third volume were printed simultane-ously. The first few sheets are signed 'Vol. II,' perhaps inad-vertently.

The work was originally planned for two volumes. It may be that the growth in the bulk of the work was the reason for the omission of much of the biographical material in the latter part of the alphabet.

As late as June 1765, Osborne advertised the remaining copies of the work for five guineas in sheets. In December 1768 and in later years, the remaining copies were advertised by Newbery and Carnan for seven pounds bound. The slow sale of the edition must have decreased Osborne's profits. Johnson's copy was sold in 1785 for £3/19/0.

This is one of the Johnsonian books in which the Dedication and the Preface have been confused. Thus G. P. R. James, the grandson of Dr. James, wrote that the Preface did not sound like Johnson and that he had found the manuscript of the whole Preface written in Dr. James's hand. (See the communication from S. M. Ellis in the *Times Literary Supplement*, 20 December 1928. Dr. Powell replied in the same publication two weeks later.) Yet at Sotheby's six months later this Preface was offered as a Johnsonian item. (10 June 1929, lot 286.)

The *Medicinal Dictionary* was translated into French by Diderot and others, 1746–8, in six folio volumes.

DEDICATION
TO DR. MEAD.

SIR,

That the *Medicinal Dictionary* is dedicated to You, is to be imputed only to Your Reputation for superior Skill in those Sciences which I have endeavoured to explain and facilitate: And You are, therefore, to consider this Address, if it be agreeable to You, as one of the Rewards of Merit; and if otherwise, as one of the Inconveniences of Eminence.

However You shall receive it, my Design cannot be disappointed; because this public Appeal to Your Judgment will shew, that I do not found my Hopes of Approbation upon the Ignorance of my Readers; and that I fear His Censure least, whose Knowledge is most extensive.

I am, SIR, Your Most Obedient, Humble Servant,

R. James.

KENNEDY'S *CHRONOLOGY*

Published: 29 March 1763 (*St. James's Chronicle*).
References: Boswell, *Life*, i:366, 547.
            Courtney, pp. 4, 101.
Johnson's Contributions: Dedication and last paragraph.
Copies: Bowdoin; Columbia; Library of Congress; New York
    Public; Yale; Bodleian; British Museum; Cambridge Univer-
    sity; Edinburgh University; Bibliothèque Nationale; R. B.
    Adam; Dr. R. W. Chapman; A. T. Hazen.

More copies might appear if collectors were to seek the book.

JOHN KENNEDY, Rector of Bradley in Derbyshire, with the assistance of his wife, studied for forty-two years to establish the
date of the creation of the world. This information, for which
we are indebted to one of Mrs. Piozzi's marginal notes,[1] is perhaps a sufficient explanation of the publication of his *Complete System of Astronomical Chronology*. In 1751 he had
published another book of a similar nature, *A New Method
of . . . Scripture Chronology upon Mosaic Astronomical
Principles*. With this earlier book Johnson had no connection.
Little is known of Johnson's friendship with Mr. and Mrs.
Kennedy. Mrs. Piozzi says that Johnson regarded the woman
highly as a Hebrew scholar, and that her husband was a better
Grecian.[1] By Dr. Chapman it has been suggested that a manuscript sermon in the Yale University Library may have been
composed by Johnson for Mr. Kennedy.[2]

Boswell indicates that Johnson had acknowledged to him
the Dedication to the King, and there has never been any
doubt of the authorship. Boswell entered in his Journal, 23
March 1772: 'I had read in his Library this forenoon the
Dedication to Kennedy's *Scripture Chronology*, which I immediately knew to be his. I said, "You cannot deny it." He
answered, "Why, I don't deny it." '[3] Boswell seems to have
been somewhat disturbed by Johnson's statement about Rolt's

1. Quoted in Boswell, *Life*, i:547 (Appendix).
2. *The Times*, 29 September 1933, p. 13.
3. *Boswell Papers*, ix:30; xi:280.

Dictionary, 'Sir, I never saw the man and I never read the book,'[4] since, concerning Kennedy's *Chronology,* hé wrote of Johnson: 'He had certainly looked at this work before it was printed; for the concluding paragraph is undoubtedly of his composition, of which let my readers judge.'[5]

Bibliographical evidence I think has never been produced to support Boswell's assertion, although it has been available. The last leaf of the text is a cancel, apparently the only one in the whole book. Although I have never seen the leaf in its uncancelled state, I feel quite confident that the cancel was printed in order to substitute the fine conclusion which Johnson had composed.

Bibliographical Description

A / Complete system / of / astronomical chronology, / unfolding the Scriptures. / In which / [*contents*] / [*rule*] / [*two Latin quotations*] / [*rule*] / By John Kennedy, / rector of Bradley in Derbyshire. / [*double rule*] / London: / Printed by E. Allen, in Bolt-Court, Fleet-Street; / for Messrs. Davis and Reymers, in Holborn; W. Owen, in Fleet-Street; / and T. Hope, behind the Royal Exchange. / [*short rule*] / M.DCC. LXII.

Facsimile of title-page, dedication, and last page in the second volume of the Catalogue of the R. B. Adam Library.

Quarto; 26.5 × 20.5 cm. Price: £1/3/0 sewed; £1/5/0 bound.

Signatures: [A](half-sheet); *,**,***,a,b,d⁴; B–Zzzz⁴; †,††²; 5 folded tables; 1 leaf.

4. Boswell, *Life,* i:359.

5. *Ibid.,* i:366. The *Critical* and *Monthly* Reviews, in May and June, 1763, devoted much space to reviews of the book. The tone of both is friendly but far from laudatory. Kenrick in the *Monthly* quotes this concluding paragraph, and remarks: 'Without paying any particular regard to such a declamatory strain of compliment, we may safely say, it is very happy for mankind in general, and the Christian cause in particular, that the inspiration of the scriptural historians, and the validity of the sacred writings, may be proved by very different and more convincing arguments.' To Ferguson, who reviewed it in the *Critical,* Kennedy replied in a scarce pamphlet. Kennedy published several other pamphlets and there were a number of replies.

The tone of Kenrick's last paragraph makes one wonder whether he knew that Johnson had written the last paragraph of Kennedy's work.

Pagination: 4 unnumbered pages, containing title-page with verso blank, and Dedication; 23 unnumbered pages, containing Analysis of the Entire Work; one blank page; [i]–xxiii Introductory Discourse; [xxiv] blank; [1]–728 Text; i–viii Tables; 5 inserted folded tables; 1 leaf of Errata with verso blank.

There are no watermarks on the half-sheets signed with daggers, on the folded tables, on the errata leaf, or on the two preliminary leaves; Sigs. B–Yy have a fleur-de-lis for watermark; Sigs. Zz–Zzzz and the six sheets of introductory matter contain a different watermark.

Leaf Zzzz4, containing on verso the concluding paragraph written by Johnson, is a cancel in each of the seven copies that I have examined.

The unusual variety of signatures doubtless reflects the several afterthoughts of the author.

Johnson's copy is in lot 64 in the *Catalogue* of his Library (1785).

The Dedication was reprinted, with slight changes in punctuation and spelling, in Gleig's edition of the *Voyage to Abyssinia,* (*Works,* Volume xv, 1789, pp. 486–7).

In my own copy, there is a handsome folded plate preceding the first page of the text, engraved by Uffington and containing a number of astronomical figures, but this appears to have been taken from some other treatise and inserted here by a previous owner.

DEDICATION

TO THE KING.

SIR,

Having by long Labour, and diligent Enquiry, endeavoured to illustrate and establish the Chronology of the BIBLE, I hope to be pardoned the Ambition of inscribing my Work to YOUR MAJESTY.

An Age of War is not often an Age of Learning; the Tumult and Anxiety of Military Preparations seldom leave Attention vacant to the silent Progress of Study, and the placid Conquests of Investigation. Yet, surely, a Vindication of the Inspired Writers can never be unseasonably offered to the DEFENDER OF THE FAITH, nor can it ever be improper to promote that Religion without which all other Blessings are Snares of Destruction, without which Armies cannot make us safe, nor Victories make us happy.

I am far from imagining that my Testimony can add any Thing to the Honours of YOUR MAJESTY, to the Splendour of a Reign crowded with Triumphs, to the Beauty of a Life dignified by Virtue. I can only wish, that Your Reign may long continue such as it has begun, and that the Effulgence of Your Example may spread its Light through distant Ages, till it shall be the highest Praise of any future Monarch, that he exhibits some Resemblance of GEORGE THE THIRD.

I am, Sir, YOUR MAJESTY's Most obedient, Most devoted, and Most humble Subject, and Servant,

JOHN KENNEDY.

[Concluding paragraph]

Thus have I endeavoured to free religion and history from the darkness and difficulties of a disputed and uncertain chronology; from difficulties which have appeared insuperable, and darkness which no luminary of learning has hitherto been able to dissipate. I have established the truth of the Mosaical account, by evidence which no transcription can corrupt, no negligence can lose, and no interest can pervert. I have shewn, that the universe bears witness to the inspiration of its historian, by the revolution of its orbs, and the succession of its seasons; *that the stars in their courses fight against* incredulity, that the works of God give hourly confirmation to the *law,* the *prophets,* and the *gospel,* of which *one day telleth another, and one night certifieth another;* and that the validity of the sacred writings never can be denied, while the moon shall encrease and wane, and the sun shall know his going down.

LAUDER'S *ESSAY ON MILTON*

Published: 14 December 1749 (*General Advertiser*).
References: Boswell, *Life,* i:227–231.
     Courtney, p. 36.
Johnson's Contribution: Preface and Postscript.
Copies: Not rare. The reissue with the New Preface of the Booksellers is in the libraries at Harvard, the British Museum, Reading University, and the London Library.

THE controversy which Lauder stirred up by his publications was continued vigorously for several years, and the *Gentleman's Magazine* for 1747 and the succeeding years contains numerous references to it. Johnson was an innocent participator, but appearances were against him and he was believed by many, doubtless, to be equally blameworthy with Lauder. The publication of Johnson's *Life of Milton* thirty years later induced Archdeacon Francis Blackburne to insert in his *Memoirs of Hollis* a long attack on Johnson as the foe of Milton.[1] The controversy gave rise to many pamphlets, of which most have now only an antiquarian interest, and I have not attempted to study the question in detail. Dr. Douglas, who exposed Lauder's forgeries, has been immortalized by a passage in Goldsmith's *Retaliation*.

The Preface in its first form was published with Lauder's *Proposals for printing by subscription Hugonis Grotii Adamus Exsul, tragoedia: with an English version, and the lines imitated from it by Milton subjoined to the pages*. These *Proposals* were issued 5 September 1747[2] and were reprinted with some changes in the *Gentleman's Magazine*, xvii(August 1747):404. Of the *Proposals* I have seen only one copy, in the British Museum: from that copy I have taken the text which is reproduced below. The two additional paragraphs in the Preface to the *Essay on Milton* do not seem to me to be Johnsonian.

In support of the performance of *Comus* for the benefit of Mrs. Foster, 5 April 1750, Johnson inserted a letter in the *General Advertiser* for April 4. This was reprinted by Boswell.[3]

1. The attack on Johnson was also published separately as *Remarks on Johnson's Life of Milton:* Johnson, when he was shown a copy of this, wrote 'In the business of Lauder I was deceived, partly by thinking the man too frantic to be fraudulent' (Boswell, *Life,* i:231, note 2, quoted from Murphy). Johnson was so diametrically opposed to Milton in his political, religious, and critical principles that his high praise of Milton was obscured and his opponents easily convinced themselves that he shared the malevolence of Lauder. See also Courtney, p. 137.

2. I have taken the date from a statement in the *Gentleman's Magazine* that the Proposals, with a specimen, will, after the 5th instant, be deliver'd out. The *Gentleman's Magazine* for August would normally have been published during the first week in September.

3. Boswell, *Life,* i:227–8. The *Prologue* which Johnson furnished for *Comus* was reprinted by the Oxford University Press in 1925, together with Johnson's *Postscript* to Lauder's *Essay*.

In November, 1750, Rev. John Douglas published *Milton Vindicated from the charge of Plagiarism,* in which he exposed Lauder's forgeries. This book was announced as published on November 26, although the title-page is dated 1751. On November 28 the booksellers, John Payne and Joseph Bouquet, wrote the following advertisement which was published in the *London Gazetteer:*

> Upon the publication of the Rev. Mr. Douglas's Defence of Milton, in Answer to Lauder, we immediately sent to Lauder, and insisted upon his clearing himself from the Charge of Forgery which Mr. Douglas has brought against him, by producing the Books in Question. *He has this Day admitted the Charge,* but with great Insensibility. We therefore disclaim all Connexion with him, and shall for the future sell his Book ONLY as a Masterpiece of Fraud, which the Public may be supplied with at 1s. 6d. stitched.

Their New Preface, which was offered to former purchasers and bound in with the remaining copies, was dated Dec. 1, 1750. It apologizes for the imposition, states that the booksellers acted in good faith, that the Rev. Mr. Douglas has exposed Lauder after ten months of insolent triumph, and that they now reissue it merely 'as a curiosity of fraud and interpolation.' In addition there was, according to Courtney (p. 37), a Postscript dated January 2, 1750–51, pp. v–viii. Of the existence of this new Postscript I have no other knowledge, and Dr. Chapman tells me that he has not found Courtney's authority for the statement.

When Lauder's fraud had been exposed, Johnson dictated to Lauder an apology in the form of a *Letter to the Reverend Mr. Douglas,* a rare pamphlet of three sheets in quarto. This is dated December 20, 1750, but I have not found it advertised earlier than 3 January 1751 (*General Advertiser*). To Johnson's letter Lauder added some testimonies concerning his character and a Postscript affirming that he had had no intention to defraud, since he undertook only to test the prejudices of the idolaters of Milton.[4]

4. There is a useful summary of Lauder's strange career in an article by A. H. Millar in *Blackwood's Edinburgh Magazine,* clxvi(Sept. 1899):381–96;

Bibliographical Description

An / Essay / on / Milton's / use / and / imitation / of the / moderns, / in his / Paradise Lost. / Things unattempted yet in prose / or rhime. Milton. / London: / Printed for J. Payne and J. Bouquet, / in Pater-noster-Row. / MDCCL.

Octavo; 21 × 12.5 cm. Originally published at 3/6, but reduced after Lauder's confession to 1/6.

Signatures: a⁸; b(half-sheet); B–L⁸; M(half-sheet).

Pagination: (Preliminary leaves unnumbered) title-page with verso blank; Dedication with verso blank; Preface (4 pp.); Extracts (10 pp.); Dates and Errata (4 pp.); Lauder's advertisement as a tutor, with advertisement by the booksellers on verso; 1–164 Text; [165–168] Postscript and notice of the Subscription for Mrs. Foster.

In one copy that I have seen, the New Preface of the Booksellers (4 pp.) is inserted between title-page and dedication, and b4 containing Lauder's advertisement is cut out. In another copy the New Preface is inserted after Johnson's Preface, and leaf b4 has not been removed.

The *Preface, Postscript,* and the dictated *Letter to Douglas* were all reprinted in Volume xiv of the *Works* (1788).

The Dedication, 'To the learned Universities of Oxford and Cambridge,' is one of the most amazing features of Lauder's boldness.

TEXT

(The text of the Preface is taken from the *Proposals* 1747)

It is now more than half a century since the *Paradise lost,* having broke through the cloud with which the unpopularity of its

but his suggestion that the letter opposing one of Lauder's schemes (*Gentleman's Magazine,* xvii:530) may have been by Johnson has no justification.

Lauder was not chastened by the exposure: in 1751 he addressed an *Apology for Mr. Lauder* to the Archbishop of Canterbury, and in 1754 he published *King Charles I vindicated from the charge of plagiarism . . . and Milton himself convicted of forgery.* The review of this in the *Gentleman's Magazine,* for February 1754, was thought by Chalmers to be Johnsonian. I find no trace of Johnson's style.

Murphy's account, differing somewhat from Boswell's, is reprinted in *Miscellanies,* i:394.

See F. Blackburne's *Mem. of Hollis* (1780),ii:*536, where a letter signed by Lauder is attributed to Johnson. *G. M.* xvii(Aug. 1747):363–4. Hardly justified.

author for a time obscured it, has attracted the general admiration of mankind, who have endeavoured to compensate the error of their first neglect by lavish praises, and boundless veneration. There seems to have arisen a contest among men of genius and literature, who should most advance its honour, or best distinguish its beauties. Some have revised editions, others have published commentaries, and all have endeavoured to make their particular studies in some degree subservient to this general emulation.

Among the inquiries to which this ardour of criticism has naturally given occasion, none is more obscure in itself, or more worthy of rational curiosity, than a retrospection of the progress of this mighty genius in the construction of his work, a view of the fabric gradually rising, perhaps from small beginnings, till its foundation rests in the centre, and its turrets sparkle in the skies; to trace back the structure through all its varieties to the simplicity of its first plan, to find what was first projected, whence the scheme was taken, how it was improved, by what assistance it was executed, and from what stores the materials were collected; whether its founder dug them from the quarries of nature, or demolished other buildings to embellish his own.

This inquiry has been indeed not wholly neglected, nor perhaps prosecuted with the care and diligence that it deserves. Several critics have offered their conjectures, but none have much endeavoured to enforce or ascertain them. Mr. *Voltaire* tells us, without proof, that the first hint of *Paradise lost* was taken from a farce called *Adamo,* written by a player; Dr. *Pearce,* that it was derived from an *Italian* tragedy called *Il paradiso perso;* and Mr. *Peck,* that it was borrowed from a wild Romance.⁵ Any of these conjectures may possibly be true, but as they stand without sufficient proof, it must be granted likewise, that they may all possibly be false, at least they cannot preclude any other opinion, which, without argument, has the same claim to credit, and may perhaps be shewn by resistless evidence to be better founded.

5. Johnson refers to the following works:

(a) Voltaire, *Essay upon the Epick Poetry of the European Nations* (London 1727), the second paragraph in the section devoted to Milton. In Voltaire's revision of the essay in French the words 'a player' were omitted.

(b) Z. Pearce, *A Review of the Text of the twelve books of Milton's Paradise Lost: in which the chief of Dr. Bentley's emendations are considered* (London 1733), Preface, p. vii.

(c) Francis Peck, *New Memoirs of Milton* (London 1740), pp. 51, 52. Or, since Peck quotes the opinions of Voltaire and Pearce, Johnson may have derived his information wholly from Peck's work.

It is related, by steady and uncontroverted tradition, that the *Paradise lost* was at first a tragedy, and therefore amongst trage- dies the first hint is properly to be sought. In a manuscript pub- lished from *Milton's* own hand, among a great number of sub- jects for tragedy, is *Adam unparadised,* or *Adam in Exile;* and this therefore may be justly supposed the embryo of this great poem. As it is observable that all these subjects had been treated by others, the manuscript can be supposed nothing more than a memorial or catalogue of plays, which, for some reason, the writer thought worthy of his attention. When therefore I had ob- served that *Adam in Exile* was named amongst them, I doubted not but, in finding the original of that tragedy, I should disclose the genuine source of *Paradise lost.* Nor was my expectation dis- appointed; for, having procured the *Adamus Exsul* of *Grotius,* I found, or imagined myself to find, the first draught, the *prima stamina* of this wonderful poem. And, as I cannot doubt but the discovery will give the same pleasure to others as to me, I hope the publick will favour this attempt, since the original is so scarce, that *Gronovius,* with all the influence that his learning gives him, was not able to procure me a printed copy, the version that will be added is new and elegant, and the question which this publication tends to illustrate, is, in the highest degree, worthy of general regard.[6]

6. The version printed in the *Gentleman's Magazine* (August 1747) divides the last sentence into two, with the period after 'a printed copy.' There are no other important differences.

As the Preface to the *Essay on Milton* this was reprinted without any revi- sion or change except in punctuation. But, since the last sentence was no longer appropriate, it was dropped, and the following paragraphs were added. They are I believe by Lauder and not by Johnson.

"Having thus traced the ORIGINAL of this work, I was naturally induced to continue my search to the COLLATERAL RELATIONS, which it might be supposed to have contracted, in its progress to MATURITY: and having, at least, per- suaded my own judgment, that the search has not been intirely ineffectual, I now lay the result of my labours before the public; with full conviction, that, in questions of this kind, the world cannot be MISTAKEN, at least cannot long continue in ERROR.

"I cannot avoid acknowledging the CANDOUR of the author of that excellent monthly book, the GENTLEMAN'S MAGAZINE, in giving admission to the speci- mens in favour of this argument; and his IMPARTIALITY, in as freely inserting the several answers. I shall here subjoin some EXTRACTS from the xvii. volume of this work, which I think suitable to my purpose. To which I have added, in order to obviate every pretence for cavil, a LIST of the authors quoted in the following ESSAY, with their respective DATES, in comparison with the DATE of PARADISE LOST."

POSTSCRIPT.

When this essay was almost finished, the splendid edition of PARADISE LOST, so long promised by the reverend Dr. *Newton,* fell into my hands; of which I had, however, so little use, that as it would be injustice to censure, it would be flattery to commend it: and I should have totally forborn the mention of a book that I have not read, had not one passage, at the conclusion of the life of MILTON, excited in me too much pity and indignation to be suppressed in silence.

"*Deborah,* MILTON's youngest daughter," says the editor, "was "married to Mr. *Abraham Clarke,* a weaver in *Spittle-fields,* and "died in *August* 1727, in the 76th year of her age. She had ten "children. *Elizabeth,* the youngest, was married to Mr. *Thomas* "*Foster,* a weaver in *Spittle-fields,* and had seven children, who "are all dead; and she herself is aged about *sixty,* and *weak* and "*infirm.* She seemeth to be a *good plain sensible woman,* and has "confirmed several particulars related above, and informed me of "some others, which she had often heard from her mother." These the doctor enumerates, and then adds; "in all probability "MILTON's whole family will be *extinct* with her, and he can *live* "only in his writings. And *such is the caprice of fortune,* this "*grand-daughter* of a MAN, who will be an everlasting glory to the "nation, has now for *some years,* with her husband, kept a *little* "*chandler's* or *grocer's shop, for their subsistence,* lately at the "lower *Holloway,* in the road between *Highgate* and *London,* "and at present in *Cock Lane,* not far from *Shoreditch Church.*"

That this relation is true, cannot be questioned:—but, surely, the honour of letters, the dignity of sacred poetry, the spirit of the *English* nation, and the glory of human nature, require—that it should be true no longer. In an age, in which statues are erected to the honour of this great writer, in which his effigy has been diffused on medals, and his work propagated by translations, and illustrated by commentaries; in an age, which, amidst all its vices, and all its follies, has not become infamous for want of charity: it may be, surely, allowed to hope, that the living remains of MILTON will be no longer suffered to languish in distress. It is yet in the power of a great people, to reward the poet whose name they boast, and from their alliance to whose genius, they claim some kind of superiority to every other nation of the earth; that poet, whose works may possibly be read when every other monument of *British* greatness shall be obliterated; to reward him—not with pictures, or with medals, which, if he sees, he sees with contempt, but—with tokens of gratitude, which he, perhaps, may even now consider as not unworthy the regard of an immortal spirit. And, surely, to those, who refuse their names to no other scheme of expence, it will not be unwelcome, that a SUBSCRIPTION is proposed, for relieving, in the languor of age, the pains of disease, and the contempt of poverty, the grand-daughter of the author of PARADISE LOST. Nor can it be questioned, that, if I, who have been marked out as the ZOILUS of MILTON, think this regard due to his posterity, the design will be warmly seconded by those, whose lives have been employed, in discovering his excellencies, and extending his reputation.[7]

LENGLET DU FRESNOY'S
CHRONOLOGICAL TABLES

Published: 19 November 1762 (*Lloyd's Evening Post*).
Johnson's Contribution: Preface.
Copies: Columbia; Illinois State Library; Library Company of Philadelphia; Library of Congress; New York Public (Vol. i); Princeton; British Museum; Edinburgh University; Glasgow University; London Library; National Library of Scotland.

OF Nicholas Lenglet du Fresnoy, through a curious oversight, there is no mention in the *Life*. Of Thomas Flloyd (or Floyd) the translator there is one brief anecdote. Yet it seems to have been by the merest chance that Boswell failed to add this to his list of Johnsonian Prefaces. At the time when he discussed these writers with Johnson, Boswell had not thought of writing the *Life of Johnson;* and when in later years he complained about the expense to which he was put by his wish to own books for which Johnson had written Prefaces or Dedications, the conversations of 1763 had been forgotten by Johnson.

The story may be told briefly. On a rainy evening, 14 July 1763, Johnson and Boswell supped by themselves at the Mitre. More than once Boswell remarked that Johnson was in

7. As I have pointed out, this Postscript was reprinted in 1925 by the Oxford University Press.

a very good humour and that he himself was more than usually at ease in the presence of his famous friend. During the conversation Johnson said:

> Idleness is a disease which must be combated; but I would not advise a rigid adherence to a particular plan of study. I myself have never persisted in any plan for two days together. A man ought to read just as inclination leads him; for what he reads as a task will do him little good.[1]

Here there is no mention of du Fresnoy. But on the next day Boswell wrote to Temple:

> Mr. Johnson was in vast good humour, and we had much conversation. I mentioned Fresnoy to him. But he advised me not to follow a plan and he declared that he himself never followed one above two days. . . . He is to give me his advice as to what books I should take with me from England.[2]

Two weeks later, in another private conversation at the Turk's Head coffee-house, they talked of Derrick, and Boswell includes the story which Johnson had once told him about Flloyd and Derrick.[3] This is separated in the *Life* by only a few pages from the account of the supper at the Mitre, and it is not impossible that the story was recalled to Johnson's mind by Boswell's inquiry about du Fresnoy and that he told the story at that time.

Proof of Johnson's contribution is scanty but certain. In the advertisement of the book in *Lloyd's Evening Post*[4] the booksellers placed at the top 'Recommended by Samuel Johnson.' This can refer only to the Preface, and the style of this Preface is indubitably Johnson's. Both from the style and from the genial thrust at the French, I think that the Dedica-

---

1. Boswell, *Life*, i:428.
2. *Letters of Boswell*, edited by C. B. Tinker (Oxford 1924), i:22.
There is of course no certainty that the reference is to Flloyd's translation, but it is the most obvious explanation. It had been published only eight months earlier, it was in English, it was known to Johnson, and the introductory matter contains 'the short method of studying history and a catalogue of books necessary for that purpose, with some remarks on them.'
3. Boswell, *Life*, i:457. Another anecdote of Flloyd is reported in *Boswell Papers*, xi:274.
4. 19 November 1762.

tion may have been revised by Johnson, and I have therefore included the text of the Dedication, but it is hardly a Johnsonian utterance.

The fact that a copy of the book was owned by Johnson tends to confirm the attribution, though the presence or absence of a book in Johnson's library can not be considered independent proof either for or against any such attribution.[5]

The bibliographical description is based on the copy in the Library of Princeton University. This copy is of more than passing interest because it has on the title-page the autograph signature of John Witherspoon, a signer of the Declaration of Independence and an early president of Princeton. Like all the copies that I have seen, it has been heavily trimmed by the binder, although it is quite certainly an original binding.

Bibliographical Description

Chronological tables / of / universal history, / sacred and profane, ecclesiastical and civil; / from the / creation of the world, / to the / year one thousand seven hundred and forty-three. / With a / preliminary discourse / on / the short method of studying history; / and / a catalogue of books necessary for that purpose; / with some remarks on them. / By Abbé Lenglet duFresnoy. / In two parts. / Translated from the last French edition, and continued down to the / death of King George II. / Part the first. / [*double rule*] / London: / Printed for A. Millar, J. Newbery, R. Baldwin, W. Johnston, / D. Wilson, S. Crowder and Co. T. Jefferys, A. Hamilton, / J. Coote, H. Payne and Co. T. Becket and Co. and J. Walter. / MDCCLXII.

Two volumes, octavo. Price: 12/– bound.
Trimmed copy: 20.6 × 13 cm.

Signatures: Vol. I: [A](half-sheet); Index(2 leaves); a–g^8; h^4; i^2; B–X^8; Y^4; Y^{*2}.
Vol. II: 2 leaves; a(half-sheet),A–Hh^8.

5. In the *Catalogue* of Johnson's Library (1785), among 'octavo et infra,' lot 29 is: 'Fresnoy's *Chronology* 2 vol.' In the same lot is Warton's *Spenser*.

Pagination: Vol. I: [i] half-title; [ii] blank; [iii] title-page; [iv] blank; [v]–vi Dedication; vii–viii Preface; *–****(4 pp.) Contents; i–cxxiii Preliminary Discourse and Catalogue of Books; [cxxiv] blank; [1]–320 Tables, etc.; 321–332 Indices (one Erratum at bottom of p. 332).

Vol. II: 2 leaves unnumbered, containing half-title and title-page, with blank versos; iii–vii Author's advertisement; viii–x Contents; [1]–437 Tables, etc.; 438–496 Indices.

The two volumes are sometimes bound together.

There are a number of printer's errors, which seem to be of no significance. For the sake of completeness they are listed: a4 verso is signed, as well as recto; d4 is not signed; L2 is signed K2 in error; P3 is signed P in error; signature marks are omitted on S4 and T2–T4 because of the crowded page (or they may have been cut off by the binder); p. 284 is incorrectly numbered 184. All these are in Vol. I.

In Vol. II, the copy at Princeton lacks the half-title and title-page, and it is probable that they were omitted by the binder. The pagination of sheet a indicates that the printer did not intend at that time to print a half-title.

The preliminary matter of Vol. I is printed on so many sheets or parts of sheets that one cannot be certain how it was grouped. I suppose that the Contents and the last two leaves of the book may have been printed together after everything else had been completed, because of the use of index and asterisk for signatures. The printer already had two series of Roman numerals in his preliminary matter, and the unusual use of asterisks to indicate pagination was probably his attempt to prevent further confusion. These two leaves signed with an index, and paged with asterisks, containing the Contents, were printed to be bound at the end of the text of the first volume, preceding the Index to the volume. The direction line on p. 320 proves this, and the pages are so bound in some copies. I have also seen them bound at the end of the volume. The binder of President Witherspoon's copy disregarded the direction line, in order to place the Contents in a more usual position.

G. Kearsly is listed as one of the booksellers in the Advertisement in *Lloyd's Evening Post;* 'H. Payne and W. Cropley' there replaces the name of H. Payne and Co.

In Vol. II, pp. 194ff., the tables are printed in four parallel columns, and the catch-word (or direction line) at the end of each page is planned for the second column of the second page

following. This is a normal but difficult procedure; mistakes however are very few.

DEDICATION

To the RIGHT HONOURABLE the EARL
OF POMFRET.

My LORD,

At the same time that I have the honour of presenting this
work to your Lordship, as an acknowledgement of your many
favours to me; I have also the pleasure of reflecting on the propriety of offering a work of literature to your Lordship; who, to
the knowledge of the modern languages, have superadded the
more learned ones. These are the acquirements of many; but the
exalted understanding, good sense, and masterly elocution which
your Lordship possesses, in so extensive a degree, are the portion
of few. The world is too sensible of the truth of this, to suspect
me of adulation.

The difficulty attending this translation hath been far from
that common to translators; the many hundreds of names of persons and places, which *French* writers are so notoriously remarkable for corrupting, have cost me time and trouble to rectify, almost equal to that of compiling the whole work.

Tho' I have taken great care, I fear some mistakes have un-
avoidably escaped me: but if my part in this work should, upon
the whole, meet with your Lordship's sanction, I am persuaded it
will receive the concurrent approbation of every other person,
whose good opinion can do any honour to him, who is,

My Lord, Your Lordship's much obliged, and most obedient
servant,

THOMAS FLLOYD.

Sept. 8, 1762.

THE PREFACE.

The necessity of Chronology to a distinct and exact knowledge
of history, is too evident to require proof. History is little more
than romance to him who has no knowledge of the succession of
events, the periods of dominion, and the distance between one
great action and another. To adjust the course of time, and to
range transactions under their proper years, has long been one of
the great employments of learned industry. With physical or as-

tronomical chronology which consults the sky, divides the seasons, and regulates the year by necessary intercalations, the following work has little connection; it contains chiefly an historical
chronology, such as all nations, by whom polite learning is cultivated, have provided for the instruction of students, and of which
we have more than one in our own language, but less copious
than that which is here offered to the public. Tabular Chronology must always have this inconvenience, that the same, or
nearly the same space upon paper being allotted to one year as to
another, some barren years will have blank columns, and some
years crouded with events, cannot be fully dilated and displayed.
This inconvenience may be observed in Dr. *Blair's*[6] tables, of
which the construction is otherwise very commodious, and the
method very clear and pleasing. This work, therefore, excels all
that have been hitherto offered to the *English* student, as it contains a more exact enumeration of events in less room. Every species of history is comprised in it; and the reader, of whatever kind
be his studies, will not often find his curiosity disappointed. If
this recommendation appear too general, it may be limited by remarking, that though this work be useful to every class of students, it is peculiarly fitted for schools, where the youth, who are
about to read history, ought to be acquainted with the great revolutions of the world, and enabled to have, from its source, the
stream of succession to the present time; and that among the
higher classes it will be found eminently useful to young clergy-
men, as being written by an Ecclesiastic, it contains a very minute
account of the history of the church.

JOHNSON AND MRS. LENNOX

SURPRISINGLY little is known now about Charlotte (Ramsay)
Lennox, and her works are read only by literary antiquarians.
Yet she was esteemed by Johnson as the most talented of his
women friends, and her original works were frequently reprinted and translated. Many readers of Boswell doubtless
know Hawkins's account of the literary banquet after the

6. John Blair, *Chronology and History of the World*. With the beginning of
this Preface, the reader may like to compare Johnson's letter to Mrs. Thrale
in 1777: 'Chronology you know is the eye of history.' (*Letters*, ii:27.)

manner of the ancients which Johnson arranged in honour of Mrs. Lennox.[1] And Boswell names three of her books which he believes owe something to Johnson. A study of her publications, however, makes it appear that Johnson wrote for her six dedications, the *Proposals* for publishing her Original Works (a Johnsonian item that has not yet been recovered), one chapter in the *Female Quixote,* and two sections of her translation of Brumoy's *Greek Theatre.*[2]

The friendships of Mrs. Lennox with literary men seem to have been established by means of her own literary work. She became acquainted with Strahan, the printer, and in that way met and married Mr. Lennox who was employed by Strahan. Probably through Strahan she made the acquaintance of Johnson.[3] When she undertook her study of Shakespeare's sources, published in *Shakespear Illustrated,* she needed some one to help her with her Italian, and her husband found Baretti at a coffee-house. She agreed to help him with his Eng-

1. Quoted in Boswell, *Life,* i:255n. Some information about her is preserved also in Volume iv, pp. 10, 275, 524.

2. One other Dedication, that in her translation of *Memoirs for the History of Mme. de Maintenon* (1757), is well written, but I think not by Johnson. Additional evidence has recently been discovered that Johnson continued to help her, in two letters written to Johnson in 1778, published in the *Bulletin of the John Rylands Library,* xvi(1932):56–7. In one she appeals to him for help about her translation of Sully which Dodsley is reprinting without consulting her; in the second, which was written at some time after March 1776, she seeks his advice (probably) about the publication of her *Works.* It is also possible that Johnson corrected some of her poems: the version of 'On Reading Hutchinson on the Passions' which is printed as a specimen in her *Proposals for printing by subscription, Poems on several occasions* (November 1752) differs greatly from the version in her *Poems on Several Occasions* (1747), which was reprinted in *Harriot Stuart* (1751). The change renders it less personal and more like Johnson's moralizing strain. This in itself might not seem significant, but Baretti (in an *Ode to Charlotte Lennox*) accuses Johnson, 'who thinks a graceful nothing a sin and a vice,' of restraining her by his influence from writing love poetry. This ode was sent by Baretti to a friend in May 1754, and it seems very probable that it refers to some of Charlotte's poems in manuscript. There is a possibility, however, that Baretti refers to an early manuscript version of *Philander* (1758). The *Ode* is discussed by Miss Miriam Small in her study of Mrs. Lennox (New Haven 1935), pp. 155–161.

3. This is the most probable tradition. Another legend, accepted by the *DNB,* is that she was introduced to Johnson by her first publisher, Samuel Paterson. Johnson introduced her to Richardson.

lish in return, but according to Baretti she did not carry out her part of the bargain. It was she who introduced Baretti to Johnson.

In the study of Mrs. Lennox's relations with Johnson I have had the advantage of numerous suggestions from Miss Miriam Small of Wells College. In particular, she directed my attention to the important second edition of *Henrietta* (1761).

BRUMOY'S *GREEK THEATRE*

Published: 21 February 1760 (*London Chronicle*).
References: Boswell, *Life,* i:345.
          Courtney, pp. 97, 163.
Johnson's Contributions: Dedication; translation of the *Dissertation upon the Greek Comedy* and of the *General Conclusion.*
Copies: Boston Public Library; Detroit Public Library; Library Company of Philadelphia; Library of Congress; New York Society Library; Peabody Institute; Princeton; University of Chicago; Yale; Bodleian; British Museum; Bibliothèque Nationale; Signet; R. B. Adam; Dr. R. W. Chapman; Col. R. H. Isham; Dr. L. F. Powell.

THIS work was apparently undertaken by Mrs. Lennox as a commission from the booksellers, and she was aided by Lord Orrery who wrote the Preface and translated certain sections, by Dr. Gregory Sharpe, Dr. Grainger, and John Bourrya, and by Dr. Johnson. The book was therefore sponsored by a formidable array of scholars, but the translation by Mrs. Lennox has been criticized and the book was never reprinted. Very probably it was because of this work that Mrs. Lennox complained to the Duchess of Newcastle of 'my present Slavery to the Booksellers, whom I have the mortification to see adding to their heaps by my labours, which scarce produce me a scanty and precarious subsistence.'[1] Whether the booksellers added greatly to their heaps by this publication may reasonably be doubted.

It seems curious that Boswell, who knew that two long dis-

1. See the whole letter in the discussion of *Henrietta* below.

sertations were translated by Johnson (he marks them 'internal evidence,' but they are acknowledged in the book itself), should never have suspected the Dedication, which is one of Johnson's best. The explanation probably is that Boswell had never seen the work but had mentioned the *Dissertation upon the Greek Comedy* and the *General Conclusion* because he had found them included in Stockdale's Volume xiv of the *Works* (1788). I believe that the Dedication has been assigned in print to Johnson only by Mr. R. B. Adam in the Catalogue of his Johnsonian Library (1929), and he lists it without apparent consciousness that it is a new attribution. I suppose that the dedication is so certainly by Johnson that Mr. Adam failed to observe that it was not mentioned by Courtney.

External evidence is slight but it tends to support the attribution. Mrs. Lennox was ill and in the country during some parts of 1759 and 1760, particularly during the winter. Johnson had already written four dedications for her, and he was assuredly quite as available for a dedication as he was for help in translating. I do not know that the long delay in publication was caused by Johnson's delay in translating, but that may have been a contributing reason. The date of the Dedication, June 4, 1759, is presumably the date of its composition, and Johnson was in London then, although he made a trip to Oxford in July.

Johnson's copy, lot 64 in the *Catalogue* (1785), was sold for 8/–. Because of the two sections which he translated he would naturally have received a copy whether or not he had furnished the Dedication.

Bibliographical Description

The / Greek theatre / of / Father Brumoy. / Translated / by Mrs. Charlotte Lennox. / [*rule*] / In three volumes. / [*rule*] / Vol. I. / [*parallel rule*] / London: / Printed for Mess. Millar, Vaillant, Baldwin, Crowder, / Johnston, Dodsley, and Wilson and Durham. / MDCCLIX.

Three volumes, quarto; 25.5 × 20.5 cm.; two guineas bound.

Signatures: Vol. I: [A],a–c⁴; d²; a–p,B–Hhh⁴.
Vol. II: [A]²; B–Yyy⁴; [Zzz]².
Vol. III: [A]²; B–Xx,*Xx,Yy–Ppp⁴.

Pagination: Vol. I: [i] title-page; [ii] blank; [iii–v] Dedication; [vi] blank; [vii] Advertisement; [viii] blank; [i]–xxviii Preface; [i]–cxx Three discourses; [1]–422 Text; one blank leaf.

Vol. II: one blank leaf, followed by title-page, with verso blank; [1]–540 Text.

Vol. III: [i] title-page; [ii] blank; [iii] Advertisement; [iv] blank; [1]–478 Text; [479] Advertisement; [480] blank. (One sheet inserted after p. 344, containing pp. 337–344 with asterisks.)

In Vol. I, pp. vi and xxviii, the running title is spelled 'Preeace.' In Vol. III, p. 341 of the extra sheet is numbered 401 in error.

The extra sheet seems to have been needed to complete *The Birds.* Apparently the printer had estimated that *The Birds* would end with sheet Xx and had therefore begun to print *The Feasts of Ceres and Proserpine* on sheet Yy. (Similar miscalculations were made in the second volume of the *Preceptor* and in the second volume of Johnson's *Dictionary*.)

The two sections of the work which Johnson translated are in the third volume, pp. 123–161 and 428–440. They were included in the first volume of Davies's *Miscellaneous and Fugitive Pieces,* 1773.

The Earl of Corke and Orrery, in his Preface, praised both the *Female Quixote* and *Henrietta.*

The copy now in the Library of Congress was presented by Mrs. Lennox to Andrew Stone, secretary and confidant of the Duke of Newcastle and his Under-Secretary of State.

DEDICATION

TO HIS ROYAL HIGHNESS GEORGE, PRINCE OF WALES.

SIR,
On the day which fills every inhabitant of Britain with expectations of continued and uniform prosperity, may it be permitted me to acknowledge, with the greatest respect, my obligations to your Royal Highness, for suffering me to introduce this translation to the public under the protection of your illustrious name.[2]

2. The fourth of June, New Style, was the birthday of the Prince of Wales.

The arts of the drama, for which I have presumed to solicit your Royal Highness's patronage, have been always honoured with the protection of princes, as the arts which add grace to precept, and teach virtue by multiplying delights.

Of the employments which engage the labours and studies of mankind, some are incited by the power of necessity, and some dictated by the love of pleasure: to works of necessity, we are driven by nature; in pursuit of pleasure, we are influenced by example. Nations may receive plenty from the cultivation of the soil, but they must owe their politeness to the refinements of the court; and the encouragement which your Royal Highness has given to the endeavours of genius, has already kindled new ardors of emulation, and brightened the prospects of the learned and the studious, who consider the birth of your Royal Highness as the birth of science, and promise to themselves and to posterity, that from this day shall be reckoned a more illustrious period of letters and of patronage.

I am, with the profoundest respect, SIR, Your ROYAL HIGH-NESS's Most obedient, and Most humble Servant,

CHARLOTTE LENNOX.

June 4.
1759.

THE FEMALE QUIXOTE

Published: Friday, 13 March 1752 (*General Advertiser*).
References: Boswell, *Life,* i:367.
            Courtney, p. 38.
Johnson's Contributions: Dedication; most of the eleventh chapter of Book IX.
Copies: Salem Athenaeum; University of Pennsylvania (Singer); Yale; Bodleian; British Museum (2 copies); R. B. Adam; Miss Miriam Small.

BOSWELL was uncertain of the date of publication of the *Female Quixote,* but he ascribed the Dedication (to the Earl of Middlesex) to Johnson on internal evidence, and it has always been accepted as Johnson's. Like so many of these miscellaneous writings, the Dedication of the *Female Quixote* was included in Volume xiv of the *Works,* and from that source Boswell may have obtained his knowledge of the book.

The Reverend John Mitford, editor of the *Gentleman's Magazine,* first pointed out that the eleventh chapter of Book IX was almost certainly by Johnson.[1] The chapter-heading reads: 'Being, in the author's opinion, the best chapter in this history,' good evidence in itself that it was not by Mrs. Lennox herself. No other odd chapter by Johnson is known to me, and I therefore believe that Fanny Burney knew of this chapter by Johnson when she wrote:

> I daresay he hardly knows himself what he has written; for he has made numerous prefaces, dedications, odd chapters, and I know not what, for other authors, that he has never owned, and probably never will own.[2]

Fielding wrote a long and discriminating review of the *Female Quixote,* and praised it highly. His conclusion is:

> Upon the whole, I do very earnestly recommend it, as a most extraordinary and most excellent performance. It is indeed a work of true humour, and cannot fail of giving rational, as well as very pleasing, amusement to a sensible reader, who will at once be instructed and very highly diverted.[3]

The rapid sale of the edition seems to indicate that the public accepted Fielding's judgment. The frequency of the later editions will show that the book continued to maintain its popularity for a century. Although it is less read now, it has a good deal that is amusing, even though the plot may seem to

1. *Gentleman's Magazine,* New Series, xx(August 1843):132, and xxi(January 1844):41. The first and last paragraphs were probably added by Mrs. Lennox. In the middle of the chapter (vol. ii, p. 314) is one sentence containing remarks about 'An admirable writer of our own time' and 'the greatest genius of the present age.' This also was inserted by the author: Miss Small has pointed out to me that the passage reads much more smoothly if this sentence is omitted. I do not know whether Johnson was guilty of 'You was' in the sixth paragraph. According to Percy Fitzgerald, in his *Critical Examination of Hill's "Johnsonian" Editions* (London 1898), p. 35, Johnson used the form 'you was' on several occasions. Boswell did so generally; Malone corrected many instances in later editions of the *Life.*

2. *Diary of Madame D'Arblay,* edited by Austin Dobson (London 1904), ii:206.

3. *Covent-Garden Journal,* Number 24, 24 March 1752. Part of Fielding's review is quoted by the *Gentleman's Magazine,* xxii(March 1752):146, in a notice which Hill attributed to Johnson.

be elaborated and the dénouement delayed too much in the manner of the old romances at which its author aimed her satire. The late Professor Lounsbury's wit betrayed his judgment when he wrote of the *Female Quixote:* 'Occasionally it is spoken of even now as a work of genius by those who have not read it.'[4]

Bibliographical Description

The / Female Quixote; / or, the / adventures / of / Arabella. / [*rule*] / In two volumes. / [*rule*] / Vol. I. / [*rule*] / [*ornament*] / [*parallel rule*] / London: / Printed for A. Millar, over-against / Catharine-street in the Strand. / [*short rule*] / M.DCC.LII.

The title-page of the second volume is all reset, and the printer's ornament is different. The easiest way to identify it is by the line-division of the imprint: Printed for A. Millar, over-against Cathe- / rine-Street in the Strand. Some of the type is different.

Two volumes, duodecimo in twelves by cutting; 16.5 × 9.7 cm. Price: 5/- sewed, or 6/- bound.

Signatures: Vol. I: A^8; B–M^{12}; N^4.
　　　　　　Vol. II: one leaf; B–O^{12}; P^6; one leaf.

Pagination: Vol. I: [i] title-page; [ii] blank; [iii]–vi Dedication; [vii–xvi] Contents (no pagination); [1]–271 Text; [272] blank.
　　　　　Vol. II: title-page with verso blank; [1]–325 Text; [326] blank.

The second volume is much more poorly printed. Prof. William M. Sale of Cornell believes that the first volume was printed by Richardson; and that, perhaps because Richardson was too busy, the second volume was 'farmed out' to another printer. An unusual feature of this second volume is that it was printed with only five press-numbers, on pp. 21, 28, 64, 93, 144.

The preliminary leaves of the first volume (containing the Contents of both volumes) must have been printed with the last four leaves of the first volume. This may account for some discrepancies in the chapter-headings of the second volume.

Miss Talbot seems to have read and enjoyed the work on the

4. T. R. Lounsbury, *Shakespeare as a Dramatic Artist* (1901), p. 289.

day that it was officially published. See *A Series of Letters between Mrs. Carter and Miss Talbot,* edited by M. Pennington (London 1809), ii:69, 76.

Editions:

The Second Edition, 'Revised and Corrected,' was announced in the *General Advertiser,* 2 July 1752, less than four months after the publication of the first edition. It is in the same format, and (nearly) a page-for-page reprint. I have never attempted to estimate the extent of the textual revision: on p. 24 the first edition reads 'For a Villain, for a Ravisher, interrupted Arabella'; while the second edition reads 'For a Ravisher, interrupted Arabella, an impious Ravisher.' I suspect that other revisions are not of much greater significance.

Other editions include:

1783—2 volumes in one, octavo; also issued as part of the *Novelist's Magazine.*

1799—Cooke's edition.

1810—2 volumes, duodecimo; also issued as Vols. xxiii & xxiv of Mrs. Barbauld's *British Novelists.*

1820—Reissue of the *British Novelists.*

Dublin 1752—2 volumes, duodecimo; reprinted from the *first* London edition.

Dublin 1763—marked 'Third edition.'

It was also translated into German, French, and Spanish.

The Dedication by Johnson was not revised.

It is very probable that Mrs. Lennox's title inspired the title of Mrs. Tabitha G. Tenney's *Female Quixotism: exhibited in the romantic opinions and extravagant adventures of Dorcasine Sheldon.* There were four editions of this American novel.

DEDICATION

TO THE RIGHT HONOURABLE THE EARL OF MIDDLESEX.

My LORD,

Such is the Power of Interest over almost every Mind, that no one is long without Arguments to prove any Position which is ardently wished to be true, or to justify any Measures which are dictated by Inclination.

By this subtil Sophistry of Desire, I have been persuaded to hope, that this Book may, without Impropriety, be inscribed to

Your Lordship; but am not certain, that my Reasons will have the same Force upon other Understandings.

The Dread which a Writer feels of the public Censure; the still greater Dread of Neglect; and the eager Wish for Support and Protection, which is impressed by the Consciousness of Imbecillity; are unknown to those who have never adventured into the World; and I am afraid, my Lord, equally unknown to those, who have always found the World ready to applaud them.

'Tis, therefore, not unlikely, that the Design of this Address may be mistaken, and the Effects of my Fear imputed to my Vanity: They who see Your Lordship's Name prefixed to my Performance, will rather condèmn my Presumption, than compassionate my Anxiety.

But, whatever be supposed my Motive, the Praise of Judgment cannot be denied me; for, to whom can Timidity so properly fly for Shelter, as to him who has been so long distinguished for Candour and Humanity? How can Vanity be so completely gratified, as by the allowed Patronage of him whose Judgment has so long given a Standard to the National Taste? Or by what other means could I so powerfully suppress all Opposition, but that of Envy, as by declaring myself,

My Lord, Your Lordship's Obliged and most Obedient Humble Servant,

The AUTHOR?

HENRIETTA

Second Edition published: 19 March 1761 (*London Chronicle*).
Johnson's Contribution: Dedication.
Copies: Harvard (lacks Dedication); Bodleian; British Museum; H. F. B. Brett-Smith; Professor C. B. Tinker.

To dedicate the second edition of a book to a patron is a proceeding sufficiently unusual to require explanation. Fortunately, Mrs. Lennox's letter to the Duchess of Newcastle explains the reason and is of sufficient interest to be quoted in full (from BM Additional MS. 33067, folio 230):

As Your Grace has been pleased to permit me to dedicate some of my works to you, I take the opportunity of a new Edition of my *Henrietta* to solicit that favour now. The first edition was so hurried Madam, that I had not time to make an application to Your Grace, I therefore sent it into the world without any dedication, for having in my own mind devoted it to so illustrious a patroness, any other name would not satisfy my ambition. The favourable reception this performance has met with, both at home, and abroad, where it has been translated several times, gives me more confidence to intreat that Your Grace will allow me to lay it at your feet. It is a debt of gratitude Madam which I am impatient to pay; I shall never forget your goodness Madam, nor the generosity with which Your Grace relieved my distress last winter, and surely providence seem'd willing to give success to the benevolent intention of Your Grace's present. I have been in the Country almost ever since, and the air, together with proper exercise has restored me to a very tollerable degree of health. I have the comfort to hear from Mr. Stone[1] that Your Grace continues your favourable intentions with regard to Mr. Lennox, and this hope supports me in my present Slavery to the Booksellers, whom I have the mortification to see adding to their heaps by my labours, which scar[c]e produce me a scanty and precarious subsistence. If Your Grace will do me the honour to signify Your pleasure to me with regard to the Dedication of *Henrietta*, a message directed for me at the Mineral Water Ware-house in Bury Street St. James's, will come safe to my hands.

> I am with the deepest respect
> Madam, Your Grace's Most grateful and
> devoted Servant
>
> Charlotte Lennox.

London Bury Street
October 6, 1760.

Now this letter, although it may not tell the whole story, explains in a satisfactory manner the issue of the first edition without a dedication, and the presence of a dedication in the second edition.

The Duchess of Newcastle did finally find a position for Mr. Lennox;[2] she acted as godmother to Mrs. Lennox's first child; through the previous winter and for much of the summer her bounty had enabled Mrs. Lennox to rest and recover her health in the country. The author, therefore, must have been anxious to present the book with as fine a dedicatory address as possible, and it is almost inconceivable that she

1. The Duke's secretary, Andrew Stone.
2. Mrs. Lennox did not rely solely on a direct application. Gray wrote to Mason, October, 1761: 'Last week I had an application from a broken tradesman (whose wife I knew) to desire my interest with the Duke of Newcastle for a tide-waiter's place.' *Letters of Gray*, ed. D. C. Tovey (London 1904), ii:238.

should not have turned to Johnson who as I believe had previously written no less than five similar addresses for her, one of them (Brumoy's *Greek Theatre*) little more than a year before.

The style of the Dedication itself is decisive; Mrs. Lennox never wrote like this:

> To obtain the approbation of a judgment like yours, it is necessary to mean well; and, to gain kindness from such benevolence, to mean well is commonly sufficient.3

Bibliographical Description

Henrietta. / By / Mrs. Charlotte Lennox. / [*rule*] / In two volumes. / Vol. I. / [*rule*] / The second edition, corrected. / [*rule*] / [*printer's flowers*] / [*parallel rule*] / London: / Printed for A. Millar, in the Strand. / MDCCLXI.

Two volumes, duodecimo; 16.9 × 10.4 cm. (British Museum). Price: 6/– bound, or 5/– in boards.

Signatures: Vol. I: A4; B–L12; M8.
Vol. II: A4; B–O12; P2.

Pagination: Vol. I: [i] title-page; [ii] blank; [iii–vi] Dedication; [vii–viii] Contents (preliminary leaves unnumbered); [1]–255 Text; [256] blank.
Vol. II: [i] title-page; [ii] blank; [iii–viii] Contents; [1]–315 Text; [316] blank.

The two volumes are bound in one in the British Museum set.

It is interesting to observe how the printer arranged the Table of Contents. In the second volume there was plenty of room available and the Table of Contents fills six pages; but in the first volume, to avoid the use of part of a new sheet, the same amount of type is compressed to two pages.

The copy at the Bodleian, bound in calf with tooled edges, is inscribed 'To her Grace the Dutchess of Leeds From the Author,' and it contains the Leeds bookplate. Observe that Mrs.

3. With this sentence, compare Johnson's Review of Jonas Hanway's *Journal of Eight Days Journey* in *Literary Magazine*, 1757 [*Works*, 1825, vi:20]: 'to mean well is a degree of merit, which overbalances much greater errours than impurity of style.' And Johnson wrote in the Dedication to Gwynn's *London and Westminster Improved*, 'those who mean well.'

Lennox wrote 'Dutchess' although at the head of the Dedication the printer has spelled it 'Duchess.'

The text is almost a page-for-page reprint of the first edition. On the second page, 'fellow' is changed to *'fellor,'* and in the course of the narrative the names of four characters are changed, as follows: Mr. Bale to Mr. Damer, Mr. Vellum to Mr. Jones, Mrs. Measure to Mrs. Cary, and Mr. Campley to Mr. Morley.

Editions:

The first edition of *Henrietta* was issued in 1758, and it was reprinted in Dublin in the same year. There were two French translations in 1760. The Second Edition, Corrected, was published 19 March 1761. When the *Sister,* based on *Henrietta,* was acted in 1769, a mild interest was aroused in *Henrietta,* and Lowndes advertised the Second Edition in the *London Chronicle,* 7 March 1769.

On the twentieth of September in the same year, Lowndes bought a one-third interest in the book itself from the Richardsons (they had acquired it at Millar's sale), and promised that if and when a new edition was required it should be reprinted by the Richardsons.[4] Presumably this new edition is that advertised in the *London Chronicle,* 24 March 1770, 'two volumes, 12mo, 6/–; Printed for T. Lowndes at his circulating library.' Since I have never seen such an edition, it is possible that this advertisement referred to the remaining copies of the second edition of 1761, despite the alterations from the advertisement of March 1769. In 1787 it was reprinted by Harrison in one volume, with dedication unchanged, and also issued as part of the *Novelist's Magazine,* volume 23.

DEDICATION

TO HER GRACE THE DUCHESS OF NEWCASTLE.

MADAM,

The condescension and benignity .with which your Grace has hitherto favoured my performances and attempts, have at last given me boldness enough to entreat your patronage for a little novel.

Those to whom this book is new, will expect the name of such a patroness to be followed by some work of deep research and elevated dignity; but they whose nearer approaches to your Grace,

4. BM Additional MS. 38730, folio 148.

have enabled them to distinguish your private virtues, will not be disappointed when they find it recommended only by purity and innocence. To obtain the approbation of a judgment like yours, it is necessary to mean well; and to gain kindness from such benevolence, to mean well is commonly sufficient.

Had your Grace resolved only to countenance those who could have enlarged your knowledge, or refined your sentiments, few could have aspired to the honour of your notice, and far had I been removed from all hope of the favours which I have enjoyed, and the expectations which I have been permitted to indulge. But true greatness is always accessible, and pride will never be confounded with dignity by those who remember that your Grace has admitted this address from,

MADAM, Your Grace's most obliged, and Most devoted Servant,

Charlotte Lennox.

London,
Nov. 20, 1760.

PHILANDER

Published: November 1757 (*Critical Review*).
Johnson's Contribution: Dedication.
Copies: Harvard; Huntington Library; Library of Congress; Yale;
   Bodleian (Malone); British Museum (two copies); Victoria and
   Albert (Dyce).

MRS. LENNOX attempted several dramatic pieces, of which none seem to have been very successful. *Philander,* a pastoral, is in a special class, and Mrs. Lennox probably planned it only for reading or recital, not for the stage. One wonders whether Johnson's gallantry was tested when he was asked to dedicate a pastoral romance.

I have found practically no external evidence for Johnson's authorship. Miss Miriam Small points out to me that Charlemont, the dedicatee, was a friend of Topham Beauclerk, and both were friends of Johnson. Charlemont was also a friend of Lord Rockingham, and it was from Lady Rockingham's protection that young Charlotte Ramsay had been dismissed a decade earlier: but this is hardly proof. Yet the style is unmistakable. No one else surely ever spoke of 'a performance of an airy and luxuriant kind,' 'restraints of regularity,' 'imputation of arrogance,' and 'a composition of little dignity in the design, and perhaps of little elegance in the execution.'

Bibliographical Description

Philander. / A / dramatic pastoral. / [*rule*] / By the author of the Female Quixote. / [*rule*] / [*ornament*] / [*parallel (pieced) rule*] / London: / Printed for A. Millar, in the Strand. / MDCCLVIII. / [Price one shilling.]

Octavo in half-sheets; 20 × 12 cm.

Signatures: [A]–F⁴.

Pagination: [i] title-page; [ii] blank; [iii]–vii Dedication; [viii] Persons of the Drama; [9]–48 Text.

The play was reprinted in Dublin in 1758.
The *Critical Review* (November) and the *Monthly Review* (December) praised the play.

DEDICATION
TO THE RIGHT HONOURABLE LORD VISCOUNT CHARLEMONT.

My Lord,

It is generally expected that there should be some relation between the character of the patron and the nature of the work, for which protection is solicited.

But this law, like many others, is broken when it opposes the gratification of passions too strong for the restraints of regularity. Ambition, which often overpowers the judgment in questions of more importance, has made me forget the disproportion between Your Lordship's name, and a Dramatic Pastoral; and I have ventured to lay before You a composition of little dignity in the design, and perhaps of little elegance in the execution.

Yet for whatever we resolve, we labour to find reasons, till in time we forget its impropriety; I begin to hope, that by offering to Your Lordship a performance of an airy and luxuriant kind, which can at best hope only for excuse, I expose myself less to the imputation of arrogance, than if I had prefixed Your name to a

piece more grave and ostentatious, which might have been suspected of pretending to approbation.

I am, my Lord, far from imagining that any of my ideas can be
new to Your extensive knowledge, or that I have attained any
beauties of style or sentiment adequate to Your delicacy of taste.
The merit of this Poem is but small in my own opinion, and yet,
of the little praise which it may receive, I must resign a part, by
confessing that the first hint was taken from the PASTOR FIDO, and
that the two songs marked with asterisks, were written by another
hand.

Whatever praise this confession may detract from my abilities,
it will add to my sincerity; and I should discover little knowledge
of Your Lordship, if I should endeavour to recommend myself,
rather by elevation of genius than by purity of manners.

I am, with great respect, My Lord, Your Lordship's Most
obliged Humble servant,

CHARLOTTE LENNOX.

London,
Nov. 20, 1757.

SHAKESPEAR ILLUSTRATED

Published: 18 May 1753 (*Public Advertiser*).
References: Boswell, *Life,* i:255.
   Courtney, p. 38.
Johnson's Contribution: Dedication.
Copies: Not rare.

MR. LENNOX, looking for an Italian teacher for his wife who
was beginning her *Shakespear Illustrated,* found Baretti at a
coffee-house. After some time Baretti was introduced to Johnson.[1] There is no reason to doubt the substantial accuracy of
this memoir of Baretti, and he must have made the acquaintance of Mrs. Lennox at some time in the year 1752. The book
has been vigorously condemned many times since 1753 as an
uncritical piece of work,[2] but it is historically significant as an

1. *European Magazine,* xv(May 1789):349*. This uncontroverted tradition
that Baretti was introduced to Johnson by Mrs. Lennox is the reason for dating Baretti's *Proposals* not earlier than 1752.
2. The *Monthly Review* praised the book, but pointed out the very criti-
cisms which have since been attacked: Mrs. Lennox's remarks, 'which are
very judicious, and truly critical, are chiefly intended to prove, that Shakespeare has generally spoiled every story on which the plays are founded, by

early study of Shakespeare's sources. In fact, Mrs. Lennox attempted the study of sources which Johnson in his Proposals

torturing them into low contrivances, absurd intrigue, and improbable incidents.' *Monthly Review,* ix(August 1753):145. Professor T. R. Lounsbury (*Shakespeare as a Dramatic Artist,* 1901, pp. 290–292) points out that Mrs. Lennox's typical words are 'absurd' and 'ridiculous,' that she followed Thomas Rymer's criticism and even left him far behind, that she made it clear that whatever Shakespeare touched he deformed, and he suggests that Mrs. Lennox missed her century, for she ought to have lived in the period immediately following the Restoration. Then, in a final burst of rhetoric, Professor Lounsbury adds, 'Had she in addition become Mrs. Rymer, the conjunction of these two stars, shooting madly from their spheres in the Shakespearean firmament, would have attracted the attention of observers for all time.' (p. 292). More recently, Professor Karl Young, in a monograph on *Shakespear Illustrated* (University of Wisconsin *Studies in Language and Literature,* 18 [1923]:146–226, 'Johnson on Shakespeare: One Aspect'), wrote of the same feature of the work: 'It must be admitted that Mrs. Lennox shows a strong affinity for Thomas Rymer, but the wonder is that this affinity was not palpably weakened through her association with Samuel Johnson.' (P. 197 of original. The page reference to the offprint is always greater by one.)

Perhaps it is not wholly fair to condemn Mrs. Lennox unreservedly: she was not a great critic, but she was often criticizing quite on Johnsonian lines. Johnson himself shows much Rymerian influence, or follows Rymer, in the beliefs that Shakespeare is greater in comedy than in tragedy, that his plots lack moral relevancy, and that he frequently violates poetic justice. Hence, when Mrs. Lennox writes of *Lear* (Volume iii, p. 291): 'Had Shakespeare followed the Historian, he would not have violated the Rules of poetical Justice: he [the historian] represents Vice punished, and Virtue rewarded; in the Play one Fate overwhelms alike the Innocent and the Guilty, and the Facts in the History are wholly changed to produce Events, neither probable, necessary, nor just,'—when she writes in this manner, she seems almost to be echoing Johnson's criticism. Similarly, *Troilus and Cressida* lacks poetical justice. (iii:92). Concerning *Othello,* indeed, Mrs. Lennox very properly refutes the ill-founded charges of Rymer. (i:129–132.) Again, there is a fine passage in praise of the comic scenes of *Much Ado* (iii:271): it is good enough to have been suggested by Johnson.

Johnson was himself bound in general by the neo-classic rules; that Mrs. Lennox accepted them ought hardly to be a reason for condemnation. Johnson's famous attack on the unities in his *Preface to Shakespeare* (1765) is almost un-Johnsonian, and he himself feels that he has done something very bold in attacking one of the central dogmas of his own school. 'I am almost frighted at my own temerity; and when I estimate the fame and the strength of those that maintain the contrary opinion, am ready to sink down in reverential silence.' (See also Professor Young's monograph, referred to above, pp. 202, 203.)

Surely it is not to be held against Mrs. Lennox that, under the influence if not under the guidance of the last of the great classical critics, she judged by the classical standards rather than by the revolutionary ideas which the first romantic critics were endeavoring to establish.

But this study is concerned chiefly with Johnsonian bibliography and not with Shakespearean criticism.

had light-heartedly promised but which in his edition was imperfectly performed.

Gordon Goodwin, in his article on Mrs. Lennox in the *Dictionary of National Biography*, asserts that some of the critical observations in *Shakespear Illustrated* were ascribed by Malone to Johnson. The authority for this statement was Lowndes, 1834. Long passages from Johnson's *Miscellaneous Observations on the Tragedy of Macbeth* (1745) are quoted by Mrs. Lennox,[3] and this fact may have been the reason for Malone's remark. Professor Young is rightly disturbed to find that Johnson, who had promised to study Shakespeare's sources, used *Shakespear Illustrated* so little in his edition.[4] Perhaps Malone was right, and the parts in *Shakespear Illustrated* which Johnson revised or added were the parts which he recalled when he was editing certain plays a few years later. I think it much more likely, however, that Johnson's editing was somewhat uneven, and that he suggested the source when it was known to him, without bothering to refer

3. *Shakespear Illustrated,* i:273–275, 280ff. The story has recently been amplified from the statements in the *DNB* or in Lowndes by a bookseller: 'In some of the notes, where Mrs. Lennox attempts to show that Shakespeare injured the stories by the introduction of absurd intrigues and improbable incidents, Malone says she was assisted, in such observations, by Johnson.' (Pickering and Chatto *Catalogue* 277, 1932, item 217.)

4. Karl Young, 'Johnson on Shakespeare: One Aspect' in University of Wisconsin *Studies* 18(1923):222–3: 'For Johnson's treatment of Mrs. Lennox's book I have no satisfactory explanation. His independence of her in literary judgments was to be expected. [To combat her opinions] . . . his gallantry presumably forbade. But for his ignoring of her materials there appears to be no reason that is creditable to him. The plain fact seems to be that a part of his avowed intention he simply abandoned.'

In *Modern Language Notes* xliii(1928):34, 35, Miss Miriam Small has called attention to a note in *Macbeth* which Johnson seems to have taken from Mrs. Lennox's *Lady's Museum* (1760).

It would not be surprising to find Johnsonian additions in Mrs. Lennox's book, for there is abundant evidence that he suggested additions and alterations in many books, but as I have glanced through *Shakespear Illustrated* nothing has seemed at all Johnsonian except perhaps the criticism of comic scenes in *Much Ado* to which I have referred in the footnote on p. 105: 'There is a great deal of true Wit and Humour in the comic scenes of this play; the characters of Benedict and Beatrice are properly marked, and beautifully distinguished.' (iii:271).

to the book for which he had written a Dedication a decade earlier.

Bibliographical Description

Shakespear illustrated: / or the / novels and histories, / on which the / plays of Shakespear / are founded, / collected and translated from the / original authors. / With / critical remarks. / In two volumes. / By the / author of the Female Quixote. / [*ornament*] / London: / Printed for A. Millar in the Strand. / MDCCLIII.

The second volume omits 'In two volumes' and adds immediately above the ornament 'Vol. II.' The third volume, published in the spring of 1754, reads, 'The third and last volume,' is dated MDCCLIV, and has a different ornament.

Two volumes, duodecimo in twelves; 17.5 × 10 cm. Price: 6/-. A third volume was issued in the same format in the spring of 1754.

Signatures: Vol. I: A⁶; one leaf; B–N¹²; O².
    Vol. II: two leaves; B–M¹²; N⁶.
    Vol. III: two leaves; B–N¹²; O¹⁰.

Pagination: Vol. I: [i] title-page; [ii] blank; [iii]–xii Dedication; [xiii–xiv] Contents; [1]–292 Text.
    Vol. II: title-page with verso blank; Contents with verso blank, [1]–274 Text; [275–278] Advertisements.
    Vol. III: title-page with verso blank; Contents on one leaf; [1]–308 Text.

Although I have never seen one, Dr. Chapman tells me that there is in some copies a blank leaf conjugate with the *Contents* leaf in the first volume.

The Dedication was first reprinted in Volume xiv of the *Works* (1788). Boswell marks it 'acknowledged.' It was reprinted from the first edition by Professor Young in his monograph.

Boswell furnished Mrs. Lennox with Proposals for a new edition in 1793 (C. C. Abbott, *Catalogue of Papers . . . found at Fettercairn House,* Oxford, 1936, p. 77), but I think the Proposals were never published.

Shakespear Illustrated was reprinted and edited in two volumes, octavo, by M. M. Noah; Philadelphia, 1809. Only the first volume was published, however.

DEDICATION

TO THE RIGHT HONOURABLE *JOHN,*
EARL OF *ORRERY.*

My LORD,

I have no other Pretence to the Honour of a Patronage, so illustrious as that of your Lordship, than the Merit of attempting what has by some unaccountable Neglect been hitherto omitted, though absolutely necessary to a perfect Knowledge of the Abilities of *Shakespear.*

Among the Powers that must conduce to constitute a Poet, the first and most valuable is Invention; and of all the Degrees of Invention, the highest seems to be that which is able to produce a Series of Events. It is easy when the Thread of a Story is once drawn to diversify it with Variety of Colours; and when a Train of Action is presented to the Mind, a little Acquaintance with Life will supply Circumstances and Reflexions, and a little Knowledge of Books, furnish Parallels and Illustrations. To tell over again a Story that has been told already, and to tell it better than the first Author is no rare Qualification; but to strike out the first Hints of a new Fable; hence to introduce a Set of Characters so diversified in their several Passions and Interests, that from the clashing of this Variety may result many necessary Incidents; to make these Incidents surprising, and yet natural, so as to delight the Imagination without shocking the Judgment of a Reader; and finally, to wind up the whole in a pleasing Catastrophe produced by those very Means which seem most likely to oppose and prevent it, is the utmost Effort of the human Mind.

To discover how few of those Writers, who profess to recount imaginary Adventures, have been able to produce any Thing by their own Imagination would require too much of that Time, which your Lordship employs in nobler Studies. Of all the Novels and Romances that Wit or Idleness, Vanity or Indigence, have pushed into the World, there are very few, of which the End cannot be conjectured from the Beginning; or where the Authors have done more, than to transpose the Incidents of other Tales, or strip the Circumstances from one Event for the Decoration of another.

In the Examination of a Poet's Character it is therefore first to

be enquired what Degree of Invention has been exerted by him.
With this View I have very diligently read the Works of *Shakespear,* and now presume to lay the Result of my Searches before
your Lordship, before that Judge whom *Pliny* himself would
have wished for his Assessor to hear a literary Cause.

How much the Translation of the following Novels will add to
the Reputation of *Shakespear,* or take away from it, You, my
Lord, and Men learned and candid like You, if any such can be
found, must now determine. Some Danger, as I am informed,
there is, lest his Admirers should think him injured by this Attempt, and clamour as at the Diminution of the Honour of that
Nation, which boasts herself the Parent of so great a Poet.

That no such Enemies may arise against me (though I am unwilling to believe it) I am far from being too confident, for who
can fix Bounds to Bigotry and Folly? My *Sex,* my *Age,* have not
given me many Opportunities of mingling in the World; there
may be in it many a Species of Absurdity which I have never
seen, and among them such Vanity as pleases itself with false
Praise bestowed on another, and such Superstition as worships
Idols, without supposing them to be Gods.

But the Truth is, that a very small Part of the Reputation of
this mighty Genius depends upon the naked Plot, or Story of his
Plays. He lived in an Age when the Books of Chivalry were yet
popular, and when therefore the Minds of his Auditors were not
accustomed to balance Probabilities, or to examine nicely the Proportion between Causes and Effects. It was sufficient to recommend a Story, that it was far removed from common Life, that its
Changes were frequent, and its Close pathetic.

This Disposition of the Age concurred so happily with the Imagination of *Shakespear* that he had no Desire to reform it, and
indeed to this he was indebted for the licentious Variety, by
which he has made his Plays more entertaining than those of any
other Author.

He had looked with great Attention on the Scenes of Nature;
but his chief Skill was in Human Actions, Passions, and Habits;
he was therefore delighted with such Tales as afforded numerous
Incidents, and exhibited many Characters, in many Changes of
Situation. These Characters are so copiously diversified, and some
of them so justly pursued, that his Works may be considered as a
Map of Life, a faithful Miniature of human Transactions and he
that has read *Shakespear* with Attention, will perhaps find little
new in the crouded World.

Among his other Excellencies it ought to be remarked, because it has hitherto been unnoticed, that his *Heroes are Men,* that the Love and Hatred, the Hopes and Fears of his chief Personages are such as are common to other human Beings, and not like those which later Times have exhibited, peculiar to Phantoms that strut upon the Stage.

It is not perhaps very necessary to enquire whether the Vehicle of so much Delight and Instruction be a Story probable, or unlikely, native, or foreign. *Shakespear's* Excellence is not the Fiction of a Tale, but the Representation of Life; and his Reputation is therefore safe, till Human Nature shall be changed. Nor can he who has so many just Claims to Praise, suffer by losing that which ignorant Admiration has unreasonably given him. To calumniate the Dead is Baseness, and to flatter them is surely Folly.

From Flattery, my Lord, either of the Dead or the Living, I wish to be clear, and have therefore solicited the Countenance of a Patron, whom, if I knew how to praise him, I could praise with Truth, and have the World on my Side; whose Candour and Humanity are universally acknowledged, and whose Judgment perhaps was then first to be doubted, when he condescended to admit this Address from,

My Lord, Your Lordship's most obliged, and most obedient, humble Servant,

The AUTHOR.

SULLY'S *MEMOIRS*

Published: 8 November 1755 (*Public Advertiser*).
Johnson's Contribution: Dedication.
Copies: Yale; Bodleian; British Museum; Miss Miriam Small.

I do not believe that this first quarto edition can be very rare, although I have found very few sets. Two sets were offered at Hodgson's, 24 October 1934.

THE proof that Johnson wrote the Dedication to the Duke of Newcastle has been involved in such obscurity that it is no longer possible to regard it as satisfactory; yet it seems quite certain that this Dedication was furnished by Johnson.

Under the year 1778, Boswell writes:

I once got from one of his friends (Percy) a list, which there was pretty good reason to suppose was accurate, for it was written down in his presence by this friend, who enumerated each article aloud, and had some of them mentioned to him by Mr. Levett, in concert with whom it was made out; and Johnson, who heard all this, did not contradict it. But when I shewed a copy of this list to him, and mentioned the evidence for its exactness, he laughed, and said, 'I was willing to let them go on as they pleased, and never interfered.' Upon which I read it to him, article by article, and got him positively to own or refuse.[1]

Concerning this list Boswell wrote in an undated letter to Percy:

> I return you the list of Mr. Johnson's writings with many thanks. I must tell you however that he allowed Levet to dictate to you several errours, as for instance the Conquest of Goree, and the Preface to Sully. He corrected these errours *himself* to me.[2]

Now the Preface to Sully is merely a translation of the French Preface and would hardly have been attributed to Johnson either by Levett or by Percy. There is, however, a Dedication to Sully which is written in Dr. Johnson's best manner. Confusion of Preface and Dedication in Johnsonian books seems to have occurred whenever it was remotely possible.[3] If people have been confused for one hundred and fifty years, it is perhaps not particularly remarkable that Mr. Levett said 'Preface' when he ought to have said 'Dedication.' When Boswell read the list to Johnson and Johnson said that he had not written the Preface to Sully, one can only suppose that he was still sufficiently amused by the whole episode to say no more than the literal truth—that he had not written the Preface.

1. Boswell, *Life*, iii:321. George Steevens seems to be referring to the same episode in his article in the *St. James's Chronicle*, 11 January 1785.

2. *Letters of James Boswell*, edited by Professor C. B. Tinker (Oxford 1924), ii:281. This letter is now in the collection of Mr. R. B. Adam. Because of the date under which Boswell inserts this episode in the *Life*, the letter is dated 1778?. In any case, the letter probably was written not very long after the list had been made out, and this must have been before the death of Garrick in January 1779. The *Conquest of Goree* I have not identified, unless it is M. Adanson's *Voyage to Senegal, the isle of Goree, and the River Gambia*. This was translated from the French, with notes by an English gentleman, in 1759. It seems hardly possible that John Lindsay's *Voyage to Africa and taking of Goree* (1759) could ever have been ascribed to Johnson.

3. Kennedy's *Astronomical Chronology*, Angell's *Stenography*, and James's *Medicinal Dictionary* are among the works which have been troublesome in this respect.

One would suppose at first glance that Boswell ought to have suspected the truth at once, for Boswell knew very well that Johnson had had some connection with the book.[4] Perhaps it is a dangerous expedient, but I am inclined to believe that Boswell was a literal-minded man, and that when Johnson asserted that he had not furnished the Preface, it never occurred to him that Johnson might very well have written the Dedication.[5] It is very possible, of course, that he had never looked at this book, and in that case he could not have known that it contained both a dedication and a preface. Many of his attributions (Brumoy's *Greek Theatre*, for instance) were obviously made without direct inspection of the works themselves. No dialectic and no ingenious excuses, however, can wholly explain away Boswell's letter.

Fortunately, in addition to the evidence of the style itself, there is some independent evidence. Tyers asserted that Johnson 'composed the Preface to the Poems of Miss Williams, to Sully's Memoirs, to Macbean's Classical Geography, and to Adams on the Globes.'[6] Since Johnson contributed to Miss Williams's *Miscellanies* an 'Advertisement,' to Macbean's *Geography* a 'Preface,' and to Adams's *Treatise on the Globes* a 'Dedication,' it is a not unreasonable assumption that Tyers intended to refer to the Dedication of Sully's *Memoirs*. Had it not been for Boswell's troublesome letter to Percy, there would have been no question about it; Tyers had known

4. Boswell indicates that the review of Sully's *Memoirs* in the *Literary Magazine* (No. vi, pp. 281–2. See Boswell, *Life*, i:309) was acknowledged by Johnson; he may have thought that Levett knew of this review and in some confused recollection dictated it to Percy as the 'Preface to Sully.' The brief review is not very distinguished, but it was probably written by Johnson.

5. I have thought for a long time that this was the only satisfactory explanation of Boswell's letter to Percy, but to make the suggestion to eager Boswellians has seemed a hazardous proceeding. Recently I have been heartened by the discovery that the late Geoffrey Scott has spoken editorially in the *Boswell Papers* (vi:157) of 'Boswell's docility and literal-mindedness.'

6. *Gentleman's Magazine*, lv(1785):87. Tyers had previously printed some additional remarks, in the Supplement to the *Gentleman's Magazine* for 1784, p. 982: 'He wrote the preface to Macbean's Biblical Geography, to Mrs. Williams's Miscellanies, and to Adams on the Globes.' Then, when he revised these notes for the first number of the new volume, he seems to have added Sully's *Memoirs*.

Johnson for a great many years, and, what is more important, he had known him when Sully's *Memoirs* was first published. He was therefore in a position to know about this book, whereas Boswell had first met Johnson seven years afterwards. There is independent evidence of Johnson's authorship in a note, which has been disregarded by later editors, in Croker's edition. Croker presumably was aware of the facts which have been presented above. With a magnificent disregard for controversial problems, he remarks, under the correct date: 'In 1755 Johnson seems to have written for Mrs. Lennox the dedication to Sully's *Memoirs*.'[7]

I have observed elsewhere that the presence of a work in Johnson's library is an added indication, but not proof, of Johnsonian authorship. The quarto edition of 1756 is listed in the *Catalogue* of Johnson's Library (lot 393), and was sold for eighteen shillings.

Bibliographical Description

Memoirs / of / Maximilian de Bethune, / Duke of Sully, / prime minister to / Henry the Great. / Containing / the history of the life and reign of that monarch, / and his own administration under him. / Translated from the French. / To which is added, / the tryal of Ravaillac for the murder of / Henry the Great. / In three volumes. / Vol. I. / London, / Printed for A. Millar, in the Strand; R. and J. Dodsley, in Pall-Mall; / and W. Shropshire, in New Bond Street. / MDCCLVI.

Three volumes, quarto; 26 × 20.5 cm. Price: two guineas bound.

Signatures: Vol. I: [A],a–c,a,B–Yyy⁴; Zzz(half-sheet).
    Vol. II: 2 leaves; a,B–Aaaa⁴; Bbbb(half-sheet).
    Vol. III: a,B–Xxx⁴; Yyy(one leaf).

7. *Life of Johnson,* edited by J. W. Croker (1831),i:287. Boswell disparages Tyers's accuracy; concerning this Croker remarks, 'There seems, on examination, no reason to doubt the accuracy of his *facts.*' (*Ibid.* i:304n.) It is not known when Tyers first met Johnson, but he says himself that his acquaintance with Johnson lasted thirty years (*Miscellanies* ii:364), which would indicate that they first met in 1754; but the statement may have been only an approximation.

Pagination: Vol. I: [i] half-title; [ii] blank; [iii] title-page; [iv] blank; [v–vii] Dedication; [viii] blank; [i]–xxiv Preface to French edition; [xxv]–xxxii Summary of Contents; [1]–540 Memoirs, Books I–X.

Vol. II: [i] half-title; [ii] blank; [iii] title-page; [iv] blank; [i]–viii Summary of Contents; [1]–555 Memoirs, Books XI–XXIII; [556] blank.

Vol. III: [i] title-page; [ii] blank; [iii]–vii Summary of Contents; [viii] blank; [1]–407 Memoirs, Books XXIV–XXX and Supplement, and Tryal of Ravaillac; [408] blank; Sheets Ggg to the end: Index (unpaged).

Dr. Chapman has found in the Bodleian the unseparated sheet Yyy of the third volume. The second and third leaves were used as cancels, to make minor textual corrections, for Yy3 and U3 respectively, in the first volume. Yyy4 was blank.

Editions:
1756—three volumes quarto; first edition; published 8 November 1755.
1757—five volumes octavo; second edition.
1761—three volumes quarto; third edition; published July 1761.
1763—six volumes duodecimo; fourth edition.
1778—six volumes duodecimo; fifth edition.
1778—five volumes octavo.
Editions in 1810 and later in the nineteenth century.
Edinburgh, 1760—five volumes duodecimo.
Edinburgh, 1773—five volumes duodecimo.
Dublin, 1781—six volumes duodecimo, marked fifth edition.
Edinburgh, 1805—five volumes duodecimo.
Philadelphia, 1817.
And doubtless other editions.

The expedient of printing in quarto and octavo was of course adopted to allow two prices. When the expensive quarto edition of 1756 was exhausted, it was reprinted in 1761. (Strahan estimated that an edition must be sold in three years to make it profitable to the bookseller. See *Letters of David Hume,* edited by J. Y. T. Greig, Oxford, 1932, ii:239.) The fourth edition, in duodecimo, which was issued in 1763, was an attempt on the part of the London proprietors, Millar, Shropshire, and the Dodsleys, to meet the competition of the cheap, pirated duodecimo edition which had been printed at Edinburgh in 1760. It was published in monthly parts. (See advertisements in *London Chronicle,* 21

July 1763 and *passim* to 6 December 1763, when the edition was completed.)

For the two London editions of 1778 the explanation is not immediately apparent. Perhaps the stock of both octavo and duo-decimo editions had become exhausted. It is likely that it was a result of some compromise among the booksellers, perhaps as a result of the protests of Mrs. Lennox. (See her letter to Johnson, published in the *Bulletin of the John Rylands Library,* xvi[1932]: 56.)

The Edinburgh editions of 1760 and 1773 were unauthorized or pirated editions. In these Johnson's dedication is not reprinted.

DEDICATION

(To Thomas Holles-Pelham, Duke of Newcastle, etc.)

MY LORD,

Authors are often unfortunate in the choice of their Patrons: and Works are devoted with great solemnity, to the use of those who cannot use them, and the pleasure of those whom they cannot please.

That I have avoided this impropriety, in dedicating to your GRACE these MEMOIRS OF THE DUKE OF SULLY, a whole Nation, whose affairs you have so long and so happily directed, will bear me witness: But then, I can claim no praise from my own discernment; because I only echo the Voice of the People, and address myself, where that leads me.

Though my sex and manner of life make[8] me a stranger to public affairs; I yet discover of myself, that the History I have translated, is not only interesting but important: and that the original author of it was not only well versed in all the prime operations of government, but that he saved a Nation, by bringing method and order into every branch of her revenues, and administring the whole with the most accurate economy.

A Book, thus filled with political wisdom, could be fitly offered only to Him, who lays out his whole time and attention, in labours of the same tendency; and for the service of a more free, and therefore a nobler People.

That Providence may co-operate with your endeavours; and that your GRACE may steer not only safely, but triumphantly, through every difficulty of the present conjuncture, are wishes so natural to all true Britons, that they cannot be thought improper

8. 'makes' in edition of 1761 and later editions.

even from a woman, and in this public manner. She is, with the profoundest Respect,

MY LORD, Your GRACE's most Obedient, and most Humble Servant,

CHARLOTTE LENNOX.

London, Sept. 5,
      1755.

LINDSAY'S *EVANGELICAL HISTORY*

Published: 16 April 1757 (*Public Advertiser*).
References: Boswell, *Life*, iv:383, 549–50.
             Courtney, p. 78.
Johnson's Contribution: Dedication.
Copies: Library Company of Philadelphia; Yale; British Museum.

THIS work is in certain respects the most puzzling item in the Johnsonian canon. Very little has been known about it, very little can be discovered about it, and copies seem to be extraordinarily rare. There are three problems: authorship (of the Dedication), editions, and a possible revision of the text of the Dedication.

Boswell denies emphatically that the Dedication can be by Johnson, 'though it has been confidently ascribed to him. . . . He was no *croaker;* no declaimer against *the times.*' He quotes a few passages and asserts, 'This is not Johnsonian. There are, indeed, in this Dedication, several sentences constructed upon the model of those of Johnson. But the imitation of the form, without the spirit of his style, has been so general, that this of itself is not sufficient evidence.'[1] This is all very persuasive, even though as Boswell admits the construction of the sentences is typical of Johnson's manner. But there is decisive evidence, which was unknown to Boswell, that Johnson did furnish this Dedication. Robert Anderson, the biographer of Johnson, wrote to Bishop Percy in 1806:

> I have lately made a discovery that will enrich my Johnson, a dedication of eleven pages, to the Parliament, prefixed to the "Evangelical

1. Boswell, *Life*, iv:383–4, note.

History Harmonized," in 2 vols. . . . . It bears on the title page, "By a Society of Gentlemen," but was the production of the Rev. John Lindsay. The dedication has escaped the diligence of Boswell and Malone, and is written in the excellent dedicator's best style of dignified remonstrance and sublime piety.

The dedication of course had not escaped the diligence of Boswell, but in other respects there is nothing in the letter that is exceptionable. As his proof, Anderson printed the following note from one C. G., who has not been identified:

> Extract from a letter of the Rev. Mr. Lindsay, upon being asked if he was concerned in compiling this work.
>
> "12th June, 1761.
> ". . . and a set of 'The Evangelical History,' (in 2 vols.) bound, are ready for packing. This latter was indeed compiled by me alone; but the bookseller, (at whose request I wrote it,) had a mind to make a *society*, by desiring Mr. Johnson, the Dictionarian, to adorn it with a Dedication, to persons with whom I never had the honour of any correspondence."

Mr. Lindsay, at same time, sent me a few copies of a new title page, of which this, on the reverse, is one, agreeable to what he wrote me above.

This specimen of a new title-page, according to Anderson, substituted the name 'John Lindsay' in place of the 'Society of Gentlemen.'[2] Unless this letter is a forgery, and there is no reason to suspect that it is, the Johnsonian authorship of the Dedication is well established.[3] The letter also establishes two other facts: that the compilation was one of Newbery's projects, and that the dedication was solicited by Newbery. Both facts fit well with what is known of Newbery's activities at that period. The author or compiler was probably the John Lindsay (1686–1768) who completed John Court's *New Testament of our Lord and Saviour Jesus Christ carefully and diligently compared*.[4] He is said to have been a corrector

---

2. The facts are printed, with references, in Dr. Powell's Appendix, Boswell, *Life*, iv:549, 550. What has since become of Anderson's copy of the book, which contained C. G.'s note, seems not to be known.

3. Independent proof is in Gleig's Volume xv of the *Works* (1789), p. 7.

4. Published in parts, 1734–6, folio. Republished in 1737 with the title, *A Critical and Practical Commentary on the New Testament;* second edition, 1740.

of the press for Bowles. Newbery perhaps turned to him as an available person who could put together a popular, as opposed to a scholarly and critical, Life of Christ. Many such were issued in the eighteenth century, and Newbery hoped to add this to his long list of successful publications. Unfortunately, the work was nothing but a compilation, and not a very good one: part of the Preface was adapted without acknowledgment from Charles Leslie's *Short and Easy Method with the Deists*. Newbery's judgment was good when he decided that a dedication by Johnson would help, for it was the dedication that was found by the reviewers to be the best part of the book.

There is much evidence that there was either another edition or another issue, or both, of this work, but I have not found any other edition. C. G. wrote, in the letter quoted above, that there was a new title-page; this, according to Anderson, had Lindsay's name on it. Yet if this issue was ever marketed, it has now disappeared, so far as I can tell. Welsh, who had access to important Newbery and Collins records, wrote of this work: 'A much earlier book, as B. Collins of Salisbury valued his fourth share in this "held of Mr. John Newbery" at £15/15/– in 1746.'[5] It is possible, but not very probable, that Welsh in some way confused this book with some similar publication. There is supplementary evidence in the *London Catalogue* for 1766, which lists:

Evangelical History of the New Testament, 2 vols. 8vo. 8/–.
———————————— Christ Harmonized, 2 vols. 8vo. 8/–.

This certainly indicates that the compilers of the *Catalogue* had a record of two anonymous publications, and the exact correspondence in format strengthens the belief that they were, essentially, two editions of the same work with a slightly altered title.[6] Whether an earlier edition will eventually be

5. C. Welsh, *A Bookseller of the last century* (London and New York 1885), p. 242.
6. The same entries are repeated in the *London Catalogue* for 1767 and 1773, which I have consulted. But the list of the earlier catalogue was prob-

discovered I do not know: in any case Johnson's Dedication probably first appeared in 1757.

One other fact that is not satisfactorily explained is that the Dedication is dated 1758 in the *Works* (Chalmers's edition, 1806, and later editions).[7]

The third problem in connection with this book is that of a possible revision of the Dedication by Johnson. The book was reviewed in the *Literary Magazine,* and the Dedication was there reprinted with some interesting changes.[8] There are, I am fairly convinced, too many such changes to be considered merely as printer's revisions. The most interesting perhaps are the use of italic type for the Biblical allusions at the end, and the alteration of 'By what methods the unenlightened ignorant may be made proper readers of the word of God, has been long and diligently considered,' to make it read 'unenlightened and ignorant.' In this revised form the phrase has a thoroughly Johnsonian sound; one wonders whether the other form might have been a misprint. I do not think that the use of 'ignorant' as a collective noun is necessarily un-Johnsonian, but it is more like an Elizabethan usage (cf. 'the vulgar') than is the revised form of the phrase.[9] If

ably never corrected in these new editions, so that the reappearance of the two items does not add to the evidence.

A work with an almost identical title, and in exactly the same format, was published by Buckland in 1777. It was compiled by Thomas Brown and is a different, though similar, work. I do not think that it had been published before 1777 (it was reprinted in 1787), so that its existence does not explain the presence of the two titles in the Catalogue of 1766.

For some bibliographical evidence of another edition, see the notes appended to the bibliographical description below.

7. There are other curious errors in dates, however: in the *Works* (ed. 1787, Vol. ix), Rolt's *Dictionary* is dated 1757 instead of 1756; and in the *Works* (ed. 1788, Vol. xiv), Adams's *Treatise on the Globes* is dated 1767 instead of 1766.

8. No. 13, April 15–May 15, 1757, Vol. ii, pp. 180–2. The *London Chronicle,* 19 May 1757, also reviewed the book, and the text is that of the *Literary Magazine,* from which it was probably copied. The text in the *Works,* 1806, where it is dated 1758, has the same revisions. The changes in the version that is printed in the *Literary Magazine* are indicated in the reproduction of the text below. Dr. L. F. Powell called to my attention the reading 'unenlightened and ignorant.'

9. I do not find 'ignorant' as a collective noun specifically authorized either by Johnson or by the *Oxford English Dictionary.* I quote a few examples of

'unenlightened ignorant' is a misprint merely, there are no revisions that alter the sense: each change is one that might well have been made by any literate person to improve the clarity or smoothness of the text. I do not find any convincing evidence that these changes were made by Johnson.

Yet there are enough to make one wonder whether Johnson himself made them. Johnson wrote numerous reviews for the *Literary Magazine:* did he suggest these changes in the text when he knew that it was to be reprinted in the Magazine? The review is certainly not by him. And why did Chalmers in the *Works* of 1806 reprint from the *Literary Magazine* rather than from the original, dating it 1758? Perhaps at some future date the answer will be found in another edition dated 1758, but it hardly seems probable that the book could have been sufficiently successful to require a second edition.

Bibliographical Description

The / Evangelical history / of our Lord / Jesus Christ / harmonized, / explained and illustrated / with variety of / notes practical, historical, and critical. / To which is sub-joined, / an account of the propagation of Christianity, / and the original settlement and state of the church. / Together with / proper prefaces, and a compleat index. / The whole dedicated to the Lords Spiritual and Temporal, / and Commons in Parliament assembled. / [rule] / By a society of gentlemen, / who are greatly alarmed at the present shameful neglect / of religion and virtue, and earnestly concerned for the / temporal and eternal happiness of mankind. / [rule] /

---

the words as adjectives: 'It is ascribed only to a people very little enlightened; and among them, for the most part, to the mean and the ignorant.' *Journey to the Western Islands,* ed. R. W. Chapman (Oxford 1924), p. 99. Compare the use of 'unlearned' in the third paragraph of the Preface to Baretti's *Introduction to the Italian Language,* p. 14 above, and the *Rambler* 180: 'A man of science is expected to excel the unlettered and unenlightened . . .' Reynolds wrote 'the ignorant and unlearned in that art' (F. W. Hilles, *Literary Career of Reynolds,* 1936, p. 78, note 3); perhaps the original of all these phrases is the well-known description (Acts 4:13) of Peter and John as 'unlearned and ignorant men.'

In two volumes. / [*rule*] / Vol. I. / [*rule*] / London: / Printed for J. Newbery at the Bible and Sun in St. Paul's / Churchyard; and B. Collins in Salisbury. / MDCCLVII.

Two volumes, octavo; 20.2 × 12.2 cm.; 8/– bound.

Signatures: Vol. I: a⁷(a8 lacking); B–Y⁸.
               Vol. II: one leaf; B–U⁸; X⁷(X8 lacking).

Pagination: Vol. I: title-page, with verso blank; 11 unnumbered pages, containing the Dedication; one blank page; [i]–xvi General Preface; [xvii]–xxiv Preface; 25–336 Text.
    Vol. II: title-page, with verso blank; [1]–286 Text and Appendix; 31 pp. of Index; one page of Errata.

Leaf C5, the first page of the Text (Vol. I), is a cancel in the copies at the British Museum and at Yale. The original leaf, in the copy owned by the Library Company of Philadelphia, was headed: 'Preface to the history of the Gospel, by the evangelists themselves.' For this the direction line on p. xxiv is correct. The cancel reads: 'A paraphrase of the several prefaces written by the evangelists themselves.' It seems surprising that the author cancelled a leaf for such a slight change, and the printer retaliated by introducing a typographical error on p. 26.

The copy in the British Museum has a different press number on p. 32 of the second volume.

Bibliographically, this work looks suspicious as a true first edition. The Preface begins on Sheet B, p. i, and the real text begins on C5, p. 25. It thus looks as if another edition had been reprinted, and that Johnson's unpaged Dedication was the only new section. The work is of an unusual nature, however, and the author may have prepared his prefaces before the printer began to print the Work. With this presumptive evidence should be considered the statement of Welsh which has already been quoted (p. 118).

The sale of the work must have been slow, for it is advertised in 1773 and again in 1778 by Newbery and Carnan. (*London Chronicle,* 31 October 1778.) It is described as two volumes bound in one, in the vellum manner, price 7/–. (For this type of binding, see discussion of the *World Displayed.*) I have not seen a copy so bound: there must be considered the bare possibility that this was the reprint from which Chalmers in 1806 derived his text and his date of 1758.

The text was reprinted in Gleig's Volume xv of the *Works* (1789), with minor changes in punctuation and spelling. It was included in Chalmers's edition of the *Works* (1806), perhaps on the suggestion of Anderson, with the text as it had appeared in the *Literary Magazine*. It is not impossible that Chalmers took his text (*Works*, 1806, iii:91–95) directly from the *Literary Magazine*, since Chalmers in his General Preface in the first volume and Anderson in his *Life* (1815, p. 257) both point out that the dedication was there reprinted when the periodical was conducted by Johnson. Similarities in wording seem to indicate that Anderson borrowed his account in part from Chalmers. Anderson wrote Percy about this Dedication soon after Chalmers wrote his Preface to the *Works*. Not even this hypothesis, however, explains the date 1758.

The use of 'hath' in the sixth paragraph of the Dedication is unusual, although it occurs a few times in acknowledged Johnsonian works.

DEDICATION

(Collated with the text in the *Literary Magazine*)

TO THE LORDS SPIRITUAL and TEMPORAL AND
COMMONS in PARLIAMENT assembled.

That we are fallen upon an age in which corruption is barely not universal, is universally confessed. Venality sculks no longer in the dark, but snatches the bribe in publick; and prostitution issues forth without shame, glittering with the ornaments of successful wickedness. Rapine preys on the publick without opposition, and perjury betrays it without enquiry. Irreligion is not only avowed but boasted; and the pestilence that used to walk in darkness, is now destroying at noonday.

Shall this be the state of the *English* nation, and shall her lawgivers behold it without regard? Must the torrent continue to roll on till it shall sweep us into the bottomless[1] gulph of perdition? Surely there will come a time when the careless shall be frighted, and the sluggish shall be roused: when every passion shall be put upon the guard by the dread of general depravity: when he who laughs at wickedness in his companion, shall start from it in his

1. 'bottomless' omitted in *Lit. Mag.* A few differences in capitalization are not noted.

child; when the man who fears not for his soul, shall tremble for his possessions: when it shall be discovered that religion only can secure the rich from robbery, and the poor from oppression; can defend the state from treachery, and the throne from assassination.

If this time be ever to come, let it come quickly: a few years longer, and perhaps all endeavours will be vain. We may be swallowed by an earthquake; we may be delivered to our enemies, or abandoned to that discord, which must inevitably prevail among men that have lost all sense of divine superintendence, and have no higher motive of action or forbearance, than present opinion of present interest.

It is the duty of private men to supplicate and propose, it is yours to hear and to do right. Let religion be once more restored, and the nation shall once more be great and happy. This consequence is not far distant: that nation must always be powerful where every man performs his duty, and every man will perform his duty that considers himself as a being whose condition is to be settled to all eternity by the laws of *Christ*.

The only doctrine by which man can be made *wise unto salvation*,[2] is the will of God, revealed in the books of the Old and the New Testament.

To study the Scriptures, therefore, according to his abilities and attainments, is every man's duty; and to facilitate that study to those whom nature hath made weak, or education has left ignorant, or indispensable cares detained[3] from regular processes of enquiry, is the business of those who have been blessed with abilities and learning, and appointed[4] the instructors of the lower classes of men, by that common Father, who distributes to all created beings their qualifications and employments; and has allotted[5] some to the labour of the hand, and some to the exercise of the mind; has commanded some to teach, and others to learn; has prescribed to some the patience of instruction, and to others the meekness of obedience.

By what methods the unenlightned[6] ignorant may be made proper readers of the word of God, has been long and diligently considered. Commentaries of all kinds have indeed been copiously produced; but there still remain multitudes to whom the labours of the learned are of little use, for whom expositions re-

2. II Timothy 3:15.   3. 'detain' in *Lit. Mag.*
4. 'and are appointed' in *Lit. Mag.*   5. 'who has allotted' in *Lit. Mag.*
6. 'unenlightned and ignorant' in *Lit. Mag.*

quire an expositor. To those indeed, who read the divine books without vain curiosity, or a desire to be wise beyond their powers, it will always be easy to discern the strait path, to find the words of everlasting life. But such is the condition of our nature, that we are always attempting what is difficult[7] to perform: he who reads the scripture to gain goodness, is desirous likewise to gain knowledge, and by his impatience of ignorance, falls into error.

This danger has appeared to the doctors of the *Romish* Church, so much to be feared, and so difficult to be escaped, that they have snatched the Bible out of the hands of the people, and confined the liberty of perusing it to those whom literature has previously qualified. By this expedient they have formed a kind of uniformity, I am afraid too much like that of colours in the dark: but they have certainly usurped a power which God has never given them, and precluded great numbers from the highest spiritual consolation.

I know not whether this prohibition has not brought upon them an evil which they themselves have not discovered. It is granted, I believe, by the *Romanists* themselves, that the best commentaries on the Bible have been the works of Protestants. I know not indeed, whether, since the celebrated paraphrase of *Erasmus,* any scholar has appeared amongst them, whose works are much valued, even in his own communion. Why have those who excell in every other kind of knowledge, to whom the world owes much of the increase of light which has shone upon these latter ages, failed, and failed only when they have attempted to explain the scriptures of God? but only because they are in their church[8] less read and less examined, because they have another rule of deciding controversies, and instituting laws.

Of the Bible some of the books are prophetical, some doctrinal, and some historical; some partly doctrinal and partly historical,[9] as the gospels, of which we have in the subsequent pages attempted an illustration. The books of the Evangelists contain an account of the life of our blessed SAVIOUR, more particularly of the years of his ministry, interspersed with his precepts, doctrines, and predictions. Each of these histories contains facts and dictates related likewise in the rest, that the truth might be established by concurrence of testimony; and each has likewise facts and dictates which the rest omit, to prove that they were wrote without communication.

7. 'what it is difficult' in *Lit. Mag.*
8. 'why but because they are in the church' in *Lit. Mag.*
9. 'some doctrinal, some historical, and some partly doctrinal and historical' in *Lit. Mag.*

These writers not affecting the exactness of chronologers, and relating various events of the same life, or the same events with various circumstances, have some difficulties to him, who, without the help of many books, desires to collect a series of the acts and precepts of *Jesus Christ,*[10] fully to know his life, whose example was given for our imitation; fully to understand his precepts, which it is sure destruction to disobey.

In this work, therefore, an attempt has been made, by the help of harmonists and expositors, to reduce the four gospels into one series of narration, to form a compleat history out of the different narratives of the evangelists, by inserting every event in the order of time, and connecting every precept of life and doctrine, with the occasion on which it was delivered; shewing, as far as history or the knowledge of ancient[11] customs can inform us, the reason and propriety of every action; and explaining, or endeavouring to explain, every precept and declaration in its true meaning.

Let it not be hastily concluded, that we intend to substitute this book for the Gospels, or intrude our own expositions as the oracles of God. We recommend to the unlearned reader to consult us when he finds any difficulty, as men who have laboured not to deceive ourselves, and who are without any temptation to deceive him: But men, however, that while[12] they mean best, may be mistaken. Let him be careful, therefore, to distinguish what we cite from the Gospels from what we offer of our own:[13] He will find many difficulties answered;[14] and if some yet remain, let him remember that God is in heaven and we upon earth, that our thoughts are not God's thoughts,[15] and that the great cure of doubt is an humble mind.

THE LITERARY MAGAZINE

First number published: 19 May 1756 (*Public Advertiser*).
References: Boswell, *Life*, i:307–316.
            Courtney, pp. 75–77.
Johnson's Contributions: Preliminary Address 'To the Public'; original articles and reviews; some editorial supervision.
Copies: Harvard (one volume); Library of Congress (one volume); Yale; Bodleian (two volumes); British Museum.

10. semi-colon in *Lit. Mag.*   11. 'antient' in *Lit. Mag.*
12. 'him; but as men, however, that, while' in *Lit. Mag.*
13. 'as our own' in *Lit. Mag.*   14. 'removed' in *Lit. Mag.*
15. 'God is in heaven . . . thoughts' in italics in *Lit. Mag.* Compare Ecclesiastes 5:2; Isaiah 55:8.

IT is difficult to determine the extent of Johnson's official connection with the *Literary Magazine,* but his position seems to
have been that of a contributing editor or literary editor.
Boswell says that Johnson 'engaged also to superintend and
contribute largely' to it. 'What were his emoluments from
this undertaking, and what other writers were employed in it,
I have not discovered. He continued to write in it, with inter-
missions, till the fifteenth number.'[1] In a letter to Robert
Chambers, Johnson seems to imply that his connection is
quite unofficial, for he writes: 'You must not tell that I have
anything in it.'[2] Two years later he wrote to Dr. Burney: 'I
have been a little engaged, from time to time, in the *Literary
Magazine,* but not very lately. I have not the collection by
me, and therefore cannot draw out a catalogue of my own
parts, but will do it, and send it.'[3] This testimony, added to
the discussion of the plans of the periodical in his Address to
the Public, indicates that Johnson was quite closely connected
with it during its first year. The list of Johnson's articles
which Boswell compiled is probably substantially correct, and
the composition of these articles and reviews must have required a substantial amount of reading.

In charge of the details of the magazine as editor was William Faden, the printer of the *Rambler.*[4] He may have been
the printer, and his name is on the imprint of the first number. Murphy and Robert Chambers seem to have been contributors, and some articles have been attributed to Gold-

1. Boswell, *Life,* i:307. Boswell correctly places the appearance of the first
number in May, although he allowed a careless error in the *Chronological
Catalogue* in 1793, where it is dated January 1756.

2. 31 July 1756. The letter, now owned by Mr. R. B. Adam, is discussed
briefly in the *Cornhill Magazine,* New Series, lxvii(1929):409.

3. *Letters,* No. 113, 8 March 1758. Reprinted in Boswell, *Life,* i:328. It is to
be wished that Johnson had drawn out a catalogue of his own parts in the
Magazine for preservation.

4. J. Hawkins, *Life of Johnson* (1787), p. 351, says that 'one Faden, a
printer, was the editor.' Faden was also co-publisher of a few numbers of the
Universal Chronicle in 1760. He was I believe associated with Newbery, a
fact which may be the explanation of Murphy's statement that the *Literary
Magazine* was under Newbery's auspices. (*Miscellanies* i:413.)

smith.[5] In the second volume were reprinted Johnson's *Proposals* for Shakespeare and the Dedication of Lindsay's *Evangelical History*.

Croker, in his edition of the *Life* (1831, i:292n), suggests that the *Literary Magazine* is the result of the plan for a *Bibliothèque* which Johnson had outlined to Dr. Adams (Boswell, *Life*, i:283–5).

The Preface was reprinted in Volume xiv of the *Works* (1788).

Bibliographical Description

The / Literary magazine: / or, / universal review: / for the year MDCCLVI. / [*rule*] / [*quotation from Virgil*] / [*rule*] / Vol. I. / [*rule*] / [*ornament*] / [*parallel rule*] / London: / Printed for J. Richardson in Pater-noster Row.

The title-page of the first number has the imprint, 'London: Printed for W. Faden, in Wine-Office-Court, Fleet-Street. MDCCLVI.'

The imprint of the second and third volumes is, 'London: Printed for J. Wilkie, behind the Chapter-House, in St. Paul's Church-yard.'

Octavo in half-sheets. Price for each number (six or seven half-sheets): six pence. Approximately 21 × 13.5 cm. (British Museum copy.)

Signatures: Vol. I: frontispiece; 3 leaves; map; B–Sss4; Ttt3.
  Vol. II: frontispiece; title-page; plate; B–4C4.
  Vol. III: title-page; map; B–Tt4; Uu3. (Maps and plates inserted in all volumes.)

Pagination: Vol. I: frontispiece; [i] title-page of volume; [ii] blank; [iii] title-page of first number; [iv] Contents of first number; [iii]–iv To the Public; map; [1]–[494] Text; 3 leaves of In-

---

5. In the *Review of English Studies*, v(1929):410–30, R. W. Seitz argues that Goldsmith wrote nothing for the *Literary Magazine*. Prior perhaps associated Newbery with the magazine because of Murphy's statement. Griffith Jones, later the editor of the *London Chronicle*, was also a contributor. (J. Nichols, *Literary Anecdotes of the Eighteenth Century*, 1812, iii:465–6.) Gordon Goodwin, in his biography of Jones in the *Dictionary of National Biography*, seems to have elaborated this remark into a suggestion that Jones was the printer of the *Literary Magazine*.

dex. (Frequent errors in pagination: 47–48 repeated, but corrected in next sheet. 335–342 repeated, but corrected in next sheet. One leaf inserted after p. 280. 121–128 repeated. Leaf Rr4 is lacking, without any break in pagination.)

Vol. II: frontispiece; title-page with verso blank; plate; [1]–[552] Text; 4 leaves of Index. (Sheet Bbb has duplicate pagination, *361–*368.)

Vol. III: title-page with verso blank; map; [1]–331 Text; [332–334] Index.

The magazine was first announced for 2 February 1756 (*Public Advertiser,* 5 January 1756). The plans were changed, however, and the magazine appeared on or about the fifteenth of each month. The first number, for April 15 to May 15, was announced on the nineteenth of May; the last number appeared in July 1758. Each number was issued 'stabbed.'

Boswell writes that Johnson's last contribution was in the fifteenth number.

Whether the imprints (Faden for the first number, Richardson for the first volume, and Wilkie for the second and third volumes) indicate actual changes of ownership or merely changes in publishing arrangements, I do not know.

The set in the Yale Library lacks the number for April 1758; the first volume lacks the frontispiece, and the map is bound between the two title-pages. The copy in the British Museum lacks the map at the beginning of the third volume.

The stub of Uu4 (Vol. III) is visible in the copy at Yale. It may have been a blank leaf, or it may have been used for a title-page. In any event, it was intended to be removed, and should probably not be included in the collation.

The printer was probably Faden. See *London Evening Post,* 25 June 1757.

The heading of each number, usually 'The Literary Magazine,' is in January 1758 'The Literary and Antigallican Magazine.'

TO THE PUBLIC.

There are some Practices which custom and prejudice have so unhappily influenced, that to observe or neglect them is equally censurable. The promises made by the Undertakers of any new Design, every Man thinks himself at liberty to deride, and yet every man expects, and expects with reason, that he who solicits the Public Attention should give some account of his pretensions.

We are about to exhibit to our Countrymen a new MONTHLY COLLECTION, to which the well-deserved popularity of the first undertaking of this kind,[6] has now made it almost necessary to prefix the name of MAGAZINE. There are already many such periodical compilations, of which we do not envy the reception, nor shall dispute the excellence. If the nature of things would allow us to indulge our wishes, we should desire to advance our own interest without lessening that of any other, and to excite the curiosity of the vacant, rather than withdraw that which other writers have already engaged.

Our design is to give the history political and literary of every month, and our Pamphlets must consist, like other Collections, of many Articles unconnected and independent on each other.

The chief political Object of an *Englishman's* attention must be the great Council of the Nation, and we shall therefore register all public Proceedings with particular care. We shall not attempt to give any regular series of debates, or to amuse our Readers with senatorial rhetoric. The speeches inserted in other papers have been long known to be fictitious, and produced sometimes by men who never heard the debate, nor had any authentic information.[7] We have no Design to impose thus grossly[8] on our Readers, and shall therefore give the naked arguments used in the discussion of every question, and add, when they can be obtained, the Names of the Speakers.

As the Proceedings in Parliament are unintelligible without a knowledge of the facts to which they relate, and of the state of the Nations to which they extend their influence, we shall exhibit monthly a View, though contracted yet distinct, of Foreign Affairs, and lay open the Designs and Interests of those Nations which are considered by the *English* either as friends or enemies.

Of transactions in our own Country curiosity will demand a more particular account, and we shall record every remarkable event, extraordinary casualty, uncommon performance, or striking novelty, and shall apply our care to the discovery of truth, with very little reliance on the daily historians.

The Lists of Births, Marriages, Deaths, and Burials will be so drawn up that we hope very few omissions or mistakes will be

6. The *Gentleman's Magazine*, 1731.
7. Principally in mind Johnson must have had his own *Parliamentary Debates* in the *Gentleman's Magazine*.
8. 'grosly' in original.

found, though some must be expected to happen in so great a variety, where there is neither leisure nor opportunity for minute information.

It is intended that LISTS shall be given of all the Officers and Persons in public employment, and that all the Alterations shall be noted as they happen, by which our LIST will be a kind of Court-Register always complete.

The literary History necessarily contains an account of the Labours of the Learned, in which whether we shall shew much judgment or sagacity, must be left to our Readers to determine; we can promise only justness and candour. It is not to be expected that we can insert extensive extracts or critical Examinations of all the writings which this age of writers may offer to our notice. A few only will deserve the distinction of criticism, and a few only will obtain it. We shall try to select the best and most important pieces, and are not without hope, that we may sometimes influence the public voice, and hasten the popularity of a valuable Work.

Our regard will not be confined to Books; it will extend to all the productions of Science. Any new calculation, a commodious instrument, the discovery of any property in nature, or any new method of bringing known properties into use or view, shall be diligently treasured up wherever found.

In a paper designed for general perusal, it will be necessary to dwell most upon things of general Entertainment. The elegant trifles of literature, the wild strains of fancy, the pleasing amusements of harmless wit, shall therefore be considered as necessary to our Collection. Nor shall we omit researches into antiquity, explanations of coins or inscriptions, disquisitions on controverted history, conjectures on doubtful geography, or any other on [corrected to 'of' in *Works*] those petty works upon which learned ingenuity is sometimes employed.

To these accounts of temporary transactions and fugitive performances, we shall add some dissertations on things more permanent and stable; some inquiries into the history of nature, which has hitherto been treated as if mankind were afraid of exhausting it. There are in our own country many things and places worthy of note that are yet little known, and every day gives opportunities of new observations which are made and forgotten. We hope to find means of extending and perpetuating physiological discoveries, and with regard to this Article, and all others, intreat the assistance of curious and candid correspondents.

We shall labour to attain as much exactness as can be expected in such variety, and shall give as much variety as can consist with reasonable exactness; for this purpose a selection has been made of men qualified for the different parts of the work, and each has the employment assigned him, which he is supposed most able to discharge.

THE LONDON CHRONICLE

First number published: 1 January 1757.

References: Boswell, *Life,* i:317.
Courtney, p. 78.
Johnson's Contribution: Preliminary Discourse.

Sets of varying degrees of completeness are not rare. The first volume is in the following American libraries: Boston Athenaeum; Boston Public Library; Brown; Cornell; Harvard; Library of Congress; Michigan; Newberry; New York Public Library; University of Illinois; Wisconsin Historical Society; Yale.

THIS newspaper was the first of many 'Chronicles,' it was one of the strongest and most respected papers of the period, and according to Boswell it was the only one which Johnson read regularly. Its title, in the early years, was 'The London Chronicle: or, Universal Evening Post.' To it Johnson contributed, in addition to the Preliminary Discourse, a review of Grainger's *Sugar-Cane* (in part), and the *Character* of the Rev. Zachariah Mudge; and in it he reprinted his *Proposals* for Shakespeare.[1]

The title-page of the first volume reads:

The / London Chronicle / for / the year 1757. / Volume I. / From January 1, to June 30. / [*rule*] / To be continued. / [*parallel rule*] / London, / sold by J. Wilkie, behind the Chapter-House, in St. Paul's Church-Yard.

It was published three times weekly; the price of each num-

1. See Courtney, pp. 78, 103, 113. Also the article on the Newspaper by D. Nichol Smith in the second volume of A. S. Turberville's *Johnson's England,* (Oxford 1933).

ber was two pence. The price was increased to two pence half-
penny in July 1759, and to three pence in July 1776. Later in-
creases are not of immediate importance. The printer was
Strahan, who also was one of the proprietors: at his death in
1785 he owned a one-ninth interest. Dodsley was one of the
principal undertakers, but he withdrew on January 24, 1757
because of the scurrilous articles which were printed in the
paper despite his protest. The firm of 'R. & J. Dodsley' appears only on the first eleven numbers. The editor was Spens.[2]

Each issue consisted of one sheet in quarto, eight pages,
with vertical chain-lines: a special paper of about twice the
usual size was utilized, of which a half-sheet was printed as a
normal quarto.

For his Introduction Johnson was paid one guinea. The Introduction was included by T. Davies in his *Miscellaneous
and Fugitive Pieces* (1773). Facsimiles of the Introduction are
in the second volume of the Catalogue of the Johnsonian Library of Mr. R. B. Adam; in Stanley Morison, *The English
Newspaper* (Cambridge 1932), p. 134; and in A. S. Turberville, *Johnson's England* (Oxford 1933), ii:347. It is therefore
unnecessary to reproduce the Introduction here. It fills the
first page of the first issue, and has no special title.

The trimmed copy of the first volume in the Yale Library
measures 27.8 × 20.5 cm.

MACBEAN'S *GEOGRAPHY*

Published: 19 June 1773 (*St. James's Chronicle*).
References: Boswell, *Life,* ii:204.
            Courtney, p.116.
Johnson's Contribution: Preface.
Copies: Boston Public Library; Harvard; New York Public Li-

2. In addition to the references already given, see [R. A. Austen-Leigh],
Story of a Printing House (London 1912), p. 24; R. Straus, *Robert Dodsley*
(London 1910), pp. 96–99; *The Library*, 4th series, iii(1922–23):269–271. Griffith Jones edited the *London Chronicle* for some years until ill-health forced
him to resign in 1779, (*Boswell Papers*, xiii:210). For a list of variants in two
sets at the Bodleian, see *Bodleian Quarterly Record*, vii(1934):517–9.

brary; Yale; Bodleian (Douce); British Museum (2 copies); Edinburgh University; Lichfield Birthplace; John Rylands Library; Signet Library; R. B. Adam; Dr. R. W. Chapman.

FOR Alexander Macbean, one of his amanuenses in the laborious task of transcribing copy for his *Dictionary,* Johnson seems ever to have retained an humane interest. His powers of discrimination and judgment were perhaps not great, but for his learning Johnson respected him; perhaps it was the insufficiency of these large general powers of mind that rendered Macbean's life little more, so far as we can determine, than an uninterrupted wretchedness.

Johnson's characterization of Macbean was recorded by Fanny Burney in 1778. To Mrs. Thrale's inquiry concerning Macbean, Johnson replied:

Madam, he is a Scotchman; he is a man of great learning, and for his learning I respect him, and I wish to serve him. He knows many languages, and knows them well; but he knows nothing of life. I advised him to write a geographical dictionary; but I have lost all hopes of his ever doing anything properly, since I found he gave as much labour to Capua as to Rome.[1]

I think it not unlikely that Mrs. Piozzi remembered imperfectly the same conversation when she wrote years later to Queeney concerning *Retrospection:*

The eternal difficulty is to judge where to contract most and where to amplify, lest one should at last resemble Johnson's Macbean, whom he set a long time ago to compile a Geographical Dictionary, and looking it over said he had dwelt too little on the Article 'Athens' — 'Ah Doctor' says the man, 'but if I make so much writing about *Athens,* what room will be left for me to talk of *Abingdon?*' — 'After this conversation' cries Johnson 'you may be sure we talked no more of work.'[2]

To Macbean's memory Johnson paid his final tribute in a letter to Mrs. Thrale at the time of Macbean's death: 'He

1. *Diary of Madame D'Arblay* (London 1842), i:93. Actually, in the *Dictionary* 31 lines are devoted to Capua, 54 lines to Rome, and 75 lines to Tarsus.
2. Letter of April 27, 1796; published in *The Queeney Letters,* edited by the Marquis of Lansdowne (New York 1934), p. 256. In editing *Letters to and from Samuel Johnson* (London 1788), i:218, Mrs. Piozzi wrote: 'Macbean was a man of great learning, with little power of bringing it into play.—He had read before he died the Hebrew Bible eleven times over.'

was very pious, he was very innocent; he did no ill, and of doing good a continual tenour of distress allowed him few opportunities: he was very highly esteemed in the house.'[3]

Boswell indicates that the Preface was acknowledged by Johnson, and Thomas Tyers wrote that Johnson 'composed the Preface . . . to Macbean's Classical Geography.'[4] It was reprinted in Volume xiv of the *Works* (1788). The volume is not uncommon in old libraries. It is bibliographically unexceptional; Dr. Chapman possesses an uncut copy. Johnson's copy is in lot 32 in the *Catalogue* of his Library (1785).

Bibliographical Description

A / Dictionary / of / ancient geography, / explaining / the local appellations in sacred, Grecian, / and Roman history; / exhibiting / the extent of kingdoms, and situations of cities, &c. / And illustrating / the allusions and epithets in the Greek and Roman poets. / The whole established by proper authorities, and designed for / the use of schools. / By Alexander Macbean, M. A. / [*rule*] / [*motto*] / [*parallel rule*] / London, / Printed for G. Robinson, in Pater Noster-Row; and T. Cadell, / in the Strand. 1773.

Octavo in half-sheets; 21.5 × 13 cm.; 7/6 bound.

Signatures: [A](quarter-sheet); B–Kkkk⁴; Llll(quarter-sheet).

Pagination: [i] title-page; [ii] blank; [iii]–iv Preface. The text of the Classical Geographical Dictionary is printed in alphabetical order, in double columns, without pagination.

PREFACE.

The necessity of Geography to historical, political, and commercial knowledge, has been proved too often to be proved again. The curiosity of this nation is sufficiently awakened, and no books are more eagerly received than those which enlarge or facilitate an acquaintance with distant countries.

But as the face of the world changes in time by the migration

3. *Letters*, 26 June 1784.   4. *Gentleman's Magazine*, lv(1785):87.

of nations, the ravages of conquest, the decay of one empire, and the erection of another; as new inhabitants have new languages, and new languages give new names; the maps or descriptions of a later age are not easily applied to the narrations of a former: those that read the Ancients must study the ancient geography, or wander in the dark, without distinct views or certain knowledge.

Yet though the Ancients are read among us, both in the original languages and in translations, more perhaps than in any other country, we have hitherto had very little assistance in ancient Geography. The treatise of Dr. Wells is too general for use, and the Classical Geographical Dictionary, which commonly passes under the name of Eachard, is little more than a catalogue of naked names.

A more ample account of the old world is apparently wanting to English literature, and no form seemed equally commodious with that of an alphabetical series. In effect, however systematically any book of General Geography may be written, it is seldom used otherwise than as a Dictionary. The student wanting some knowledge of a new place, seeks the name in the index, and then by a second labour finds that in a System which he would have found in a Dictionary by the first.

As Dictionaries are commodious, they are likewise fallacious: he whose works exhibit an apparent connexion and regular subordination cannot easily conceal his ignorance, or favour his idleness; the completeness of one part will show the deficiency of another: but the writer of a Dictionary may silently omit what he does not know; and his ignorance, if it happens to be discovered, slips away from censure under the name of forgetfulness.

This artifice of Lexicography I hope I shall not often be found to have used. I have not only digested former Dictionaries into my alphabet, but have consulted the ancient Geographers, without neglecting other authors. I have in some degree enlightened ancient by modern Geography, having given the situation of places from later observation. Names are often changing, but place is always the same, and to know it exactly is always of importance: there is no use of erring with the ancients, whose knowledge of the globe was very imperfect; I have therefore used ancient names and modern calculations. The longitude is reckoned from London to the east and west.

A work like this has long been wanted: I would willingly flatter myself that the want is now supplied; and that the English student will for the future more easily understand the narratives of ancient historians, the reasonings of ancient statesmen, and the descriptions of ancient poets.

MAURICE'S *POEMS*

Published: May 1780 (*Monthly Review*).[1]
References: Boswell, *Life,* iii:370, note 2.
       Courtney, p. 129.
Johnson's Contributions: Preface to the *Oedipus Tyrannus;* and probably assistance with the Dedication of the volume.
Copies: Library Company of Philadelphia; New York Public Library; Yale (2 copies); British Museum; R. B. Adam; Dr. R. W. Chapman.

REVEREND THOMAS MAURICE, in charge óf a country parish in Essex, published numerous volumes of poetry, but I believe only a single sermon, which was judged by the reviewer to be 'a judicious discourse.'[2] Of his friendship with Johnson little is known beyond what Maurice himself says in the Advertisement to a new edition of the poems.[3] Since this Advertisement contains proof of Johnson's assistance, and since its style offers a guide to aid in assigning the Dedication to Johnson, I shall reproduce it.

The following arduous attempt to give the finest drama of Sophocles an English dress, was commenced by me at a very juvenile period, when at Stanmore, under my revered friend and preceptor Dr. PARR: at whose august tribunal most of the choruses were *shewed up* (to use a school term) as EXERCISES. The accustomed candour of that liberal and enlightened scholar induced him to receive with complacency, my well-intended, however inadequate efforts. The work, when finished, afterwards passed under the eye of another revered friend of my youth, Dr. SAMUEL JOHNSON, who condescended to write the Preface, and which

1. The Dedication is dated 15 June 1779. Maurice apologizes in his general preface for the long delay.
2. Kenrick's *London Review,* ix(June 1779):467. The sermon was published by Kearsly.
3. T. Maurice, *Westminster Abbey with other Poems* (1813), p. 122. This book is now not very commonly to be found. The translation of *Oedipus Tyrannus,* with Johnson's preface, was reprinted separately in 1822. It was Dr. Parr who introduced Maurice to Johnson. See E. H. Barker, *Parriana* (1828) i:432. There are references to Johnson and to this translation, but little new information, in the *Monthly Mirror,* viii(Nov. 1799):259ff. and in Maurice's *Memoirs,* Part One (1819), p. 73.

bears internal evidence of its origin. As only a few copies were at that time printed off, it is here again, with diffidence, submitted to that public, whose indulgence my early productions have already so amply experienced.

This apologetic Advertisement is so unlike anything that Johnson wrote that I much doubt whether Maurice, thirty years earlier, could have composed the fine Dedication to the Duke of Marlborough without very large assistance from Johnson. To be sure, Maurice makes no mention of that Dedication, which is not reprinted, but since there was no occasion to speak of it, his omission can not be considered an indication that Johnson did not help with the Dedication.

The Dedication to the volume published in 1813, in keeping with the trend of the period, is merely a brief statement of the fact of dedication, not a dedicatory epistle: it therefore proves little or nothing. In general Johnson avoided the use of classical tags, so that the use of 'stupet in titulis'[4] in the first paragraph of the Dedication might arouse suspicion; yet Windham has the following note of Johnson's conversation at Ashbourne in 1784: '*Qui stupet* in statuis, applied to Joseph Warton's admiration of fine passages. His taste is amazement.'[5] The archaic form 'hath' is seldom used in Johnson's acknowledged dedications, whether by chance or by conscious avoidance I know not. The form 'hath' is used in the Dedication to Lenglet du Fresnoy's *Chronological Tables;* as in the case of that Dedication, I believe that the dedicator wrote this one, with generous assistance from Johnson. Note that 'hath' is employed twice in the last paragraph of the Preface below.[6]

Bibliographical Description

Poems / and / miscellaneous pieces, / with a / free translation / of the / Oedipus Tyrannus of Sophocles. / By / the Rev.

4. Horace, *Satires*, Book One, vi:17.
5. From Windham's Diary, quoted in *Letters*, ii:441.
6. 'Hath' is also used in the Dedication of the *Evangelical History*, and in the *Proposals* for the *Harleian Miscellany*.

Thomas Maurice, A. B. / of / University College, Oxford. / London, / Printed for the author; / and sold by J. Dodsley, Pall-Mall;. G. Kearsly, in Fleet-street; / Messrs. Fletcher, Prince, Parker and Bliss, Oxford; and / Messrs. Woodyer and Merryl, in Cambridge. / M.DCC.LXXIX.

Facsimile of Preface in the second volume of the Catalogue of the R. B. Adam Library.
Quarto; 26 × 20.5 cm. Price: 10/6.

Signatures: A⁴; [a]²; B–Hh⁴. (Fleur-de-lis watermark in sheets B–Aa.)

Pagination: [i] title-page; [ii] blank; iii–iv Dedication; v–vi Preface; vii–x Subscribers; [xi] Contents; [xii] blank; [1]–237 Text; [238] blank. (Pp. 231–2 repeated in the numbering; Johnson's Preface is on pp. 149–152.)

Three hundred copies were for the subscribers.

Johnson and Percy were among the subscribers. The first poems in the book are addressed to Johnson and Percy, respectively. Boswell saw the Verses to Dr. Johnson, in manuscript, in 1776.[7] It seems surprising that he did not suspect Johnson's assistance in the book, which he might easily have seen at Johnson's house. When the book was first published, however, Boswell was in Scotland.

Johnson's copy is in lot 326 in the *Catalogue* of his Library (1785).

Messrs. James Tregaskis & Son had in 1936 (*Catalogue* 1021) a presentation copy in which the numbering of pp. 118 and 119 had been corrected. In other copies these pages are misnumbered 105 and 112 respectively. There is another very slight variation in one of the copies at Yale, in which the initial T on p. 149 does not appear.

DEDICATION

TO HIS GRACE THE DUKE OF MARLBOROUGH.

MY LORD,

To animate mankind to the practice of virtue, and the conquest of those passions which are most detrimental to society, by

---

7. *Boswell Papers,* xi:202, Lichfield, 26 March 1776. Boswell neglected to mention this in the *Life.*

holding forth examples taken from real life, either of vice degraded or triumphant virtue, hath ever been the chief aim of those who duly considered the nature and origin of theatrical composition. While Comedy holds the mirror to folly, it is the office of Tragedy to expose to public detestation those vices, to which the distinguished rank of the offender, or the nature of the offence itself, sanctified by the "stupet in titulis" of popular delusion, may have given a long and secure dominion over the human mind.

SOPHOCLES, my Lord, hath given us in the following pages a lively and pathetic instance of the destructive nature of ambition, of the instability of human grandeur, and of the disasters too generally consequent when the passions are not under the due subordination of reason. I am convinced I shall offend no person except yourself, when I add that the steady and tranquil happiness which hath ever attended your Grace in the exercise of every social and domestic virtue, and the universal respect paid to that integrity which neither interest could ever allure, nor ambition ever shake from the basis whereon it is fixed, will be the best proof and the strongest confirmation of the doctrine which this great master of tragic writing and morality hath thus endeavoured to establish.

At a period when the most solemn ties, both religious and civil, are treated with such avowed contempt, to behold those, who are most eminent among our nobility, steadily adhering to the dictates of virtue, and setting so conspicuous an example of parental duty and conjugal affection, must, while it abashes the front of vice, excite in the breast of every good man the sublimest satisfaction, accompanied with the heartiest wishes for its long continuance among mankind.

I have the honour to be, My Lord, Your Grace's most obliged And most devoted servant,

THOMAS MAURICE.

Woodford, 15th June, 1779.

PREFACE.

The Tragedy of which I have attempted to convey the beauties into the English language in a free translation, stands amidst the foremost of the classical productions of antiquity. Of tragical writing it has ever been esteemed the model and the master-piece. The grandeur of the subject is not less eminent than the dignity of the personages who are employed in it; and the design of the whole can only be rivalled by that art with which the particular parts are conducted. The subject is a nation labouring under calamities of the most dreadful and portentous kind; and the leading character is a wise and mighty prince, expiating by his punishment the involuntary crimes of which those calamities were the effect. The design is of the most interesting and important nature, to inculcate a due moderation in our passions, and an implicit obedience to that providence of which the decrees are equally unknown and irresistable [*sic*].

So sublime a composition could not fail to secure the applause, and fix the admiration of ages. The philosopher is exercised in the contemplation of its deep and awful morality; the critic is captivated by its dramatic beauties, and the man of feeling is interested by those strokes of genuine passion which prevail in almost every page—which every character excites, and every new event tends to diversify in kind or in degree.

The three grand unities of time, place, and action,[8] are observed with scrupulous exactness. However complicate its various parts may on the first view appear, on a nearer and more accurate examination we find every thing useful, every thing necessary; some secret spring of action laid open, some momentous truth inculcated, or some important end promoted: not one scene is superfluous, nor is there one Episode that could be retrenched. The successive circumstances of the play arise gradually and naturally one out of the other, and are connected with such inimitable judgment, that if the smallest part were taken away the whole would fall to the ground. The principal objection to this tragedy is, that the punishment of Oedipus is much more than adequate to his crimes: that his crimes are only the effect of his ignorance, and that consequently the guilt of them is to be imputed not to Oedipus, but Apollo, who ordained and predicted them, and that he is only *Phœbi reus,* as Seneca expresses himself. In vindication of Sophocles, it must be considered that the conduct of Oedipus is by no means so irreproachable as some have contended: for though his public character is delineated as that of a good king, anxious for the welfare of his subjects, and ardent in his endeavours to appease the gods by incense and supplication, yet we find him in private life choleric, haughty, inquisitive; impatient of controul, and impetuous in resentment. His character, even as a king, is not free from the imputation of imprudence, and our

8. Compare Johnson's *Preface to Shakespeare* (1765).

opinion of his piety is greatly invalidated by his contemptuous treatment of the wise, the benevolent, the sacred Tiresias. The rules of tragic art scarcely permit that a perfectly virtuous man should be loaded with misfortunes. Had Sophocles presented to our view a character less debased by vice, or more exalted by virtue, the end of his performance would have been frustrated; instead of agonizing compassion, he would have raised in us indignation unmixed, and horror unabated. The intention of the poet would have been yet more frustrated on the return of our reason, and our indignation would have been transferred from Oedipus to the gods themselves—from Oedipus, who committed parricide, to the gods who first ordained, and then punished it. By making him criminal in a small degree, and miserable in a very great one, by investing him with some excellent qualities, and some imperfections, he at once inclines us to pity and to condemn. His obstinacy darkens the lustre of his other virtues; it aggravates his impiety, and almost justifies his sufferings. This is the doctrine of Aristotle and of nature, and shews Sophocles to have had an intimate knowledge of the human heart, and the springs by which it is actuated. That his crimes and punishment still seem disproportionate, is not to be imputed as a fault to Sophocles, who proceeded only on the antient and popular notion of Destiny; which we know to have been the basis of Pagan theology.

It is not the intention of the Translator to proceed farther in a critical discussion of the beauties and defects of a Tragedy which hath already employed the pens of the most distinguished commentators; which hath wearied conjecture, and exhausted all the arts of unnecessary and unprofitable defence. The Translator is no stranger to the merits of Dr. Franklin; whose character he reveres, and by whose excellent performance he has been animated and instructed. He thinks it necessary to disclaim every idea of rivalship with an author of such established and exalted reputation. The present translation, though it be executed with far less ability than that of Doctor Franklin, may deserve some notice, because professedly written on very different principles. The Doctor was induced by his plan, and enabled by his erudition, to encounter all the difficulties of *literal* translation. This work will be found by the reader, what it is called by the writer, a *free* translation. The Author was not fettered by his text, but guided by it; he has however not forgotten the boundaries by which liberal translation is distinguished from that which is wild and licentious. He has always endeavoured to represent the sense of his original, he hopes sometimes to have caught its spirit, and he throws himself without reluctance, but not without diffidence, on the candour of those readers who understand and feel the difference that subsists between the Greek and English languages, between antient and modern manners, between nature and refinement, between a Sophocles who appeals to posterity, and a writer who catches at the capricious taste of the day.

PAYNE'S *NEW TABLES OF INTEREST*

Published: 28 February 1758 (*London Chronicle*).
Reference: Courtney, p. 79.
Johnson's Contribution: Preface.
Copies: British Museum; Professor C. B. Tinker. One of the rarest of Johnsonian books.

JOHN PAYNE was employed for many years in the Bank of England, where he rose to the position of Chief Accountant. It is therefore not surprising that he should have prepared these Tables for sale, and doubtless the statement on the title-page, that the author was 'of the Bank of England,' was intended to convey to the purchasers a sense of authoritativeness and official approbation. John Payne was also a bookseller and the publisher of the *Rambler* and of the *Universal Chronicle;* with Joseph Bouquet he published Lauder's *Milton.* As a friend of Johnson and as a fellow-member of the Ivy-Lane Club, it was not unnatural that he should ask his famous friend for a recommendatory Preface. Only one personal anecdote of Payne seems to be recorded, that of his footrace with Dr. Johnson.[1] He died unmarried in 1787.

The Preface to the *Tables of Interest* is not mentioned by Boswell. It was first included in Johnson's *Works* by Alexander Chalmers in 1806. Courtney cites only the authority of

---

1. *Letters,* ii:363, n. 1. Hill quotes from Croker's edition. Croker says that the anecdote appeared first in the *European Magazine.*

To distinguish the confusing names of three different families of Paynes, see J. Nichols, *Literary Anecdotes of the Eighteenth Century* (London 1812), iii:223, 462, 660, 736, and vi:439.

the Catalogue of the British Museum Library. That it was written by Dr. Johnson there can be, I think, little doubt.

Bibliographical Description

New tables / of / interest. / By John Payne, / of the Bank of England. / [*mottoes*] / London: / Printed by D. Leach for J. Payne, at Pope's Head / in Pater-noster-Row. / M DCC LVIII.

Broad (oblong) sextodecimo in four signatures; 9 × 12 cm. Publication price: 4/0. (It was offered for 3/– in 1759.)

Signatures: a,b⁴; c²; A–U⁴; X–Aa⁴; Bb²; X–Ee⁴. (The four and one-half sheets after Signature U are signed in brackets.)

Pagination: (Preliminary matter not paginated) [i] title-page; [ii] author's signature; [iii–vii] Preface; [viii] Erratum and notice to the binder; [ix–xx] Explanation of Contents; [1]–196 + 64 unnumbered pages, Tables.

No other book is known to me in exactly this format, though it was probably used occasionally. The format may be identified with certainty by matching the vertical chain-lines. The watermark is near the bottom of the inner edge, and can occur only on the second and third leaves of a gathering (or on leaves one and four).

Each copy was signed by the author, on the verso of the title-page, as an added assurance of accuracy and authenticity. This practice, though not frequent, was not unknown in the eighteenth century; only a few months later John Angell signed and numbered each copy of his *Stenography, or Short-hand Improved.*

I have noted two typographical errors: (1) in the next to the last paragraph of the Preface, the word 'take' is in Roman type (perhaps intentionally); (2) the fourth line of c1 verso reads '5 per eent.'

The Preface, except the quotation from Pope, is printed in italic type.

PREFACE.

Among the writers of fiction, whose business is to furnish that entertainment which Fancy perpetually demands, it is a standing plea, that the beauties of nature are now exhausted, that imitation has exerted all its power, and that nothing more can be done for the service of their mistress, than to exhibit a perpetual transposition of known objects, and draw new pictures, not by introducing new images, but by giving new lights and shades, a new arrangement and colouring to the old. This plea has been chearfully admitted; and Fancy, led by the hand of a skilful guide, treads over again the flowery path she has often trod before, as much enamoured with every new diversification of the same prospect, as with the first appearance of it.

In the regions of Science, however, there is not the same indulgence: the Understanding and the Judgment travel there in the persuit of Truth, whom they always expect to find in one simple form, free from the disguises of dress and ornament; and, as they travel with laborious step and a fixed eye, they are content to stop when the shades of night darken the prospect, and patiently wait the radiance of a new morning, to lead them forward in the path they have chosen, which, however thorny or however steep, is severely preferred to the most pleasing excursions that bring them no nearer to the object of their search. The plea, therefore, that nature is exhausted, and that nothing is left to gratify the mind but different combinations of the same ideas, when urged as a reason for multiplying unnecessary labours among the sons of Science, is not so readily admitted: the Understanding, when in possession of Truth, is satisfied with the simple acquisition; and not, like Fancy, inclined to wander after new pleasures in the diversification of objects already known, which, perhaps, may lead to Error.

But notwithstanding this general disinclination to accumulate labours for the sake of that pleasure which arises merely from different modes of investigating Truth, yet, as the mines of Science have been diligently opened, and their treasures widely diffused, there may be parts chosen, which, by a proper combination and arrangement, may contribute not only to entertainment but use; like the rays of the sun, collected in a convex[2] mirrour, to serve particular purposes of light and heat.

The power of Arithmetical numbers has been tried to a vast extent, and variously applied to the improvement both of business and science. In particular, so many calculations have been made with respect to the value and use of money, that some serve only for speculation and amusement; and there is great opportunity for selecting a few that are peculiarly adapted to common

2. Corrected in ink to 'concave.'

business, and the daily interchanges of property among men. Those which happen in the Public Funds are, at this time, the most frequent and numerous; and to answer the purposes of that business, in some degree more perfectly than has hitherto been done, the following Tables are published. What that degree of perfection above other Tables of the same kind may be, is a matter, not of opinion and taste in which many might vary, but of accuracy and usefulness with respect to which most will agree. The approbation they meet with will, therefore, depend upon the experience of those for whom they were principally designed, the Proprietors of the Public Funds, and the Brokers who transact the business of the Funds, to whose patronage they are chearfully committed.

Among the Brokers of Stocks are men of great honour and probity, who are candid and open in all their transactions, and incapable of mean and selfish purposes: and it is to be lamented, that a market of such importance as the present state of this nation has made theirs, should be brought into any discredit by the intrusion of bad men, who, instead of serving their country, and procuring an honest subsistence in the army or the fleet, endeavour to maintain luxurious tables and splendid equipages by sporting with the public credit.

It is not long since the evil of Stock-jobbing was risen to such an enormous height, as to threaten great injury to every actual proprietor; particularly to many widows and orphans, who being bound to depend upon the Funds for their whole subsistence, could not possibly retreat from the approaching danger. But this evil, after many unsuccessful attempts of the Legislature to conquer it, was, like many other, at length subdued by its own vio lence; and the reputable Stock-brokers seem now to have it in their power effectually to prevent its return, by not suffering the most distant approaches of it to take footing in their own practice, and by opposing every effort made for its recovery by the desperate sons of fortune, who, not having the courage of highwaymen, *take* 'Change-alley rather than the road, because, tho' more injurious than highwaymen, they are less in danger of punishment by the loss either of liberty or life.

With respect to the other patrons to whose encouragement these Tables have been recommended, the proprietors of the Public Funds who are busy in the improvement of their fortunes; it is sufficient to say—that no motive can sanctify the accumulation of wealth, but an ardent desire to make the most honourable and

virtuous use of it, by contributing to the support of good government, the increase of arts and industry, the rewards of genius and
virtue, and the relief of wretchedness and want.

> What GOOD, what TRUE, what FIT, we justly call,
> Let this be all our care—for this is All;
> To lay this TREASURE up, and hoard with haste
> What *ev'ry day* will want, and most the *last*.
> This done, the poorest can no wants endure;
> And this not done, the richest must be poor.   POPE.

JOHNSON AND WILLIAM PAYNE

IT is disappointing to be forced to admit that nothing is
known of William Payne beyond the information of the title-
pages of his books and Boswell's brief mention of him. More
facts may in time be recovered, but I have thus far been unsuccessful in my inquiries. Boswell remarks that he was the
brother of the respectable bookseller of that name, and Dr.
Hill took this to mean John Payne of the Bank of England.[1]
This was one of Hill's few errors, for Boswell must certainly
have meant Thomas Payne, who was not related to John. It
is not that John Payne was not a respectable bookseller, but
he had died in 1787 and in any event Boswell would presumably have thought of him as the Accountant of the Bank
of England or perhaps as the publisher of the *Rambler*,[2]
whereas 'honest Tom Payne' could be identified completely
as the 'respectable bookseller.' Furthermore, Thomas Payne
was the publisher of all the books written by William Payne,
while John Payne's name appears in the imprint of the *Game
of Draughts* only. In 1779, Thomas Payne sold to Lowndes
the right to print in Hoyle's *Games* 'a Pamphlet called the
Game of Drafts as written by my late Brother William
Payne.'[3]

1. Boswell, *Life*, i:317.
2. That John Payne was the publisher of the *Universal Chronicle* seems
not to have been known by Boswell.
3. British Museum, Additional Manuscript 38728, folio 165. It is dated 11
February 1779. Payne must therefore have died between 1773 and 1779.

It is my belief that William Payne made the acquaintance of Johnson through his brother Thomas Payne, who may have solicited Johnson's help, but manuscript records of Thomas Payne which might have contained references to the matter have been lost. Therefore one can maintain with assurance only that William Payne was a teacher of mathematics and a student of the games of Whist and Draughts. He published four books, three of which are of interest to Johnsonians: *An Introduction to the Game of Draughts* (1756), *An Introduction to Geometry* (1767, enlarged edition 1768), *Elements of Trigonometry* (1772), and *Maxims for Playing the Game of Whist* (published anonymously 1773). The last of these books needs no further discussion.

Each of the three acknowledged books contains a dedication and a preface. In each case I believe that the dedication was furnished by Johnson and the preface by Payne. The reasons for this statement require to be investigated. Boswell marks both the Dedication and Preface to the *Game of Draughts* as acknowledged, and both were included in Volume xiv of the *Works*. The Dedication is unmistakable, but the Preface, despite some good sentences, seems to me very doubtful, especially the last paragraph. It seems to me highly probable that this Preface was included because of a mistake which caused confusion between Dedication and Preface, a mistake which has been amazingly frequent in Johnsonian bibliography.[4] The text of the Preface will be included, that

4. This confusion has arisen in connection with Mrs. Lennox's translation of Sully's *Memoirs*, Dr. James's *Medicinal Dictionary*, and Kennedy's *Astronomical Chronology*, and one cannot feel very certain that the same or other mistakes will not continue to cause confusion in the future.

It is not without interest that Chalmers, who reprinted the Dedication in the *Works* (1806), did not include the Preface. Furthermore, I learn from Professor D. N. Smith that in Mrs. Thrale's list of Johnson's writings (*Thraliana*, end of 1777) the Dedication is included but not the Preface.

The Prefaces of Payne's books have sentences scattered through them that seem quite Johnsonian, but the author thoughtfully included in each instance some passages that are distinctly not Johnsonian. For example, this sentence from the *Geometry* seems to me to pass any test for Johnsonian style and content: 'No man ought to increase the croud of books, without some prospect of increasing or facilitating knowledge.' But the next sentence is impossible.

my judgment may be corroborated or refuted by qualified judges. No copy was catalogued with Johnson's library.

The *Introduction to Geometry* and the *Elements of Trigonometry* are not mentioned by Boswell. Both are represented in the *Catalogue* of Johnson's Library, one copy of the first edition and one of the second edition of the *Geometry,* and two copies of the *Trigonometry*. This is sufficiently surprising, despite Johnson's fondness for mathematical books, to make one wonder. Mr. R. B. Adam recently attributed the Dedication of the *Geometry* to Johnson, and it has been unhesitatingly accepted by Dr. Powell in his revision of the *Life*.[5] There can be, I think, no doubt that it is wholly by Johnson. In the second edition, the Dedication was unchanged, while the Preface was considerably altered, and this evidence of revision is an additional reason for deciding against a possible Johnsonian authorship of this Preface, and, by analogy, of the Preface to the *Game of Draughts*.

The Dedication to the *Trigonometry* is a slighter work, yet it seems to me that each of its three brief sentences has a Johnsonian ring. Perhaps I am too sanguine, yet both external and internal evidence have 'emboldened' me to include the book here rather than in an appendix of doubtful and spurious works. Further study of Payne's prose and of the facts of his life by practised Johnsonians is needed.

Bibliographical Description of the GAME OF DRAUGHTS

An / Introduction / to the game of / draughts. / Containing / fifty select games, / together with / many critical situations for drawn games, / won games, and fine strokes. / The whole designed for the instruction of / young players, in this innocent and / delightful amusement. / [*rule*] / By William Payne, / teacher of mathematics. / [*parallel rule*] / London, / Printed for the author at the Golden Ball in Bedford-street, /

5. Boswell, *Life,* ii:481–2. This dedication, however, was twice mentioned in the nineteenth century as a Johnsonian piece. See *Notes and Queries,* First Series, i:259 (Mr. Bolton Corney); and H. B. Wheatley, *The Dedication of Books* (London 1887), p. 184.

Covent-Garden: and sold by T. Payne, at the Meuse-Gate / in Castle-street; J. Marks, in St Martin's-lane; J. Jackson, / in St James's-street; W. Shropshire, in New Bond-street; / W. Owen, in Fleet-street; J. Payne, in Pater-noster-Row; / and J. Brotherton, in Cornhill. / M DCC LVI. / [Price two shillings and sixpence.]

Published: January, 1756 (*Gentleman's Magazine*).[6]
References: Boswell, *Life,* i:317.
         Courtney, p. 74.
Johnson's Contribution: Dedication.
Copies: Boston Public Library; Library of Congress; British Museum (two copies); Cambridge University; R. B. Adam; Professor C. B. Tinker. Rare: three of the copies listed are in poor condition.

Facsimile of Dedication in the second volume of the Catalogue of the R. B. Adam Library.
Octavo; 18.3 × 11.3 cm.

Signatures: A–I4; K2.

Pagination: (preliminary leaves unnumbered) [i] title-page; [ii] blank; [iii–v] Dedication; [vi] blank; [vii–viii] Preface; [1]–67 Text; [68] blank.

There is also a spurious edition, with the same date on the title-page. Of this I have examined two copies, and a third was offered in the Isham Sale.[7] It seems, therefore, to be fully as rare as the original edition. Signatures A, H, I, and K are printed on wove paper, and the type is not like any in use in the eighteenth century. It must have been printed soon after 1800. I am not at all sure that it was done with intent to deceive.

This edition may be easily distinguished from the original: it was all re-set, and every page shows differences. The easiest 'point' of differentiation is line 7 of the title-page: in the original this line reads 'Together with,' while in the spurious edition it is printed in capitals 'TOGETHER WITH.' The spurious edition has numerous misprints, of which the most striking on the title-page are 'Teacher of the mathematics' and 'Bedford-sttreet,' and on the second page of the Dedication, line 7, 'to take it its Fate.'

6. It is listed in the *Universal Magazine,* February, 1756.
7. American Art Association–Anderson Galleries, 4 May 1933.

Both Dedication and Preface were included in Volume xiv of the *Works* (1788), and in Twiss's *Miscellanies*.[8]

DEDICATION

TO THE RIGHT HONOURABLE WILLIAM-
HENRY EARL OF ROCHFORD, &c.

My LORD,
    When I take the Liberty of addressing to Your Lordship *A Treatise on the Game of* DRAUGHTS, I easily foresee that I shall be in danger of suffering Ridicule on one Part, while I am gaining Honour on the other, and that many who may envy me the Distinction of approaching You, will deride the Present I presume to offer.
    Had I considered this little Volume as having no Purpose beyond that of teaching a Game, I should indeed have left it to take its Fate without a Patron. Triflers may find or make any Thing a Trifle; but since it is the great Characteristic of a wise Man to see Events in their Causes, to obviate Consequences, and ascertain Contingencies, your Lordship will think nothing a Trifle by which the Mind is inured to Caution, Foresight, and Circumspection. The same Skill, and often the same Degree of Skill, is exerted in great and little Things, and your Lordship may sometimes exercise, at a harmless Game, those Abilities which have been so happily employed in the Service of your Country.
    I am, *My LORD, Your Lordship's Most Obliged Most Obedient, and most Humble Servant,*
                                          William Payne.

PREFACE.

It is natural for a Man to think well of the Art which he professes to teach, and I may therefore be expected to have some Esteem for the Play of DRAUGHTS. I would not, however, be thought to over-rate it. Every Art is valued in a joint Proportion to its Difficulty and Usefulness. The Use of DRAUGHTS is the same with that of any other Game of Skill, that it may amuse those Hours for which more laudable Employment is not at Hand, and happy is the Man whose equability of Temper and constancy of Perseverance in better Things, exempt him from the Need of such Reliefs.
    Whatever may be determined concerning its Use, its Difficulty

8. See Courtney, p. 74.

is incontestible; for among the Multitudes that practise it, very few understand it. There are indeed not many who by any frequency of Playing can attain a moderate Degree of Skill without Examples and Instructions. I have therefore here given a Collection of the most artful Games, the most critical Situations, and the most striking Revolutions, that have fallen within my Notice; which are such as may, in some Respects, set this Game even equal with that of *Chess.*

There is indeed one Secret boasted in the World which I cannot teach. Some Men pretend to an infallible Method, by which he that moves first shall win the Game; but no such Hero has it ever been my fortune to encounter, and no such do I expect to find. Nor can it be proved that the first Mover has any considerable Advantage over a Person equally skilful with himself. In this Opinion I have the Concurrence of those excellent Players Mr *James Randell,* Captain *John Godfrey,* and Mr *William Wolly,* my intimate and worthy Friends, whose Examples have greatly contributed to my skill in the Game; but in particular those of the great *Randell,* of whom it may with probability be asserted, that what he could not attain will never be discovered.

Bibliographical Description of the GEOMETRY

An / Introduction / to / geometry. / Containing / the most useful propositions in Euclid, / and other authors. / Demonstrated in a clear and easy method, for the use / of learners. / [*rule*] / By William Payne. / [*rule*] / [*printer's flowers*] / [*parallel rule*] / London: / Sold by T. Payne, at the Mews Gate; J. Marks, in / St. Martin's Lane; and M. Hingeston, at Temple / Bar. MDCCLXVII.

Published: April 1767 (*London Magazine*).
Reference: Boswell, *Life,* ii:481–2 (Appendix).
Johnson's Contribution: Dedication.
Copies: Boston Athenaeum; British Museum; Edinburgh University; R. B. Adam; Dr. R. W. Chapman.

Facsimile of Dedication in the second volume of the Catalogue of the R. B. Adam Library.
Small quarto; 19.1 × 15 cm. Price 7/6.

Signatures: A3; B–Gg4.

Pagination: (preliminary leaves unnumbered) [i] title-page; [ii]

blank; [iii–iv] Dedication; [v] Preface; [vi] Corrections; [1]–232 Text.

There are three cancels—leaves B1, K2, and X2.

There was a second edition, fully as rare now as the first, in 1768. This was a small octavo; the Preface was extensively revised, but the Dedication was unchanged. To this edition was added a section on Measuring and a Table of Weights: the same sheets were also issued separately, for the benefit of those who had purchased the first edition, with the title-page *An Introduction to the mensuration of superficies and solids.*

DEDICATION
TO HIS ROYAL HIGHNESS THE DUKE OF YORK.
SIR,

They who are permitted to prefix the names of Princes to treatises of science, generally enjoy the protection of a patron, without fearing the censure of a judge.

The honour of approaching your Royal Highness, has given me many opportunities of knowing that the work which I now presume to offer, will not partake of the usual security. For as the knowledge which your Royal Highness has already acquired of GEOMETRY extends beyond the limits of an introduction, I expect not to inform you; I shall be happy if I merit your approbation.

An address to such a patron admits no recommendation of the science. It is superfluous to tell your Royal Highness that GEOMETRY is the primary and fundamental art of life; that its effects are extended through the principal operations of human skill; that it conducts the soldier in the field, and the seaman in the ocean; that it gives strength to the fortress, and elegance to the palace. To your Royal Highness all this is already known; GEOMETRY is secure of your regard, and your opinion of its usefulness and value has sufficiently appeared, by the condescension in which you have been pleased to honour one who has so little pretension to the notice of Princes, as,

SIR, Your Royal Highnesses Most obliged, Most obedient, And most humble Servant,

William Payne.

Bibliographical Description of the TRIGONOMETRY

Elements / of / trigonometry, / plain and spherical; / applied to the most useful problems in / heights and distances, astronomy, / and navigation: / for the use of learners. / [*rule*] / By William Payne. / [*rule*] / London: / Printed by H. Hart, in Popping's Court, Fleet-Street: / and sold by T. Payne, at the Mews Gate; / and M. Hingeston, at Temple Bar. / [*short rule*] / M DCC LXXII.

Published: February 1772 (*Gentleman's Magazine*).
Johnson's Contribution: Dedication.
Copies: Columbia; Harvard; British Museum; Edinburgh University; Trinity College, Dublin.

Octavo; Copy at Edinburgh measures 21.3 × 12.6 cm.
Published price: 5/– in boards. Two parts bound together.

Signatures: 4 leaves; B–O⁸; P⁴; A–I⁸; K⁴; L².

Pagination: [i] title-page; [ii] blank; [iii–iv] Dedication; i–ii Preface; i–ii Contents; 1–215 Text; [216] Corrections.

Leaf (*13–*14) inserted between pp. 14 and 15.
Plate inserted between L2 and L3
Plate inserted between N3 and N4
Plate inserted between O6 and O7
O4 is signed N4 in error.

Pagination (Second Part): [1]–156 Tables.

I have seen the Dedication bound after the Preface and Contents, but this was probably a binder's error when it was rebound. It is probable that the preliminary leaves were not printed in one half-sheet; this might account for the peculiarities in pagination.

DEDICATION

TO THE RIGHT HONOURABLE WILLIAM HENRY NASSAU DE ZULEISTEIN, EARL OF ROCHFORD, VISCOUNT TUNBRIDGE, AND ONE OF HIS MAJESTY'S PRINCIPAL SECRETARIES OF STATE.

My Lord,
The great and various advantages derived from the mathematicks in general, are universally acknowledged by the intelligent.

Among the several branches, the excellence of Trigonometry, and its usefulness to the commerce of mankind, are so apparent; that it is not unworthy the attention of persons in the most elevated stations.

This consideration added to my long experience of your Lordship's goodness and condescension, emboldens me to address this treatise to your Lordship; and I shall think myself happy, if my endeavours to establish the elementary principles of the science, obtain the sanction of your Lordship's approbation.

I have the honour to be, With the greatest respect, My Lord, Your Lordship's much obliged, And most obedient Servant,

WILLIAM PAYNE.

PEARCE'S *FOUR EVANGELISTS*

Published: 18 January 1777 (*St. James's Chronicle*).
References: Boswell, *Life,* ii:446; iii:112–3; 489–90.
            Courtney, p. 128.
Johnson's Contributions: Dedication; Life of Bishop Pearce.
Copies: Boston Public Library; Library Company of Philadelphia; Library of Congress; Newberry Library; New York Public Library; Princeton; Salem Athenaeum; Yale; Aberdeen; Bodleian; British Museum; Cambridge University; Edinburgh University; Glasgow University; National Library of Scotland; John Rylands Library; Trinity College, Dublin; Dr. R. W. Chapman.

BISHOP PEARCE belonged to an earlier generation, for he had contributed to the *Spectator* and the *Guardian,* and he had never been well known to Johnson. The first mention of Pearce in Boswell is in connection with his discussion of Johnson's translation of the *History of the Council of Trent.* This project was dropped because a similar edition was planned by another Samuel Johnson; this latter editor was patronized by Zachary Pearce.[1] Many years later, Johnson told Boswell that Pearce's twenty etymologies were his only help on the *Dictionary;* his correspondent was at that time unknown to Johnson.[2] In his Preface to Lauder's *Milton* in 1750, Johnson referred to Pearce's suggestion concerning the

1. Boswell, *Life,* i:135.   2. *Ibid.,* i:292.

source for *Paradise Lost*.3 When Johnson undertook to prepare a life of Bishop Pearce, therefore, he was forced to rely
almost wholly on an autobiographical memoir that Pearce
had left in manuscript. The Bishop's chaplain and literary
executor, John Derby, was able to add very little. 'The chaplain of Dr. Pearce, the late Bishop of Rochester,' said Johnson, 'whom I was to assist in writing some memoirs of his
Lordship, could tell me almost nothing.'4

In his list of Johnson's contributions, Boswell is slightly inconsistent, but it was probably an oversight. The Chronological List contains both the 'Dedication' and 'Additions to the
Life,' and both are marked *acknowledged;* in the text Boswell marks them with daggers, his symbol for an ascription
based on internal evidence. Furthermore, Boswell is ambiguous concerning the life of the Bishop, to which, he says,
'Johnson made some valuable additions.'5 In a letter to
Temple he was more explicit, asserting that Johnson 'wrote
all the *Life* . . . except what his Lordship wrote himself.'6
There can be no doubt that the *Life* is by Johnson—those
parts of it which are not quoted exactly from the manuscript
of the Bishop. It has never been reprinted in Johnson's
*Works,*7 although among other matters it has some interesting
criticism of Longinus. Near the beginning Johnson inserted
a graceful tribute to the help which Pearce had offered him
twenty-five years earlier. In telling of Pearce's early education
in the classics, he wrote: 'To this long continuance of his
initiatory studies, he was perhaps indebted for the philological reputation by which he was afterwards so happily distinguished.' The Dedication, though it is by no means the last

3. *Ante,* p. 81.
4. *Boswell Revised,* p. 37; in the published book the name is omitted. Boswell, *Life,* ii:446.
5. Boswell, *Life,* iii:112, 113.
6. *Letters of Boswell,* edited by C. B. Tinker, ii:287. See also *Boswell Papers,* xii:212; xiii:68.
7. It was included, however, in the first volume of the *Lives of Dr. Edward
Pocock, Dr. Pearce, Dr. Newton, and Mr. Skelton* (London 1816). An extract
from the *Life of Pearce* is in the *London Chronicle,* 23 January 1777.

that Johnson composed, is the last on Boswell's list, and perhaps the best on that list. Boswell quoted the whole Dedication, and it was recently praised by Dr. Chapman as the best of Johnson's Dedications.[8]

Johnson's copy of this work is listed in lot 431 in the *Catalogue* of his Library (1785).

Bibliographical Description

A / Commentary, / with / notes, / on the / Four Evangelists / and the / Acts of the Apostles; / together with a new translation of / St. Paul's First Epistle to the Corinthians, / with a / paraphrase and notes. / To which are added other / theological pieces. / By Zachary Pearce, D. D. / late Lord Bishop of Rochester. / To the whole is prefixed, / some account of his Lordship's life and character, / written by himself. / [*rule*] / Published from the original manuscripts, / by John Derby, A. M. / His Lordship's Chaplain, and Rector of Southfleet and Longfield. / [*rule*] / [*Greek and Latin mottoes*] / [*rule*] / In two volumes. / [*rule*] / Vol. I. / [*double rule*] / London: Printed by E. Cox; / for T. Cadell, in the Strand. / M DCC LXXVII.

(The whole title-page, except for mottoes, is printed in capitals. The second volume omits 'In two volumes' and the rule below it, and reads 'Vol. II.')

Two volumes, large quarto; 29.8 × 23 cm.
Published price: £2/4/0 in boards. (Two guineas in sheets.)

Signatures: Vol. I: [A],a–h,B–4G⁴.
　　　　　Vol. II: [A](half-sheet); B–3P⁴; 3Q(half-sheet).
　Note: In Vol. II, Sig. I was imposed with pages interchanged
　　　diagonally on the inner form, so that the pagination is: 57,
　　　62, 63, 60, 61, 58, 59, 64.

8. *London Mercury*, xxi(1930):444. Dr. Parr was one who recognized the style of the Dedication. Calling upon Johnson soon after Pearce's *Commentary* had been published, Dr. Parr mentioned that he had been reading, with great delight, his dedication to the king.—'My dedication!' exclaimed Dr. Johnson; 'how do you know it is mine?' 'For two reasons,' replied Dr. Parr: 'the first, because it is worthy of you; the second, because you only could write it.' See W. Field, *Memoirs of Samuel Parr* (1828), i:159.

Pagination: Vol. I: [i] half-title; [ii] blank; portrait inserted;
[iii] title-page; [iv] blank; [v]–vi Dedication; [vii] Advertisement; [viii] Advertisement of Pearce's Sermons, soon to be published (actually 30 January 1779); [i]–xlv Life of the Author;
[xlvi] blank; [xlvii]–lx Dissertation; [lxi–lxiii] Chronological
tables; [lxiv] blank; [1]–599 Text; [600] blank.

    Vol. II: [i] half-title; [ii] blank; [iii] title-page; [iv] blank;
[1]–481 Text; [482] blank; [483] Errata; [484] blank.

These volumes offer no bibliographical problem other than the
error in imposition of the inner form of Signature I in Vol. II.
The copy in the Public Library in New York lacks the frontispiece and half-titles. The Advertisement on p. vii explains that
the whole impression was burned by a fire in the printing office of
Messrs. Cox and Bigg in March, 1776, but that the original manuscripts were preserved because they were at the time in the hands
of the editor.

DEDICATION

TO THE KING.

SIR,

    I presume to lay before Your Majesty the last Labours of a
learned Bishop, who died in the Toils and Duties of his Calling.
He is now beyond the Reach of all earthly Honours and Rewards; and only the Hope of inciting others to imitate Him,
makes it now fit to be remembered, that he enjoyed in his Life
the Favour of Your Majesty.

    The tumultuary Life of Princes seldom permits them to survey
the wide Extent of national Interest, without losing Sight of private Merit; to exhibit Qualities, which may be imitated by the
highest and the humblest of mankind; and to be at once amiable
and great.

    Such Characters, if now and then they appear in History, are
contemplated with Admiration. May it be the Ambition of all
your Subjects to make Haste with their Tribute of Reverence;
and, as Posterity may learn from Your Majesty how Kings should
live, may they learn likewise from your People, how they should
be honoured.

    I am, May it please Your Majesty, With the most profound Re-
spect, Your Majesty's Most dutiful and devoted Subject and
Servant,

                                 JOHN DERBY.

Southfleet in Kent,
January 6, 1777.

PERCY'S *RELIQUES*

Published: 12 February 1765 (*London Chronicle*).
References: Boswell, *Life*, i:553–5; ii:1; iv:555.
  Courtney, p. 111.
Johnson's Contribution: Dedication.
Copies: Harvard (2 copies); Library Company of Philadelphia;
  Newberry Library; University of Iowa; Wellesley; Yale; Bod-
  leian; British Museum; London Library; Glasgow University;
  Victoria and Albert (Dyce); R. B. Adam; Dr. R. W. Chapman;
  Dr. L. F. Powell; V. Rothschild; Professor C. B. Tinker. Not
  rare, but a collector's item.

THE story of the preparation for publication of the contents
of Percy's battered Folio Manuscript has been told in detail
in recent years, so that a short summary will provide all the
needed information concerning Johnson's participation.[1]

It is probable that Johnson first suggested the publication[2]
and offered to be of help, but Johnson was unexpectedly occupied during the next few years with his edition of Shakespeare, which had dragged on for a much longer time than
had been expected either by Johnson or by his subscribers.

---

1. There are two careful studies to which frequent reference will be made
in the following pages. 1. An article by Dr. L. F. Powell in *The Library*, IV,
9(1928):113–137. 2. An unpublished dissertation (1932) at Yale by Irving L.
Churchill, *The Early Literary Career of Thomas Percy*. The student of Percy
will in them find complete details. The summary which is presented is based
almost wholly on their work, which has greatly facilitated the preparation of
this chapter. A few errors in bibliographical description have been corrected.

Some additional information is contained in two articles by Miss Leah Dennis, in the *Publications of the Modern Language Association*, xlvi(1931):1166–
1201 and xlix(1934):81–97.

2. Percy wrote to Shenstone that Johnson had urged him to publish the
ballads, and had offered his assistance. Percy is perhaps unnecessarily but un-
derstandably provoked by Johnson's failure to keep his promise. See the letters in H. Hecht, *Percy und Shenstone*, in Volume ciii of Brandl's *Quellen
und Forschungen* (Strassburg 1909), pp. 5, 9.

Johnson, Shenstone, and others urged the publication of the ballads. Who
first suggested it may never be known. Dr. Churchill believes that Johnson
deserves that honor. (See his convincing summary of the evidence in *PMLA*,
li(December 1936):96off.)

Laetitia Hawkins said: 'It was, I believe, my father who suggested to Dr.
Percy the compilation of his *Reliques of Ancient English Poetry*.' (L. M.
Hawkins, *Gossip about Dr. Johnson*, edited by F. H. Skrine [London 1926],
p. 126.)

The most active helper, until his death in 1763, was William Shenstone, who was largely responsible for the selection and arrangement of the volumes. He has been criticized for his advice, which Percy eventually followed, to edit and modernize the ballads to some degree in order to render the collection more readily salable. (That this was done to a very considerable extent may be ascertained by consulting a modern edition,[3] in which the changes are indicated.) In 1765 the public still needed to be convinced of the importance of the ballads, and it seems clear that the changes which Percy called 'a few slight corrections or additions'[4] helped greatly to procure the favorable response of the public to his volumes. Shenstone perceived that rather extensive emendation would be necessary to render the work generally interesting, and his insistence finally convinced Percy, who followed Shenstone's advice after a year of hesitancy. Then, with commendable caution, he wrote: 'In a polished age, like the present, I am sensible that many of these reliques of antiquity will require great allowances to be made for them. Yet have they . . . a pleasing simplicity, and many artless graces.'[5]

Other contributors included Percy's near neighbor and intimate friend, Reverend Edward Lye, whom Percy called 'the first etymologist of the age'; Dr. Thomas Birch; Thomas Astle; Richard Farmer, whose aid was invaluable on the Shakespearean material; and David Dalrymple, who helped especially with the Scottish ballads. In 1762 Percy enlisted the aid of Thomas Warton by a skilful letter in which he praised

3. The best in English is an annotated edition by H. B. Wheatley, published at London in 1876–7. Poems which were extensively revised were marked by Percy with three asterisks. Dr. Churchill has called to my attention Percy's belated explanation of this symbol in the Preface to the Fourth Edition of the *Reliques* (1794), p. xvii.

4. Percy's Preface (Fourth Edition), p. xvi. The Postscript to Percy's first letter to Warton reveals that he then planned to publish 'in three neat vols. 12mo.' Shenstone at first was doubtful whether enough ballads of literary merit could be gathered to fill a third volume. (*Publications of the Modern Language Association*, xlvi[1931]:171n. Dr. Churchill's Dissertation, pp. 180, 311.) The work was published in three volumes, small octavo.

5. Percy's Preface, p. x.

the latter's *Observations on the Faerie Queene* and offered to help in the forthcoming revision of it (then at press), and then asked Warton's advice about his ballads.

It was in the autumn of 1760 that Percy began to do serious work on the ballads and to plan for publication along lines which were proposed by Shenstone. He had expected that the work would be published by the Dodsleys, but he broke off negotiations with them when he found Robert Dodsley too practical a man of business. Johnson then interviewed Andrew Millar to discuss a publishing agreement with him.[6] In 1761, however, Percy went up to London, talked with Johnson, and concluded the bargain with Dodsley after all. The printing of the first volume (third as finally published) began in the spring of 1762, but it proceeded slowly. Scarcely two thirds of it had been completed when Shenstone died, 11 February 1763. One delay had been caused by a surprising lack of knowledge on the part of Shenstone: he held the proof-sheets for a long time in the belief that they were completed parts of the volume. Despite all the delays and uncertainties progress was made, and two volumes had been completed by February, 1764.

In the summer of 1764 Johnson made a visit of some weeks at Easton Maudit, and it was during this period that the Dedication was composed.[7] In June Percy had decided to interchange Volumes I and III, very probably because he had received permission to dedicate the work to the Countess of Northumberland. (He had previously planned to dedicate to the memory of his friend Shenstone.) The change in the order of the volumes was appropriate, in any case, for the first two poems in the new Volume I (originally the third volume and so signed at the bottom of the first page of each sheet) are *Chevy-Chase* and the *Battle of Otterbourne*. These memorials

6. *Letters*, i:89; 29 November 1760. See also the letter in *Modern Language Notes*, December 1935.

7. Johnson, accompanied by Miss Williams, stayed from 25 June until 18 August. The details of this visit, amounting almost to a day-by-day record, may be studied in Dr. Powell's article in the *Library*, IV, 9(1928):119ff. See also Boswell, *Life*, i:553–5.

of the Percy family would be of peculiar interest to the
Countess of Northumberland who was, in her right, Baroness
Percy.[8]

The story of the Dedication has been often told, but it can
hardly be omitted with propriety at this point. That the
Dedication as it stands is substantially the composition of
Johnson there can be no doubt. Percy may well have suggested the general sentiments which he wished to express, and
it is possible that David Dalrymple altered it after Johnson
wrote it, although if it is recalled that Johnson read and corrected Dalrymple's *Annals of Scotland* a few years later, it is
hard to believe that Dalrymple would have undertaken to
correct Johnson's prose.[9]

Boswell's statement that the Dedication was furnished by
Johnson is on a page which was cancelled. The original reads:

He furnished . . . Percy with a Dedication . . . to his collection of
"Reliques of ancient English Poetry." . . . Reynolds, who we shall
afterwards see accepted of the same kind of assistance, . . . Though the
loftiness of his mind prevented him from ever dedicating in his own
person, he wrote a great number . . . for others. After all the diligence
I have bestowed, some of them have escaped my inquiries.

In the final form, the first two sentences were omitted, and instead of the last sentence, Boswell wrote:

Some of these, the persons who were favoured with them are unwill-

8. The problem of arrangement had bothered Percy for a long time. He
first considered a completely chronological arrangement in one series, but this
would have brought most of the less interesting pieces together at the beginning of the book, and might have proved fatal to its popularity. Arrangement
by subjects would probably have bored readers by the sameness of successive
poems. It was Shenstone who suggested an arrangement in nine parallel series.
to be approximately chronological within each Book. The curiously minded
reader will observe that this problem of arrangement which disturbed Percy
is the same problem that Johnson had discussed in his Introduction to the
Harleian Miscellany. *Ante*, p. 59.

9. Percy wrote to Dalrymple, 23 October 1764: 'Inclosed I send a proof
Copy of my Dedication, which I beg the favour of you to examine and
wherever you think requisite to correct and alter.' British Museum Additional
MS 32331, folio 63.

If the style of this Dedication should be considered inadequate proof of
Johnson's authorship, a study of Percy's very different style in the Dedication
to his edition of Mallet's *Northern Antiquities* (1770) will be convincing.

ing should be mentioned, from a too anxious apprehension, as I think, that they may be suspected of having received larger assistance.

The reason for this change is made clear in a letter from Boswell to Malone, 29 January 1791:

> I am to cancel a leaf of the first volume, having found that though Sir Joshua certainly assured me he had no objection to my mentioning that Johnson wrote a dedication for him, he now thinks otherwise.[10]

There is here no mention of Percy, so that it might be supposed that Reynolds only had objected. Percy's name was left in the Index by an oversight, however, and Percy suspected it to have been a deliberate act. Fortunately Boswell and Malone were able to explain the mistake satisfactorily. Finally, Percy produced the proof of Johnson's contribution ten years later,[11] when he wrote in 1800:

> I must ingenuously confess that the former Dedication, though not wholly written by him, owed its finest strokes to the superior pen of Dr. Johnson; and I could not any longer allow myself to strut in borrowed feathers.[12]

In addition to the Dedication, Johnson gave some other help while he was at Easton Maudit in 1764. In a letter to Dalrymple, Percy wrote:

> In the Glossary I have denoted by red lines such words & phrases as I am either ignorant or doubtful of: and have written in the margin

10. *Letters of Boswell,* edited by Professor C. B. Tinker (Oxford 1924), p. 417.

11. In the *European Magazine* [vii(March 1785):191] a contributor had suggested that Johnson had helped Percy with this Dedication and Mrs. Thrale listed the Dedication as Johnson's in 1777 (*Thraliana,* unpublished).

12. Quoted by Robert Anderson, in his *Life of Johnson* (3rd edition, 1815), p. 309.
Percy had been able to strut in borrowed feathers through three editions—until the death of the Countess made a new Dedication advisable. It was this new Dedication, 'To the Memory of Elizabeth of Northumberland,' that Sir John Squire once quoted, in a careless moment, as a Johnsonian dedication. (*London Mercury* 1928.)
The discussion of the reasons for this cancel has been adapted from *Boswell Revised,* pp. 45–48; the story is also told in Boswell, *Life,* i:553ff., and in an article by G. B. Hill in the *Johnson Club Papers* (London 1899), pp. 69, 70.

most of the passages wherein they occur. Shall I intreat your Assistance & that of your friends, for the removing these obscurities? Mr. Johnson . . . who has been with me for 2 months past on a Visit & left me but last week, gives them up as inexplicable: and as he has a good deal of *Glossarizing* knowledge, it will be some honour to succeed, after he has given them over.[13]

This summary, brief as it is, will indicate that Percy was quite correct when he acknowledged that to Johnson he owed 'many valuable hints for the conduct of the work.'[14]

Bibliographical Description

Reliques / of / ancient English poetry: / consisting of / old heroic ballads, songs, and other / pieces of our earlier poets, / (chiefly of the lyric kind.) / Together with some few of later date. / Volume the first. [second, third] / [*Engraving*] / London: / Printed for J. Dodsley in Pall-Mall. / M DCC LXV.

Facsimile of title-page in the *Library*, IV, 9(1928):113.
Three volumes, small octavo in eights; no watermarks, vertical chain-lines.
Trimmed copy: 17.8 × 11.2 cm. Price: 10/6, bound.

Signatures: Vol. I: A⁸; b⁶; B–Y⁸; Z⁴; 2 leaves (which are sometimes, though less frequently, bound at the end of Vol. III).
    Vol. II: A (half-sheet); B–Z,Aa⁸; 1 leaf.
    Vol. III: A (half-sheet); b⁸; c⁴; B–P,[2d P],Q–X⁸; Y⁵; Z⁸.

Pagination: Vol. I: [i–ii] blank leaf (often lacking); engraved frontispiece inserted as a plate, with recto blank; [iii] title-page; [iv] blank; [v]–viii Dedication; ix–xiv Preface; xv–xxiii Essay; [xxiv] blank; [xxv–xxviii] Contents, etc.; [1]–329 Text; [330]–344 Glossary; 2 inserted leaves (with horizontal chain-lines), containing Errata, Advertisement, To the Binder.
    Vol. II: [i–iv] half-title and title-page, with blank versos; i–iii Contents; [iv] quotation from Selden's *Table Talk;* [1]–371 Text; [372]–384 Glossary and Postscript; one leaf of music, with verso blank. (Pp. 113–128 are omitted in the numbering.)
    Vol. III: [i–iv] half-title and title-page, with blank versos; i–iii Contents; [iv] quotation from *Spectator;* [i]–xxiv On the Ancient Metrical Romances, etc.; [1]–323 Text; [324]–331 Glos-

13. Quoted by L. F. Powell in the *Library*, IV, 9(1928):122.
14. Percy's Preface, p. xiii.

sary; 332–346 Additions and Corrections. (Pp. 225–240 bracketed are inserted after p. 224, representing Sig. '2d P.')

Cancels:
   Vol. I: C2, C7, G4, G5.
   Vol. II: N7, U2–U7, X4.
   Vol. III: B1, B3, G3–G6, H4, P3, T6, T7, Y2.

The great number of cancels demonstrates the care with which Percy prepared his ballads.[15] Most of them are easily to be identified: they usually have, irregularly, a volume signature and leaf signature; in some cases the chain-lines are horizontal.

In Vol. I, only the preliminary leaves are at all troublesome. The last two leaves of Sheet b were clearly cut away (and probably used elsewhere in the book), since the sewing is between b4 and b5. The first sheet has caused some difficulty, and Dr. Churchill followed Dr. Powell in supposing that the copper-plate engraving for the frontispiece was printed on the verso of the first leaf. This would be a proceeding somewhat out of the ordinary, although not at all without precedent. (It was done in the second edition of 1767, on the verso of the second leaf.) If however the frontispiece is held to be A1, the stub which appears in some copies between A7 and A8 must be explained. For this reason, I suppose, Dr. Powell assumed that A8 was in some copies a cancel, although the text was identical in all copies. But a study of the chain-lines proves conclusively that the frontispiece is inserted, and that the stub in front of A8 is in reality the turn-over of the frontispiece. A1, which I had thought would contain the half-title, is blank in the two copies in which I have found it preserved. Why it was not used for a half-title, as in the other volumes, I am not able to say; it is not improbable that it was an oversight.[16]

15. The reasons for most of the cancels have been discovered by Dr. Powell, both by ingenious surmise and by comparison with the Farmer-Douce copy. See the *Library*, IV, 9(1928):129ff. For the cancels in the first volume, see the *Literary Supplement* of the London *Times*, 31 October 1936, p. 892.

16. There are minor variations in different copies, but they appear to be of no significance; it is possible that a half-title may have been printed in some sheets, although in that case I do not think that it would have disappeared so completely from the knowledge of students. The second edition should have half-titles in all volumes.

I have very recently come upon an unexpected corroboration of my description of Signature A. In Messrs. Dobell's Catalogue for September, 1930, is listed an uncut copy of the *Reliques* at £30. The note which is appended reads: 'Wanting the frontispiece (which has clearly never been in this copy).' No better proof could be required.

In Vol. II, all the inner leaves of Sig. U were removed, and six leaves of a new sheet were substituted. It is difficult to determine conjugate leaves in an octavo without weakening the binding of the book, but the chain-lines can be matched at the top, according to the normal folding, without difficulty; and the format is thus understandable.[17]

In Vol. III, Y6–Y8 were cut away, but since this must have been done before Sheet Z had been printed (or at least it had been determined that they were to be removed), and Z1 continues without a break from Y5 verso, I have not considered them to be cancels.[18] A3, which is signed irregularly 'Vol. I A2,' was suspected to be a cancel both by Dr. Powell and by Dr. Churchill. This is hardly possible, since the chain-lines indicate that A3 and A4 are in the same sheet, and since A3 is conjugate with the title-page.

Besides the cancels, there are some other irregularities, although none seem to be of any special significance. Catchwords are frequently omitted and are sometimes incorrect; in some cases this was because of changes in the text or arrangement of the poems. Page xi, of Vol. I, is unnumbered; pp. 145, 153, and 299, of Vol. II, are incorrectly numbered; pp. 153, 173, and 206, of Vol. III, are incorrectly numbered. In Vol. III, leaf P2 is incorrectly signed Q2.

One of the most attractive features of the *Reliques* is the series of engravings: these comprise the frontispiece, vignette on title-page, headpiece for the Dedication, a headpiece for each of the nine Books, and a tailpiece at the end of each volume. They were engraved by Charles Grignion from designs by Samuel Wale.[19]

The reception of the *Reliques* was somewhat guarded at first,

17. I have been constrained to this remark by the jaunty manner in which bibliographers discuss conjugate leaves (with vertical chain-lines) of bound volumes. Placed in this obscure position, the statement will be, I trust, sufficiently innocuous. A final decision about conjugate leaves is to be made only by taking the book apart, as Dr. Powell has recently done in order to verify my contention that A8 (Vol. I) is not a cancel.

18. Dr. W. W. Greg does not allow odd numbers in the indices of collation, but he has not convinced Dr. McKerrow that his stand is logical. (The *Library*, xiv[1934]:378.)

19. The same two artists prepared the fine title-page of the Catalogue of the Society of Artists, in 1762. Dr. Churchill has described the designs in detail. Not only the pictures themselves but the instructions which Percy gave to Wale demonstrate how fully Percy was dominated by the Gothic revival. (See Churchill's *Percy*, pp. 253ff. and Appendix.) Some additional discussion of the title-page may be found in the *Library* for December, 1933, pp. 294–5, by Dr. Warren H. Smith, 'Architectural Design on English Title-Pages.'

although more editions could perhaps have been sold had Percy been at liberty to prepare them. The reviewers inserted some of the ballads in the magazines, but the sturdy Augustans hesitated to admit this contraband. The final triumph of the Romantics raised the *Reliques* to a position of honor, and no doubt Wordsworth was justified when he wrote: 'I do not think that there is an able writer in verse of the present day who would not be proud to acknowledge his obligation to the *Reliques*.'[20]

Editions:
1765: First Edition; octavo; published 12 February; price: 10/6.
1766: Dublin; duodecimo (quite rare, cheaply printed, probably
      unauthorized).
1767: Second Edition; octavo; published in December.
1775: Third Edition; octavo.
      The Dedication by Johnson was printed in all these editions. The three London editions were published by the Dodsleys.
1790–91: Frankfort; printed without the Dedication, and probably pirated.
1794: Fourth Edition; Rivington; probably not issued until 1795. This was the last edition to be prepared by Percy, who was assisted by his nephew. The Dedication is to the memory of the Countess of Northumberland. In later editions, the original Dedication has been frequently reprinted.

The text of the Dedication offers no problem. It was unchanged in the Second Edition, except for punctuation. It doubtless represents the ideas of Percy as they were modified by the suggestions of Johnson; the result is one of Johnson's masterpieces in this style of composition. No one will ever attempt to deny to Johnson the credit for the expression of these ideas.

Percy had apologized in his Preface for the rude antiquarianism of the book, and the Dedication makes a specific apology to the Countess of Northumberland. Percy's anxiety about the matter is so well illustrated by his letter to Dalrymple, from which I have already quoted one sentence (p. 161, note 9), that it is worth quoting fully.

Inclosed I send a proof Copy of my Dedication, which I beg the favour of you to examine and wherever you think requisite to correct and

20. *Essay Supplementary to the Preface* (1815) of the *Lyrical Ballads*.

alter. Lady Northumberland has very obligingly taken the book under her patronage, and I am only afraid lest she should expect the contents to be of a higher nature than she will find them to be. To prepare her for this was therefore what I had principally in view. Along with the printed Leaves, I send some written alterations which have been proposed by some of my friends: I was afraid lest they should seem too pompous, therefore did not adopt them. Please to favour me with your opinion of them.

As I shall mention in my Preface the favours I have received from Mr. John Davidson and Mr. MacGowan, please to give me their additions &c. as they ought to appear in print. May I beg the favour of a speedy answer as the press waits?

(British Museum Additional MS 32331, folio 63.)

DEDICATION

TO THE RIGHT HONOURABLE ELIZABETH COUNTESS OF NORTHUMBERLAND: IN HER OWN RIGHT BARONESS PERCY, LUCY, POYNINGS, FITZ-PAYNE, BRYAN, AND LATIMER.

MADAM,

Those writers, who solicit the protection of the noble and the great, are often exposed to censure by the impropriety of their addresses: a remark that will perhaps be too readily applied to him, who having nothing better to offer than the rude songs of ancient minstrels, aspires to the patronage of the Countess of NORTHUMBERLAND, and hopes that the barbarous productions of unpolished ages can obtain the approbation or the notice of her, who adorns courts by her presence, and diffuses elegance by her example.

But this impropriety, it is presumed, will disappear, when it is declared that these poems are presented to your LADYSHIP, not as labours of art, but as effusions of nature, shewing the first efforts of ancient genius, and exhibiting the customs and opinions of remote ages: of ages that had been almost lost to memory, had not the gallant deeds of your illustrious ancestors preserved them from oblivion.

No active or comprehensive mind can forbear some attention to the reliques of antiquity: It is prompted by natural curiosity to survey the progress of life and manners, and to inquire by what gradations barbarity was civilized, grossness refined, and ignorance instructed: but this curiosity, MADAM, must be stronger in those, who, like your LADYSHIP, can remark in every period the influence of some great progenitor, and who still feel in their effects the transactions and events of distant centuries.

By such Bards, MADAM, as I am now introducing to your presence, was the infancy of genius nurtured and advanced, by such were the minds of unlettered warriors softened and enlarged, by such was the memory of illustrious actions preserved and propagated, by such were the heroic deeds of the Earls of NORTHUMBERLAND sung at festivals in the hall of ALNWICK: and those songs, which the bounty of your ancestors rewarded, now return to your LADYSHIP by a kind of hereditary right; and, I flatter myself, will find such reception, as is usually shewn to poets and historians, by those whose consciousness of merit makes it their interest to be long remembered.

I am, MADAM, Your LADYSHIP's Most Humble And most devoted Servant,

THOMAS PERCY.

REVIEW OF GRAINGER'S *SUGAR-CANE*

Grainger's *Sugar-Cane* published: 26 May 1764 (*London Chronicle*).

Percy's Review (first three paragraphs by Johnson): *London Chronicle*, 5 July 1764, p. 12 (continued pp. 20, 28). (Johnson reviewed the poem in the *Critical Review*, October, 1764.)

References: Boswell, *Life*, i:481, 553; ii:453.
        Courtney, p. 103.

ALTHOUGH not strictly an introduction, it seems not improper to include Johnson's three paragraphs in this study. It is in addition not unpleasing to read a little of Johnson's prose when he writes playfully. For one could be sure that these paragraphs were written in jest even if his own conversation did not prove the fact. In diction and content, however, these paragraphs are still 'Johnsonese,' and the remarks on America retain more than a passing interest. These three paragraphs have not (I think) been reprinted in any edition of Johnson's *Works*.

The proof of Johnson's authorship is contained in the proof-sheets of the *Life*. In a leaf which was afterwards changed, Boswell quotes Johnson thus:

Percy was angry with me for laughing at the Sugar-Cane; for he had a mind to make a great thing of Grainger's rats. There was a review of it in 'the London Chronicle,' said to be written by me; but I only helped Percy with it, and was in jest.[1]

In revising, Boswell kept only the first of these two sentences. Under the year 1764, however, he had written of Johnson:

He wrote a review of Grainger's *Sugar Cane, a Poem,* in the *London Chronicle.* He told me, that Dr. Percy wrote the greatest part of this review; but, I imagine, he did not recollect it distinctly, for it appears to be mostly, if not altogether, his own.[2]

In this instance, Johnson's memory was more accurate than Boswell thought. The review was prepared, I have no doubt, during Johnson's visit to Percy at Easton Maudit.

Johnson's holograph manuscript is in the possession of Dr. A. S. W. Rosenbach. Like the manuscript of the Dedication to *Jerusalem Delivered* [pp. 63, 64 *supra*], it shows Johnson's method of composition and revision. There are numerous differences of punctuation and capitalization, undoubtedly printer's changes. But there are several false starts and deleted or inserted words, which show that Johnson was composing and revising sentence by sentence. A few of these alterations are of sufficient general interest to be listed: in the third sentence, 'barbarous' was changed to 'uncivilized'; in the next sentence, 'unsupplied' was altered to 'unprovided' and this was erroneously read by the printer as 'unfriended'; the following clause was changed slightly several times before Johnson was satisfied; in the second sentence of the second paragraph, the manuscript is, 'we see these deserts of obscurity trodden by a man': this is unchanged and unambiguous in the manuscript and hence must have been altered by another, perhaps by Percy when he copied it, and the revision then botched by the printer, for no printer would have attempted such a change on his own responsibility; in the next sentence

1. *Boswell Revised,* pp. 48, 49; Boswell, *Life,* ii:453. For additional details of interest see Boswell, *Life,* ii:532–4. Percy, Shenstone, Lord Kames, and Johnson saw the poem in manuscript.
2. Boswell, *Life,* i:481.

the manuscript is defective: Johnson apparently intended 'curiosity' to be parallel with 'attention,' for the manuscript reads 'and by its physical [*small hole in MS*] curiosity of a philosophical nation'; the printer, finding something needed to be supplied, may have used his own judgment by inserting 'that' and thus altering the construction.

TEXT

To travel usefully in any country, requires a course of study and disposition of mind suited to the objects which that country particularly presents to curiosity. Holland will be most properly surveyed by the merchant and politician, and Italy by the antiquary and virtuoso. America is well known to be the habitation of uncivilized nations, remarkable only for their rudeness and simplicity. The plains and mountains of the Western hemisphere afford no monuments of ancient magnificence, nor any exhibitions of modern elegance: the life of their vagrant inhabitants, insecure and unfriended,[3] can only shew how labour may supply the want of skill, and how necessity may inforce expedients. But Nature has filled these boundless regions with innumerable forms, to which European eyes are wholly strangers. *In passing down the river of Amazons,* says Condamine, *I saw new plants, new animals, and new men.*[4]

The qualifications of an American traveller are knowledge of Nature, and copiousness of language, acuteness of observation, and facility of description. It is therefore with that pleasure which every rational mind finds in the hope of enlarging the empire of science, that we see these enlightened[5] regions visited by a

3. The reading of the manuscript, 'unprovided,' was probably misread by the printer. Twenty years later, in his Dedication for Burney's *Commemoration of Handel,* Johnson used the same word to suggest the privations of uncivilized people in 'those lands of unprovided wretchedness.'

4. La Condamine's *Relation abrégée* of his trip down the Amazon was published in 1745, in the *Mémoires* of the Academy and in a separate volume. An English translation was published in London in 1747. The quotation is from p. 24 of the translation (p. 47 in the French).

5. A Communication in the *Gentleman's Magazine* (from J. B. N[ichols]) for September, 1847, p. 252, suggests the emendation 'delightful.' Either that or 'unenlightened' would seem to be more appropriate.

It is unfortunate that any one ever attempted to improve the reading in Johnson's manuscript, which is quite different: 'we see these deserts of obscurity trodden by a man.'

man who examines them as a philosopher, and describes them as a poet.

The subject which he has chosen to illustrate, demands by its commercial value the attention of a mercantile, and by its physical curiosity, that of a philosophical nation. And it is reasonable to expect, that all to whom SUGAR contributes usefulness or pleasure, will be willing to know from what it is produced, and how it is prepared.

THE PRECEPTOR

Published: 7 April 1748 (*General Advertiser*).
References: Boswell, *Life,* i: 192.
    Courtney, p. 21.
Johnson's Contributions: Preface; Hermit of Teneriffe.
Copies: Library Company of Philadelphia (Loganian); U. S. Bureau of Education; Bodleian (2 copies); British Museum; Edinburgh University; Glasgow University (2 copies); National Library of Scotland (first volume); Trinity College, Dublin; R. B. Adam; Dr. R. W. Chapman; Professor C. B. Tinker.

IN December 1744 John Newbery obtained the King's Licence to publish the *Circle of the Sciences,* a series of miniature volumes each of which dealt with the elements of its particular subject. These volumes were published irregularly in 1745 and the subsequent years, and were several times reprinted. That the enterprise was successful is indicated by the extreme rarity of those little books. Newbery proved that there was a ready market for textbooks suitable for home instruction.

No less enterprising than Newbery was Robert Dodsley: there can be no question that the purpose of the *Preceptor* was to bring to Dodsley a share in the profit that Newbery was earning from the sale of his *Circle of the Sciences.* The close correspondence of the subjects included in the *Preceptor* and in Newbery's series is strong evidence that Dodsley intended to divert some of the income by means of a rival publication; still better evidence is the specific reference in Johnson's Preface, 'It must not be expected, that in the following pages should be found a complete Circle of the Sciences.'[1]

Like Newbery, Dodsley obtained a royal licence which was worded much like Newbery's, to the effect that since he had been at considerable trouble and expense to prepare the work, it was the King's pleasure that he should be allowed to reap his reward and that no one else should attempt to hinder him by reprinting without authorization. This licence is dated February 4, 1748.

It is difficult to ascertain the extent of Johnson's connection with the project. He furnished the *Hermit of Teneriffe,* which he had composed in one night after finishing an evening in Holborn.[2] The Preface shows that Johnson knew precisely the contents, and it would seem probable that Dodsley had advised with Johnson concerning the plans for the book. Yet Dodsley was himself quite as much a literary projector as Crokatt or Newbery and quite capable of planning and editing (and to some extent writing) such a compilation; Johnson could have written the Preface after the printed sheets of the text had been shown to him. I think that Johnson was much more intimately connected with the editing of this book than he was with Newbery's *World Displayed,* but I know of no internal or external evidence that is conclusive. The fact of the revision of the Preface seems to me an indication that his connection was more than casual.

In the second edition, published in June 1754, besides some revisions and additions in the text, Johnson's Preface is extensively revised. The spelling and punctuation, which were changed by the printer in the fifth edition, are almost unchanged in the second edition. But in the second edition there are about thirty important verbal changes, and there

1. Vol. I, p. xv, the eleventh paragraph of the Preface. The discussion in David Fordyce's *Dialogues on Education* may also have suggested the inclusion of certain topics.

2. Tyers, in the *Gentleman's Magazine* for December 1784, p. 901. He adds that Johnson sat up a whole night to compose the Preface. For Johnson's high opinion of the *Hermit of Teneriffe* see Percy's letter, quoted in Boswell, *Life,* i:537.

was never any other verbal revision. That these revisions are by Johnson I am convinced. No one else would (or could) have changed 'the same progressive order obtains in the motions of intellect' to 'the motions of intellect proceed in the like imperceptible progression'; or 'the impression of just sentiments and illustrious examples' to 'the impression of just sentiments, and recommendation of illustrious examples.'[3]

The contributors, so far as I have ascertained them, were these:

Part I, Section II, *On Speaking*
> There are thirteen speeches selected from the first four books of Nathaniel Hooke's *Roman History* (1738–45). Then there are ten selections from Shakespeare, and passages from Pope, Gay, and Milton.

Part II, *Geometry*
> This is a new translation of Sébastien Le Clerc's *Pratique de la Géométrie*, first published in 1669. (See Johnson's Preface, p. xviii.)

Part V, *On Rhetoric and Poetry*
> With slight alterations, it is from the second part of Anthony Blackwall's *Introduction to the Classics* (1718, sixth edition 1746).

Part VII, *On Logic*
> The first publication of William Duncan's *Elements of Logic*. This was published separately on June 17, 1748, and was many times reprinted.

Part IX, *On Ethics, or Morality*
> The first publication of David Fordyce's *Elements of Moral Philosophy*. This was published separately in 1754.

Part XII,
> The *Hermit of Teneriffe* is by Johnson.
> The *Choice of Hercules* is by Bishop Robert Lowth. It had been published in Spence's *Polymetis* (1747) and in the third volume of Dodsley's *Collection* (January 1748).
> The *Picture of Human Life*, from Cebes, is by Joseph Spence. It had been published in Dodsley's *Museum* (edited by Akenside) in 1747.

Some of the unidentified sections were doubtless written by Dodsley himself. The second and later editions included as an Introduction to Part I the substance of John Mason's *Essay*

3. A collation of the important changes is included with the text of the first edition, which is reproduced below. The fact of this revision of 1754 is important, as I have pointed out in the Introduction, because in 1754 Johnson made a final revision of the *Rambler*, and his *Vanity of Human Wishes* was revised for the fourth volume of Dodsley's *Collection of Poems* (1755).

on Elocution, and there were other additions. The *Hermit of Teneriffe* is reprinted in the *Gentleman's Magazine,* April 1748. There is also a summary of the contents of the *Preceptor.*

Bibliographical Description

The / Preceptor: / containing / a general course of education. / Wherein / the first principles / of / polite learning / are laid down / in a way most suitable for trying the genius, / and advancing the instruction of / youth. / [*rule*] / In twelve parts. / [*rule*] / [*List of the twelve parts*] / [*rule*] / Illustrated with maps and useful cuts. / [*rule*] / Volume the first. / [*rule*] / London: / Printed for R. Dodsley, at Tully's-Head in Pall-Mall. / M DCC XLVIII.

Two volumes, octavo; 19.7 × 12.2 cm. Price: 12/–.
Title-page in red and black.

Signatures: Vol. I: A,b,B–Bb⁸.
　　Vol. II: B–Ñn⁸.
　　Frontispiece (by Hayman and Grignion) and title-page inserted at beginning of each volume.

Pagination: Vol. I: [i] royal licence; [ii] blank; [iii]–vii Dedication; [viii] blank; ix–xxxi Preface by Johnson; [xxxii] blank; [1]–384 Text.
　　Vol. II: [1]–556 Text; one leaf containing advertisements of books.

The first leaf of Vol. I, containing the royal licence, usually precedes the frontispiece and title-page.

In addition to the frontispieces, there are in Vol. I fifteen maps and plates, and thirteen folded drawings at the end. Vol. II has five plates, and an engraved headpiece by Fourdrinier for the *Choice of Hercules.*

The second volume was probably set up in three sections simultaneously: two leaves (signed kk) are inserted after Sig. Kk to complete this Part; the last seven pages of the *Elements of Logic* (pp. 186–192, Sig. N) are printed in smaller type and the title-page of the next Part, *Natural History,* is omitted, in order to complete the *Elements of Logic;* on page 540 the direction-line (catchword) is wrong, probably because of crowding.

Some copies are corrected in manuscript on p. 533 of the second volume, where the type had twisted and failed to print. Since other copies are clearly printed, this type must have collapsed after some sheets had been printed, or else it was corrected at press.

There are some errors of no importance: page xiii is numbered 'xi,' and leaf I3 is signed 'K3.' In the second volume, sheet Aa begins with p. 351 (repeating two pages of the previous sheet) and this error is carried on: this accounts for the apparent shortage of two pages in the collation.

Two issues have been distinguished from the difference in title-pages. All copies have in red: Preceptor, Polite Learning, Youth, London, and the date. In addition some copies have in red the line 'Illustrated with maps and useful cuts.' I note also that in Sheet C of the first volume, the press number (of the outer form) may appear on C4 verso or on C5 recto, indicating two impressions of this form. There are two issues, similarly, of the *Voyage to Abyssinia* (1735).

Professor Tinker's copy of the *Preceptor* has the name and bookplate of Sir Archibald Grant of Monymuske, four times married, lastly to the widow of Andrew Millar. His great hobby, the planting of trees, seemed a needless extravagance and folly to his fourth wife. Hume observed that by her attitude 'she will check the poor man in the only laudable thing he has ever done.' (*Letters of Hume,* edited by J. Y. T. Greig, Oxford 1932, in a letter to Strahan, 5 June 1770. See also Boswell, *Life,* iii:103, 486.)

The Preface was included by Davies in his *Miscellaneous and Fugitive Pieces* (1773).

An interesting article, arguing for the influence of Johnson's Preface on American educational theory, was published by T. Hornberger in the *Penna. Magazine of Hist. and Biog.* lviii (1934):370 ff.

Editions:
1748: first edition, 7 April.
1754: second edition, June.
1758: third edition.
1763: fourth edition.
1769: fifth edition, September.
1775: sixth edition.
1783: seventh edition.
1793: eighth edition.
(Dublin 1750?—it is advertised by Faulkner at the end of his edi-

tion of Berkeley's *Querist*, but may have been published before 1750.)

PREFACE.

The Importance of Education is a Point so generally understood and confessed, that it would be of little use to attempt any new Proof or Illustration of its Necessity and Advantages.

At a time when so many Schemes of Education have been projected, so many Proposals offered to the Publick, so many Schools opened for general Knowledge, and so many Lectures in particular Sciences attended; at a time when Mankind seems intent rather upon familiarising than enlarging the several Arts; and every Age, Sex, and Profession is invited to an Acquaintance with those Studies, which were formerly supposed accessible only to such as had devoted themselves to literary Leisure, and dedicated their Powers to philosophical Enquiries; it seems rather requisite that an Apology should be made, for any farther[1] Attempt to smooth a Path so frequently beaten, to recommend Attainments so ardently pursued, and so officiously directed.

That this National[2] Desire may not be frustrated, our Schools seem yet to want some Book, which may excite Curiosity by its Variety, encourage Diligence by its Facility, and reward Application by its Usefulness. In examining the Treatises hitherto offered to the Youth of this Nation, there appeared none that did not fail in one or other of these essential Qualities; none that were not either unpleasing, or abstruse, or crouded with Learning very rarely applicable to the Purposes of common Life.

Every Man, who has been engaged in Teaching, knows with how much Difficulty youthful Minds are confined to close Application, and how readily they deviate to any thing, rather than attend to that which is imposed as a Task. That this Disposition, when it becomes inconsistent with the Forms of Education, is to be checked, will readily be granted; but since, though it may be in some Degree obviated, it cannot wholly be suppressed, it is surely rational to turn it to Advantage, by taking Care that the Mind shall never want Objects on which its Faculties may be usefully employed. It is not impossible, that this restless Desire of Novelty, which gives so much Trouble to the Teacher, may be

---

In the notes to this Preface, the verbal changes of the second edition (1754) are listed, without comment. The printer of the second edition consistently omitted the 'Saxon k' of Public. See Introduction, p. xv.

1. further.   2. general.

often the Struggle of the Understanding starting from that, to which it is not by Nature adapted, and travelling in Search of something on which it may fix with greater Satisfaction. For without supposing each Man, particularly marked out by his Genius for particular Performances, it may be easily conceived, that when a numerous Class of Boys is confined indiscriminately to the same Forms of Composition, the Repetition of the same Words, or the Explication of the same Sentiments, the Employment, must either by Nature or Accident be differently received by them;[3] that the Ideas to be contemplated, may be too difficult for the Apprehension of some, and too obvious for that of others:[4] they may be such as some Understandings cannot reach, though others look down upon them as below their Regard. Every Mind in its Progress through the different Stages of scholastic Learning, must be often in some of these Circumstances,[5] must either flag with the Labour, or grow wanton with the Facility of the Work assigned; and in either State it naturally turns aside from the Track before it. Weariness looks out for Relief, and Leisure for Employment, and surely it is rational to indulge the Wanderings of both. For the Faculties which are too lightly burthen'd with the Business of the Day, may with great Propriety add to it some other Enquiry; and he that finds himself over-wearied by a Task, which perhaps, with all his Efforts, he is not able to perform, is undoubtedly to be justified in addicting himself rather to easier Studies, and endeavouring to quit that which is above his Attainment, for that which Nature has not made him incapable of pursuing with Advantage.

That therefore this roving Curiosity may not be unsatisfied, it seems necessary to scatter in its Way such Allurements as may withhold it from an useless and unbounded Dissipation; such as may regulate it without Violence, and direct it without Restraint; such as may suit every Inclination, and fit every Capacity; may employ the stronger Genius, by Operations of Reason, and engage the less active or forcible Mind, by supplying it with easy Knowledge, and obviating that Despondence, which quickly prevails, when nothing appears but a Succession of Difficulties, and one Labour only ceases that another may be imposed.

A Book intended thus to correspond with all Dispositions, and afford Entertainment for Minds of different Powers, is necessarily

3. less suitable to some than others.
4. Apprehension of one, and too obvious for that of another.
5. in one of these Conditions.

to contain Treatises on different Subjects. As it is designed for Schools, though for the higher Classes, it is confined wholly to such Parts of Knowledge as young Minds may comprehend; and as it is drawn up for Readers yet unexperienced in Life, and unable to distinguish the useful from the ostentatious or unnecessary Parts of Science, it is requisite that a very nice Distinction should be made, that nothing unprofitable should be admitted for the sake of Pleasure, nor any Arts of Attraction neglected, that might fix the Attention upon more important Studies.

These Considerations produced the Book which is here offered to the Publick, as better adapted to the great Design of pleasing by Instruction, than any which has hitherto been admitted into our Seminaries of Literature. There are not indeed wanting in the World Compendiums of Science, but many were written at a Time when Philosophy was imperfect, as that of *G. Valla;* many contain only naked Schemes, or Synoptical Tables, as that of *Stierius;* and others are too large and voluminous, as that of *Alstedius;* and, what is not to be considered as the least Objection, they are generally in a Language, which, to Boys, is more difficult than the Subject; and it is too hard a Task to be condemned to learn Science[6] in an unknown Tongue. As in Life, so in Study, it is dangerous to do more Things than one at a time; and the Mind is not to be harrassed with unnecessary Obstructions, in a Way, of which the natural and unavoidable Asperity is such as too frequently produces Despair.

If the Language however had been the only Objection to any of the Volumes already extant, the Schools might have been supplied at a small Expence by a Translation; but none could be found that was not so defective, redundant, or erroneous, as to be of more Danger than Use. It was necessary then to examine, whether upon every single Science there was not some Treatise written for the Use of Scholars, which might be adapted to this Design, so that a Collection might be made from different Authors, without the Necessity of writing new Systems. This Search was not wholly without Success; for two Authors were found, whose Performances might be admitted with little Alteration. But so widely does this Plan differ from all others, so much has the State of many kinds of Learning been changed, or so unfortunately have they hitherto been cultivated, that none of the other Subjects were explained in such a Manner as was now required; and therefore neither Care nor Expence has been spared to ob-

6. to learn a new Science.

tain new Lights, and procure to this Book the Merit of an Original.

With what Judgment the Design has been formed, and with what Skill it has been executed, the Learned World is now to determine. But before Sentence shall pass, it is proper to explain more fully what has been intended, that Censure may not be incurred by the Omission of that which the original Plan did not comprehend; to declare more particularly who they are to whose Instruction these Treatises pretend, that a Charge of Arrogance and Presumption may be obviated; to lay down the Reasons which directed the Choice of the several Subjects; and to explain more minutely the Manner in which each particular Part of these Volumes is to be used.

The Title has already declared, that these Volumes are particularly intended for the Use of Schools, and therefore it has been the Care of the Authors to explain the several Sciences, of which they have treated, in the most familiar Manner; for the Mind used only to common Expressions, and inaccurate Ideas, does not suddenly conform itself to scholastic Modes of Reasoning, or conceive the nice Distinctions of a subtile Philosophy, and may be properly initiated in speculative Studies by an Introduction like this, in which the Grossness of vulgar Conception is avoided, without the Observation of Metaphysical Exactness. It is observed, that in the Course of the natural World no Change is instantaneous, but all its Vicissitudes are gradual and slow; if the same progressive Order obtains in the Motions of Intellect,[7] and proper Degrees of Transition from one Study to another be therefore necessary, let it not be charged[8] upon the Writers of this Book, that they intended to exhibit more than the Dawn of Knowledge, or pretended to raise in the Mind any nobler Product than the Blossoms of Science, which more powerful Institutions may ripen into Fruit.

For this Reason it must not be expected, that in the following Pages should be found a complete Circle of the Sciences; or that any Authors, now deservedly esteemed, should be rejected to make Way for what is here offered. It was intended by the Means of these Precepts, not to deck the Mind with Ornaments, but to protect it from Nakedness; not to enrich it with Affluence, but to supply it with Necessaries. The *Enquiry* therefore cannot have been, what Degrees[9] of Knowledge are desirable, but what are by

7. the Motions of Intellect proceed in the like imperceptible Progression.
8. are therefore necessary; but let it not be charged.
9. The Enquiry therefore was not what Degrees.

many Characters and Employments indispensably required;[10] and the *Choice* was determined not by the Splendor of any Part of Literature, but by the Extent of its Use, and the Inconvenience which its Neglect was likely to produce.

I. The Prevalence of this Consideration appears in the first Part, which is appropriated to the humble Purposes of teaching to *Read,* and *Speak,* and *write Letters;* an Attempt of little Magnificence, but in which no Man needs to blush for having employed his Time, if Honour be estimated by Use. For Precepts of this Kind, however neglected, extend their Importance as far as Men are found who communicate their Thoughts one to another; they are equally useful to the highest and the lowest; they may often contribute to make Ignorance less inelegant; and may it not be observed, that they are frequently wanted for the Embellishment even of Learning?

In order to the Application of this Part,[11] which consists of various Exemplifications of such Differences of Stile as require correspondent Diversities of Pronunciation, it will be proper to inform the Scholar, that there are in general three Forms of Stile, each of which demands its particular Mode of Elocution: the *Familiar,* the *Solemn,* and the *Pathetic.* That in the *Familiar,* he that reads is only to talk with a Paper in his Hand, and to indulge himself in all the lighter Liberties of Voice, as when he reads the common Articles of a News-Paper, or a cursory Letter of Intelligence or Business. That the *Solemn* Stile, such as that of a serious Narrative, expects an uniform Steddiness of Speech,[12] equal, clear, and calm. That for the *Pathetic,* such as an animated Oration, it is necessary the Voice be regulated by the Sense, varying and rising with the Passions. These Rules, which are the most general, admit a great Number of subordinate Observations, which must be particularly adapted to every Scholar; for it is observable, that though very few read well, yet every Man errs in a different Way. But let one Remark never be omitted: inculcate strongly to every Scholar the Danger of copying the Voice of another; an Attempt, which though it has been often repeated, is always unsuccessful.

The Importance of writing Letters with Propriety justly claims to be consider'd with care, since next to the Power of pleasing with his Presence, every Man would wish to be able to give De-

10. what are in most Stations of Life indispensably required.
11. In order to shew the proper use of this Part.
12. exacts an uniform Steadiness of Speech.

light at a Distance. And[13] this great Art should be diligently taught, the rather, as[14] of those Letters which are most useful, and by which the general Business of Life is transacted, there are no *Examples* easily to be found. It seems the general Fault of those who undertake this Part of Education, that they propose for the Exercise of their Scholars, Occasions which rarely happen; such as Congratulations and Condolances, and neglect those without which Life cannot proceed. It is possible to pass many Years without the Necessity of writing Panegyrics or Epithalamiums; but every Man has frequent Occasion to state a Contract, or demand a Debt, or make a Narrative of some minute Incidents of common Life. On these Subjects therefore young Persons should be taught to think justly, and write clearly, neatly, and succinctly, lest they come from School into the World without any Acquaintance with common Affairs, and stand idle Spectators of Mankind, in Expectation that some great Event will give them an Opportunity to exert their Rhetoric.

II. The second Place is assigned to *Geometry;* on the Usefulness of which it is unnecessary to expatiate in an Age, when Mathematical Studies have so much engaged the Attention of all Classes of Men. This Treatise, is one of those which have been borrowed, being a Translation from the Work of Mr. *Le Clerc;* and is not intended as more than the first Initiation. In delivering the fundamental Principles of *Geometry,* it is necessary to proceed by slow Steps, that each Proposition may be fully understood before another is attempted. For which Purpose it is not sufficient, that when a Question is asked in the Words of the Book, the Scholar likewise can in the Words of the Book return the proper Answer; for this may be only an Act of Memory, not of Understanding; it is always proper to vary the Words of the Question, to place the Proposition in different Points of View, and to require of the Learner an Explanation in his own Terms, informing him however when they are improper. By this Method the Scholar will become cautious and attentive, and the Master will know with Certainty the Degree of his Proficiency. Yet, though this Rule is generally right, I cannot but recommend a Precept of *Pardie's,* that when the Student cannot be made to comprehend some particular Part, it should be, for that Time, laid aside, till new Light shall arise from subsequent Observation.

When this Compendium is completely understood, the Scholar may proceed to the Perusal of *Tacquet,* afterwards of *Euclid* him-

13. 'And' omitted.   14. because.

self, and then of the modern Improvers of *Geometry,* such as Barrow, Keil and particularly[15] Sir *Isaac Newton.*

III. The Necessity of some Acquaintance with *Geography* and *Astronomy* will not be disputed. If the Pupil is born to the Ease of a large Fortune, no Part of Learning is more necessary to him, than the Knowledge of the Situation of Nations, on which their Interests generally depend; if he is dedicated to any of the Learned Professions, it is scarcely possible that he will not be obliged to apply himself in some Part of his Life to these Studies, as no other Branch of Literature can be fully comprehended without them; if he is designed for the Arts of Commerce, or Agriculture, some general Acquaintance with these Sciences will be found extremely useful to him; in a word, no Studies afford more extensive, more wonderful, or more pleasing Scenes; and therefore there can be no Ideas impressed upon the Soul, which can more conduce to its future Entertainment.

In the Pursuit of these Sciences it will be proper to proceed with the same Gradation and Caution as in *Geometry.* And it is always of Use to decorate the Nakedness of Science, by interspersing such Observations and Narratives, as may amuse the Mind and excite Curiosity. Thus, in explaining the State of the Polar Regions, it might be fit to read the Narrative of the *Englishmen* that wintered in *Greenland,* which will make young Minds sufficiently curious after the Cause of such a Length of Night, and Intenseness of Cold; and many Stratagems of the same Kind might be practised to interest them in all Parts of their Studies, and call in their Passions to animate their Enquiries. When they have read this Treatise, it will be proper to recommend to them *Varenius*'s Geography, and *Gregory*'s Astronomy.

IV. The Study of *Chronology* and *History* seems to be one of the most natural Delights of the Human Mind. It is not easy to live without enquiring by what Means every thing was brought into the State in which we now behold it, or without finding in the Mind some Desire of being informed concerning the Generations of Mankind, that have been in Possession of the World before us, and[16] whether they were better or worse than ourselves; or what good or evil has been derived to us from their Schemes, Practices, and Institutions. These are Enquiries which *History* alone can satisfy; and *History* can only be made intelligible by some Knowledge of *Chronology,* the Science by which Events are ranged in their Order, and the Periods of Computation are

15. 'particularly' omitted.   16. 'and' omitted.

settled; and which therefore assist the Memory by Method, and enlighten the Judgment, by shewing the Dependence of one Transaction on another. Accordingly it should be diligently inculcated to the Scholar, that unless he fixes in his Mind some Idea of the Time in which each Man of Eminence lived, and each Action was performed, with some Part of the contemporary History of the rest of the World, he will consume his Life in useless reading, and darken his Mind with a Croud of unconnected Events, his Memory will be perplexed with distant Transactions resembling one another, and his Reflections be like a Dream in a Fever, busy and turbulent, but confused and indistinct.

The Technical Part of Chronology, or the Art of computing and adjusting Time, as it is very difficult, so it is not of absolute Necessity, but should however be taught, so far as it can be learned without the Loss of those Hours which are required for Attainments of nearer Concern. The Student may join with this Treatise *Le Clerc*'s *Compendium of History,* and afterwards may, for the Historical Part of *Chronology,* procure *Helvicus*'s and *Isaacson*'s Tables; and if he is desirous of attaining the technical Part, may first peruse *Holder*'s *Account of Time, Hearne*'s *Ductor Historicus, Strauchius,* the first Part of *Petavius*'s *Rationarium Temporum;* and at length *Scaliger de Emendatione Temporum.* And for Instruction in the Method of his Historical Studies, he may consult *Hearne*'s *Ductor Historicus, Wheare*'s Lectures, *Rawlinson*'s *Directions for the Study of History:* and for Ecclesiastical History, *Cave* and *Dupin.*[17]

V. *Rhetoric* and *Poetry* supply Life with its highest intellectual Pleasures; and in the Hands of Virtue are of great Use for the Impression of just Sentiments and illustrious Examples.[18] In the Practice of these great Arts, so much more is the Gift of Nature than the Effect of Education, that nothing is attempted here but to teach the Mind some general Heads of Observation, to which the beautiful Passages of the best Writers may commonly be reduced. In the Use of this it is by no Means proper,[19] that the Teacher should confine himself to the Examples before him, for by that Method he will never enable his Pupils to make just Applications[20] of the Rules; but having once[21] inculcated the true Meaning of each Figure, he should require them to exemplify it

17. *Cave* and *Dupin, Baronius* and *Fleury.*
18. Impression of just Sentiments, and Recommendation of illustrious Examples.
19. it is not proper.   20. Application.
21. 'once' omitted.

by their own Observations, pointing to them the Poem, or, in longer Works, the Book or Canto in which an Example may be found, and leaving them to discover the particular Passage by the Light of the Rules which they have lately learned.

For a farther Progress in these Studies they may consult *Quintilian* and *Vossius*'s Rhetoric; the Art of Poetry will be best learned from *Bossu* and *Bohours* in *French,* together with *Dryden*'s Essays and Prefaces, the critical Papers of *Addison, Spence* on *Pope*'s *Odyssy,*[22] and *Trapp*'s *Prælectiones Poeticæ;* but a more accurate and Philosophical Account is expected from a Commentary upon *Aristotle*'s Art of Poetry, with which the Literature of this Nation will be in a short Time augmented.*

VII.[23] With regard to the Practice of *Drawing,* it is not necessary to give any Directions, the Use of the Treatise being only to teach the proper Method of imitating the Figures.[24] It will be proper to incite the Scholars to Industry, by shewing in other Books the Use of the Art, and informing them how much it assists the Apprehension, and relieves the Memory; and by obliging them sometimes[25] to *write* Descriptions of Engines, Utensils, or any complex Pieces of Workmanship, by which[26] they will more fully apprehend the Necessity of an Expedient which so happily supplies the Defects of Language, and enables the Eye to receive what cannot be conveyed to the Mind any other Way. When they have read this Treatise, and practis'd upon these Figures, their Theory may be improved by the *Jesuit's Perspective,* and their manual Operations by other Figures which may be easily procured.

VII. *Logic,* or the Art of arranging and connecting Ideas, of forming and examining Arguments, is universally allow'd to be an Attainment in the utmost Degree worthy the Ambition of that Being, whose highest Honour it is to be endued with Reason; but it is doubted, whether that Ambition has yet been gratified, and whether the Powers of Ratiocination have been much improved by any Systems of Art or methodical Institutions. The *Logic* which for so many Ages kept Possession of the Schools, has at last been condemned as a meer[27] Art of Wrangling, of very little Use in the Pursuit of Truth; and later Writers have contented themselves with giving an Account of the Operations of the Mind,

---

* This may be a reference to William Collins. See Johnson's *Life of Collins.*
22. *Odyssey.*　　　　　　　　　　23. VI (*correctly*).
24. the Figures which are annex'd.　25. and if they are oblig'd sometimes.
26. 'by which' omitted.　　　　　　27. mere.

marking the various Stages of her Progress, and giving some general Rules for the Regulation of her Conduct. The Method of these Writers is here followed; but without a servile Adherence to any, and with Endeavours to make Improvements upon all. This Work however laborious, has yet been fruitless, if there be Truth in an Observation very frequently made, that Logicians out of the School do not reason better than Men unassisted by those Lights which their Science is supposed to bestow. It is not to be doubted but that Logicians may be sometimes overborn by their Passions, or blinded by their Prejudices; and that a Man may reason ill, as he may act ill, not because he does not know what is right, but because he does not regard it; yet it is not more the Fault of his Art that it does not direct him when his Attention is withdrawn from it, than it is the Defect of his Sight that he misses his Way when he shuts his Eyes. Against this Cause of Error there is no Provision to be made, otherwise than by inculcating the Value of Truth, and the Necessity of conquering the Passions. But *Logic* may likewise fail to produce its Effects upon common Occasions, for want of being frequently and familiarly applied, till its Precepts may direct the Mind imperceptibly as the Fingers of a Musician are regulated by his Knowledge of the Tune. This Readiness of Recollection is only to be procured by frequent Impression; and therefore it will be proper when *Logic* has been once learned, the Teacher take frequent occasion, in the most easy and familiar Conversation, to observe when its Rules are preserved and when they are broken, and that afterwards he read no Authors, without exacting of his Pupil an Account of every remarkable Exemplification or Breach of the Laws of Reasoning.

When this System has been digested, if it be thought necessary to proceed farther in the Study of Method, it will be proper to recommend *Crousaz, Watts, Le Clerc, Wolfius,* and *Locke*'s Essay on Human Understanding; and if there be imagined any Necessity of adding the Peripatetic Logic, which has been perhaps condemned without a candid Trial, it will be convenient to proceed to *Sanderson, Wallis, Crackanthorp* and *Aristotle.*

VIII. To excite a Curiosity after the Works of God, is the chief Design of the small Specimen of *Natural History* inserted in this Collection; which, however, may be sufficient to put the Mind in Motion, and in some measure to direct its Steps; but its Effects may easily be improved by a Philosophic Master, who will every Day find a thousand Opportunities of turning the Attention of his Scholars to the Contemplation of the Objects that surround them, of laying open the wonderful Art with which every Part of the Universe is formed, and the Providence which governs the Vegetable and Animal Creation. He may lay before them the *Religious Philosopher, Ray, Derham's Physico-Theology,* together with the *Spectacle de la Nature;* and in time recommend to their Perusal, *Rondoletius* and *Aldrovandus.*

IX. But how much soever the Reason may be strengthened by *Logic,* or the Conceptions of the Mind enlarged by the Study of Nature, it is necessary the Man be not suffered to dwell upon them so long as to neglect the Study of himself, the Knowledge of his own Station in the Ranks of Being, and his various Relations to the innumerable Multitudes which surround him, and with which his Maker has ordained him to be united for the Reception and Communication of Happiness. To consider these aright is of the greatest Importance, and a Duty from which he cannot deviate without much Danger.[28] *Ethics* or *Morality,* therefore, is one of the Studies which ought to begin with the first Glimpse of Reason, and only end with Life itself. Other Acquisitions are merely temporary Benefits, except as they contribute to illustrate the Knowledge, and confirm the Practice of Morality and Piety, which extend their Influence beyond the Grave, and increase our Happiness through endless Duration.

This great Science therefore must be inculcated with Care and Assiduity, such as its Importance ought to incite in reasonable Minds; and for the Prosecution of this Design, fit Opportunities are always at hand. As the Importance of *Logic* is to be shown,[29] by detecting false Arguments, the Excellence of Morality is to be displayed, by proving the Deformity, the Reproach, and the Misery of all Deviations from it. Yet it is to be remembered, that the Laws of mere Morality are of no coercive Power; and however they may by Conviction of their Fitness please the Reasoner in the Shade, when the Passions stagnate without Impulse, and the Appetites are secluded from their Objects, they will be of little force against the Ardour of Desire, or the Vehemence of Rage, amidst the Pleasures and Tumults of the World. To counteract the Power of Temptations, Hope must be excited by the Prospect of Rewards, and Fear by the Expectation of Punishment; and Virtue may owe her Panegyrics to Morality, but must derive her Authority from Religion.

28. the greatest Importance, since from these arise Duties which he cannot neglect.
29. shewn.

When therefore the Obligations of Morality are taught, let the Sanctions of Christianity never be forgotten; by which it will be shown,[30] that they give Strength and Lustre to each other, Religion will appear to be the Voice of Reason, and Morality the Will of GOD. Under this Article one cannot sufficiently recommend[31] *Tully's Offices, Grotius, Puffendorff, Cumberland's Laws of Nature,* and the excellent Mr. *Addison's Moral* and *Religious Essays.*

X. Thus far the Work is composed for the Use of Scholars, merely as they are Men. But it was thought necessary to introduce something that might be particularly adapted to the Advantage of that Country[32] for which it is designed; and therefore a Discourse has been added upon *Trade* and *Commerce,* of which it becomes every Man of this Nation to understand at least the general Principles, as it is impossible that any should be high or low enough, not to be in some degree affected by their Declension or Prosperity. It is therefore necessary that it should be universally known among us, what Changes of Property are advantageous, or when the Balance[33] of Trade is on our Side; what are the Products or Manufactures of other Countries; and how far one Nation may in any Species of Traffick obtain or preserve Superiority over another. The Theory of Trade is yet but little understood, and therefore the Practice is often without real Advantage to the Publick: But it might be carried on with more general Success, if its Principles were better considered; and to excite that Attention, is our chief Design. To the Perusal of this Book may succeed that of *Mun* upon Foreign Trade, Sir *Josiah Child, Locke* upon *Coin, Davenant's* Treatises, the *British Merchant, Dictionaire de Commerce,* and for an Abstract or Compendium *Gee,* and an Improvements[34] that may hereafter be made upon this Plan.

XI. The Principles of *Laws* and *Government,* come next to be consider'd;[35] by which Men are taught to whom Obedience is due, for what it is paid, and in what Degree it may be justly required. This Knowledge by peculiar Necessity constitutes a Part of the Education of an *Englishman,* who professes to obey his Prince according to the Law, and who is himself a secondary Legislator, as he gives his Consent by his Representative, to all the Laws by

30. shewn.
31. Under this Article must be recommended.
32. adapted to that Country.
33. 'Balance' is divided at the end of a line in the original, and therefore acquires an extra 'l.'
34. Improvement.   35. considered.

which he is bound, and has a Right to petition the great Council of the Nation, whenever he thinks they are deliberating upon an Act detrimental to the Interest of the Community. This is therefore a Subject to which the Thoughts of a young Man ought to be directed; and that he may obtain such Knowledge as may qualify him to act and judge as one of a Free People, let him be directed to add to this Introduction, the Lord Chancellor[36] *Fortescue's Treatises, N. Bacon's Historical Discourse on the Laws and Government of England, Temple's Introduction, Locke on Government, Harrington's Oceana,[37] Plato Redivivus, Gurdon's History of Parliaments,* and *Hooker's Ecclesiastical Polity.*

XII. Having thus supply'd[38] the young Student with Knowledge, it remains now, that he learns its Application; and that thus qualified to act his Part, he be at last taught to chuse it. For this Purpose a Section is added upon *Human Life* and *Manners;* in which he is cautioned against the Danger of indulging his *Passions,* of vitiating his *Habits,* and depraving his *Sentiments.*

He[39] is instructed in these Points by three Fables, two of which are[40] of the highest Authority, in the ancient *Pagan* World. But at this he is not to rest, for if he expects to be Wise and Happy, he must diligently study the SCRIPTURES of GOD.

Such is the Book now proposed, as the first Initiation into the Knowledge of Things, which has been thought by many to be too long delayed in the present Forms of Education. Whether the Complaints be not often ill-grounded, may perhaps be disputed; but it is at least reasonable to believe, that greater Proficiency might sometimes be made; that real Knowledge might be more early communicated; and that Children might be allowed, without Injury to Health, to spend many of those Hours upon useful Employments, which are generally lost in Idleness and Play; therefore the Public will surely encourage an Experiment, by which, if it fails, nobody is hurt, and if it succeeds all the future Ages of the World may find Advantage; which may eradicate or prevent Vice, by turning to a better use those Moments in which it is learned or indulged; and in some Sense lengthen Life by teaching Posterity to enjoy those Years which have hitherto been lost. The Success, and even the Trial of this Experiment, will de-

36. 'the Lord Chancellor' omitted.
37. '*Zouch's Elementa Juris Civilis*' substituted for '*Harrington's Oceana.*'
38. supplied.
39. This short paragraph is joined to the preceding paragraph in the second edition.
40. were.

pend upon those to whom the Care of our Youth is committed; and a due Sense of the Importance of their Trust, will easily prevail upon them to encourage a Work which pursues the Design of improving Education. With this View,[41] if any Part of the following Performance shall upon Trial be found capable of Amendment, if any thing can be added or alter'd, so as to render the Attainment of Knowledge more easy; the Editor will be extremely oblig'd[42] to any Gentleman, particularly those who are engag'd[43] in the Business of Teaching, for such Hints or Observations as may tend towards the Improvement of this Book,[44] and will spare neither Expence nor Trouble in making the best use of their Informations.

PROCEEDINGS OF THE COMMITTEE FOR CLOATHING FRENCH PRISONERS

Published: August 1760.[1]

References: Boswell, *Life,* i:353; iv:97, 491.

Courtney, p. 99.

Johnson's Contribution: Introduction.

Copies: Aberdeen University; Bodleian; British Museum (2 copies); Edinburgh University; Glasgow University; Trinity College, Dublin; R. B. Adam; Dr. R. W. Chapman; Dr. L. F. Powell; Professor C. B. Tinker.

THIS is one of the books that Boswell almost overlooked, for he added in his Revise at the end of 1760:

Johnson who was ever awake to the calls of humanity wrote this year

41. 'With this View' omitted.   42. obliged.
43. engaged.
44. 'of this Book' omitted (perhaps in error).

1. The date is an approximation. The last action by the Committee was taken on July 23, when much of the book must have been nearly ready for the press. Mrs. Carter wrote to Miss Talbot, 1 September 1760: 'I have lately received an account of the subscription to the French prisoners, for which I believe I am to thank you; the preface extremely pleased me.' Miss Talbot, on September 17, replied that she had not sent the book, but that she had also received a copy. *A Series of letters between Mrs. Elizabeth Carter and Miss Catherine Talbot,* edited by M. Pennington (London 1809), ii:349, 351. One of the handsomely bound presentation copies (Bodleian) contains a pencilled note: 'Rec. Novr. 28, 1760 Entered.'

an Introduction to the proceedings of the Committee for clothing the french prisoners.

To the printer he added:

N. B. I have *catched* a small fugitive piece in 1760, which *must* be put into its place on the next page.²

It is now a rare book, and I think that the impression was not a large one. Boswell's attention was perhaps drawn to it by the following passage in the *Memoirs of Thomas Hollis:*

In the autumn of this year [1759] was projected the plan for cloathing the French prisoners by subscription, of which Mr. Hollis was an active and zealous promoter, and to which he was a bountiful contributor [fifty guineas]; on December 18th, he attended a meeting for that purpose, 'when,' as he says, 'the whole plan was sketched out nobly for immediate and effectual execution.' When the subscription was filled to a considerable amount, it was thought proper to publish it; and on that occasion, Mr. (now Dr.) Johnson was requested by Mr. Hollis to compose a short preface or introduction to that publication, which, being approved of by the curators of that charity, was accordingly prefixed to the published account of it, and a present of five guineas given by Mr. Hollis to Dr. Johnson for his trouble.³

The preparation and publication of the *Proceedings* were in charge of John Payne, assisted by a sub-committee.⁴ The last resolution of the Committee (July 23) was:

That printed copies of the proceedings of this charity should be deposited in the British Museum, and in the several Universities of the British Empire.⁵

2. *Boswell Revised,* p. 26. Boswell later altered his phrasing slightly, and moved it to the beginning of 1760. Boswell, *Life,* i:353. I doubt whether Boswell ever saw the original pamphlet.

3. F. Blackburne, *Memoirs of Hollis* (1780), i:88. Members of the Hollis family were for eighty years notable benefactors of Harvard College. (Cotton Mather tried to induce the first Thomas Hollis, uncle of Johnson's acquaintance, to give to Yale.)

On another occasion when Hollis appealed to Johnson, through John Payne, for a dissertation, he was less successful: see Boswell, *Life,* iv:97, 491.

4. *Proceedings,* p. xii. It was voted that the publication of the proceedings should be committed to the care of Mr. Payne. He lived at the Herald's College on Bennet's Hill, where the sub-committee met. There can be little doubt that John Payne of the Bank, an expert accountant and friend both to Johnson and to Hollis, is meant.

5. *Proceedings,* p. xiii.

Each of the copies that were presented to the Universities was bound with Belleisle's *Letters to Contades* (1759), in a tooled binding, with a suitable inscription. A presentation copy to Sterne is now in the Johnsonian Library of Mr. R. B. Adam. I doubt whether any copies were offered for sale.

Bibliographical Description

Proceedings of the committee / appointed to manage the contributions / begun at London Dec. XVIII MDCCLVIIII / for cloathing French prisoners of war. / [*Latin motto between rules*] / London / Printed by order of the committee / MDCCLX.

Small folio; Bodleian copy (the tallest that I have examined): 31.3 × 20 cm.
Facsimile of title-page and Introduction in second volume of the Catalogue of the R. B. Adam Library.

Signatures: [A],B,C²; D(one leaf); A–O².

Pagination: [i] title-page; [ii] blank; [iii–iv] Introduction; [v]–xiii Proceedings; [xiv] blank; 28 leaves unnumbered, containing four Appendices: List of Subscribers, Thanks of French Prisoners, General Account, Account of Collections.

The book is carefully printed on a fine watermarked paper, of mixed stock.

The public libraries, lacking the name of the author, have catalogued the book in various ways, so that it is a puzzling book to trace. For example, Glasgow enters it under 'Proceedings'; Edinburgh under 'London, Committee'; the British Museum under 'London, Miscellaneous, Comm.'; Bodleian (Printed Catalogue) under 'Prisoners'; and Bodleian (Manuscript Catalogue) under 'Committee.'

The Introduction was reprinted in the *Miscellaneous and Fugitive Pieces* published in 1773 by T. Davies.

INTRODUCTION.

The Committee intrusted with the money contributed to the relief of the subjects of France, now prisoners in the British Dominions, here lay before the public an exact account of all the sums received and expended; that the donors may judge how properly their benefactions have been applied.

Charity would lose its name, were it influenced by so mean a motive as human praise: it is, therefore, not intended to celebrate, by any particular memorial, the liberality of single persons, or distinct societies; it is sufficient, that their works praise them.

Yet he who is far from seeking honour, may very justly obviate censure. If a good example has been set, it may lose its influence by misrepresentation; and to free charity from reproach, is itself a charitable action.

Against the relief of the French, only one argument has been brought; but that one is so popular and specious, that if it were to remain unexamined, it would by many be thought irrefragable. It has been urged, that charity, like other virtues, may be improperly and unseasonably exerted; that while we are relieving Frenchmen, there remain many Englishmen unrelieved; that while we lavish pity on our enemies, we forget the misery of our friends.

Grant this argument all it can prove, and what is the conclusion? – – – that to relieve the French is a good action, but that a better may be conceived. This is all the result, and this all is very little. To do the best, can seldom be the lot of man; it is sufficient if, when opportunities are presented, he is ready to do good. How little virtue could be practised, if beneficence were to wait always for the most proper objects, and the noblest occasions; occasions that may never happen, and objects that never may be found?

It is far from certain, that a single Englishman will suffer by the charity to the French. New scenes of misery make new impressions; and much of the charity which produced these donations, may be supposed to have been generated by a species of calamity never known among us before. Some imagine that the laws have provided all necessary relief in common cases, and remit the poor to the care of the public; some have been deceived by fictitious misery, and are afraid of encouraging imposture; many have observed want to be the effect of vice, and consider casual almsgivers as patrons of idleness. But all these difficulties vanish in the present case: we know that for the prisoners of war there is no legal provision; we see their distress, and are certain of its cause; we know that they are poor and naked, and poor and naked without a crime.

But it is not necessary to make any concessions. The opponents of this charity must allow it to be good, and will not easily prove it not to be the best. That charity is best, of which the consequences are most extensive: the relief of enemies has a tendency to unite mankind in fraternal affection; to soften the acrimony of adverse nations, and dispose them to peace and amity: in the mean time, it alleviates captivity, and takes away something from the miseries of war. The rage of war, however mitigated, will always fill the world with calamity and horror: let it not then be unnecessarily extended; let animosity and hostility cease together; and no man be longer deemed an enemy, than while his sword is drawn against us.

The effects of these contributions may, perhaps, reach still further. Truth is best supported by virtue: we may hope from those who feel or who see our charity, that they shall no longer detest as heresy that religion, which makes its professors the followers of HIM, who has commanded us to "do good to them that hate us."

THE PUBLISHER

Published: December 1744 to February 1745, fortnightly.
Johnson's Contribution: Account of the Design.
Copies: Yale (3 numbers); University of Iowa; British Museum; Dr. L. F. Powell; Professor G. W. Sherburn.

THE Proposals for the *Publisher* are dated 24 September 1744. This single leaf folio was discovered by Dr. R. W. Chapman and attributed by him to Johnson in 1930.[1] When the *Publisher* was issued, Johnson's Account of the Design was reprinted as a Preface.

I see no reason to doubt that J. Crokatt was the principal undertaker and the publisher of this Miscellany, although T. Cooper's widow is the only person named in the imprint. She seems to have acted as a distributor for many publications which she could hardly have initiated. Crokatt acted as Secretary or agent of the Society of Booksellers for Promoting Learning. This Society was apparently the sponsor of the *Universal (Ancient) History* in seven folio volumes: Crokatt's

1. The *London Mercury,* xxi(March 1930):438–441. This copy of the original Proposals, now owned by Mr. Victor Rothschild, is the only one at present recorded.

name is in the imprint of all but the last volume. Crokatt was also, as agent for the same Society, associated with Osborne in the publication of Dr. James's *Medicinal Dictionary,* in three large folios.[2] The sale of the *Universal History* probably was slow, and that of James's *Dictionary* certainly was. Crokatt had therefore found by experience that 'a great book is a great evil,' and he asserted frankly that he undertook the *Publisher* in the hope of compensating himself for the losses which he had suffered. He wrote, or Johnson wrote of him, in the Account of the Design that he was a man 'who having impaired his Fortune in the Promotion of Literature, and found by Experience that a *Great Book is a great Evil,*[3] is now endeavouring to retrieve, by a periodical Pamphlet, those Losses which he has suffered by expensive Volumes.' It is to be feared that he was unsuccessful, for the *Publisher* appears to have survived for four numbers only.

When the Account of the Design was reprinted as the Preface to the *Publisher,* it was not revised.[4] Since the original *Proposals* were reissued in collotype facsimile by the Oxford University Press in 1930 and are readily available, it is not necessary to reproduce them.

Bibliographical Description

The / Publisher: / containing / miscellanies / in / prose and verse. / [*rule*] / Collected by J. Crokatt, Bookseller. / [*rule*] / Numb. I. / [To be continued every fortnight. Price sixpence.] / [*rule*] / [*ornament*] / [*parallel rule*] / London: / Printed for M. Cooper, at the Globe, in Pater- / noster-Row. MDCCXLV. / Where letters and parcels for the editor are received.

Octavo in half-sheets; 19.3 × 12 cm. (trimmed).

2. Crokatt attempted a second periodical in 1752, *The Repository.* (C. H. Timperley, *Encyclopaedia of Literary and Typographical Anecdote* [1842], p. 667, and H. R. Plomer, *Dictionary of Printers* [Oxford 1932], pp. 66–67.)
3. Callimachus, Fragment 359.
4. The spelling of three words is altered, one capital is reduced, and the end of the second paragraph is spoiled by a careless introduction of a superfluous 'less.'

Each number contained three sheets (actually five and one-half half-sheets with a separate title-page), and sold for sixpence.

First number advertised in *Daily Post,* 20 December 1744, to be published on the twenty-fifth of December. It was probably published soon afterwards, since the second number was advertised 12 January 1745 (*Westminster Journal*).

Facsimile of the *Proposals,* containing Johnson's Account of the Design, published by Oxford University Press in 1930.

Number I: title-page with verso blank; Account of the Design with verso blank; B–F4; F2: comprising 44 pp.

Number II: title-page with verso blank; G–L4; M2: comprising pp. 45–88.

Number III: title-page with verso blank, counted in the numeration as pp [89–90]; N–R4; S2: comprising pp 91–134.

Number IV: title-page with verso blank; T–Z4; Aa2: comprising pp. 135–178.

The separate title-pages after the first would not usually have been preserved when the book was bound, but in the copy at Yale they are preserved with the second and third numbers, so that I have assumed a similar title-page for the fourth number.

The pagination at the beginning of the third number was probably a careless error.

The Account of the Design is bound at the end of the first number in the copy at Yale.

In the advertisement of the first number (*Daily Post*) the statement is made that 'The avowed design of this Undertaking is the Promotion of scientific and polite literature, in order to form a supplement to the "Acta Eruditorum magnae Britanniae." ' This title I assume to be Crokatt's name for the *Bibliothèque Britannique, ou Histoire des ouvrages des savans de la Grande Bretagne,* which was published from 1733 to 1747 by P. De Hondt at La Hague; or he may have had in mind *The History of the Works of the Learned . . . in Great Britain and foreign parts,* a similar publication which, under various titles, was published from 1728 to December 1743, at London.

REYNOLDS, *SEVEN DISCOURSES*

Published: 19 May 1778 (*Public Advertiser*).
References: Boswell, *Life,* ii:2; iii:524, 529–530; iv:556.
       Courtney, p. 129.
Johnson's Contribution: Dedication.
Copies: Not rare.

THE story of the cancelled leaf which contains the proof of Johnson's authorship of this Dedication has been told with sufficient detail in the discussion of Percy's *Reliques,* and need not be repeated. It is the only Dedication, with the exception of Percy's, for which the exact date of Johnson's composition is known: for I think that Johnson referred to the Dedication for Reynolds when he wrote,

Yesterday I rose late having not slept ill. Having promised a Dedication, I thought it necessary to write, but for some time neither wrote nor read.[1]

That Johnson also read the manuscript of the *Seven Discourses* is a belief of long standing, and that it is a justifiable belief seems to be indicated by a letter which Reynolds wrote to Johnson:

I am making additions and should wish you to see it all together. If I sent it to you now, I must send it again when those additions are finished, I have not courage enough to appear in public without your imprimatur.

I am very much obliged to you for thinking about it, on Friday next I hope to send to Southwark.[2]

It would seem that Reynolds's 'too anxious apprehension that he might be suspected of having received larger assistance' than the Dedication was not without foundation.

The Dedication has been often reprinted, with the *Discourses* alone and with the *Works* of Sir Joshua. It was quoted by the *Monthly Review* for September, 1778, and by the *Gentleman's Magazine* for December, although the reviewers gave no hint that they recognized the style. Some additional discussion of Johnson and Reynolds has been included in connection with the *Catalogue* of the Society of Artists.

Bibliographical Description

Seven / discourses / delivered in the / Royal Academy / by

1. In *Prayers and Meditations,* entry for Easter Day, 19 April 1778. See *Miscellanies,* i:83.
2. Printed by Professor F. W. Hilles, *Letters of Reynolds* (1929), p. 57. He dates it 17 December 1777 in order to agree with the time when Reynolds was revising his Discourses. The letter is also reprinted in Boswell, *Life,* iii:530.

the / President. / [*rule*] / [*motto*] / [*parallel rule*] / London: / Printed for T. Cadell, in the Strand, bookseller / and printer to the Royal Academy. / M DCC LXXVIII.

Octavo; 22 × 13.5 cm. Price: 5/– sewed.

Signatures: [A](half-sheet); B–X⁸; Y(half-sheet).

Pagination: [i] half-title; [ii] blank; [iii] title-page; [iv] blank; [v–viii] Dedication; [i]–iv, 5–326 Text; [327–328] List of books sold by Cadell.

The book is not very rare, and it offers no bibliographical problems. Further details concerning this publication and its translations (particularly the difficulties that beset Baretti's Italian translation) may be found in F. W. Hilles, *Literary Career of Reynolds* (1936), pp. 46–68, 285–6.

DEDICATION

TO THE KING.

The regular progress of cultivated life is from Necessaries to Accommodations, from Accommodations to Ornaments. By Your illustrious Predecessors were established Marts for Manufactures, and Colleges for Science; but for the Arts of Elegance, those Arts by which Manufactures are embellished, and Science is refined, to found an Academy was reserved for Your Majesty.

Had such Patronage been without Effect, there had been reason to believe that Nature had, by some insurmountable impediment, obstructed our proficiency, but the annual improvement of the Exhibitions which Your Majesty has been pleased to encourage, shews that only Encouragement had been wanting.

To give Advice to those who are contending for Royal Liberality, has been for some years the duty of my station in the Academy; and these Discourses hope for Your Majesty's acceptance as well-intended endeavours to incite that emulation which Your Notice has kindled, and direct those studies which Your Bounty has rewarded.

May it please Your MAJESTY, Your MAJESTY's most dutiful servant, and most faithful subject,

Joshua Reynolds.

ROLT'S *DICTIONARY OF TRADE AND COMMERCE*

Published: 12 February 1756 (*London Evening-Post*).
References: Boswell, *Life*, i:358–9.
      Courtney, p. 74.
Johnson's Contribution: Preface.
Copies: Bowdoin; Library of Congress; Library Company of Philadelphia; Mercantile Library of Philadelphia; Yale; British Museum; National Library of Scotland; Signet Library.

DESPITE minor inaccuracies, there is probably a degree of truth in the following anecdote from Kearsley's *Life of Johnson*, from which it appears that Johnson had some thought of compiling a Dictionary of Commerce in 1755 or 1756.

Johnson, soon after the publication of his English Dictionary, made a proposal to a number of Booksellers convened for that purpose, of writing a *Dictionary of Trade and Commerce*. This proposal went round the room without any answer, when a well-known son of the trade since dead, remarkable for the abruptness of his manners, replied, 'Why, Doctor, what the D——l do you know of trade and commerce?' The Doctor very modestly answered, 'Why, Sir, not much I confess in the *practical* line—but I believe I could glean, from different authors of authority on the subject, such materials as would answer the purpose very well.'[1]

Perhaps Rolt also made his offer at about the same time, though it may be doubted whether he knew much more in the *practical* line than Dr. Johnson himself; or perhaps the booksellers preferred to utilize Johnson's talents for the composition of a general Preface, so that they then made inquiries for another compiler. In any case, Johnson wrote the Preface to the book, which, without having seen it, he thought better adapted to the needs of English merchants than the French Dictionary by Savary. Boswell once inquired about the book, and was disturbed when Johnson answered:

1. Quoted in *Miscellanies*, ii:162. Dr. Hill has pointed out that parts of the anecdote are manifestly incorrect. It is not impossible that it is a corrupted version of the same story that Boswell tells (*Life*, i:359), confused with Johnson's remarks on his qualifications as a writer of prefaces. (*Life*, i:292.) See also Murphy's story in his Life of Johnson (*Miscellanies*, i:412).

Sir, I never saw the man and never read the book. The booksellers wanted a Preface to a Dictionary of Trade and Commerce. I knew very well what such a Dictionary should be, and I wrote a Preface accordingly.[2]

Despite Johnson's confidence in the book, and the claims to superiority made for it in the Dedication to Lord Anson, it never superseded the Dictionary of Savary. The same sheets were reissued with a new title-page in 1761,[3] whereas the Dictionary of Savary, translated by Postlethwayt, experienced the luxury of a third edition in 1769. In February 1757, the booksellers attempted to sell the remainder in weekly parts, but this scheme seems to have been dropped after the first two numbers. This book, therefore, like Johnson's editions of Browne's *Christian Morals* and the *English Works of Ascham,* was sold only by the expedient of a cancel title-page.

The Preface was reprinted in the third volume of Davies's *Miscellaneous and Fugitive Pieces* (1774).

Bibliographical Description

A New / dictionary / of / trade and commerce, / compiled from / the information of the most eminent merchants, / and from / the works of the best writers on commercial subjects, / in all languages. / [*Outline of contents*] / For the use of the / merchants and tradesmen of Great Britain, / as well as of private gentlemen. / [*rule*] / By Mr. Rolt, / with the assistance of several eminent merchants. / [*parallel rule*] / London: / Printed for T. Osborne and J. Shipton; J. Hodges; J. Newbery; / G. Keith; and B. Collins. / MDCCLVI.

Folio, with horizontal chain-lines; printed on half-sheets of double-size paper.
Trimmed copy: 35 × 22.5 cm. Publication price: £1/10/– bound. Title-page in red and black.

Signatures: 2 prelim. leaves; A–10T².

2. Boswell, *Life,* i:359. See above in the discussion of Kennedy's *Astronomical Chronology,* pp. 74–5. Boswell's date is that of the second edition.
3. The second edition does have some maps.

No pagination: title-page (with verso blank); Dedication (2 pp.); Preface (4 pp. — Sig. A); Text (Sigs. B–10T).

Frontispiece facing title-page: wanting in the copy at Yale.

Since the Preface contains no textual problems, it has been omitted to save space.

SOCIETY OF ARTISTS, *CATALOGUE*

Published: 17 May 1762 (date of Exhibition).

References: Boswell, *Life,* i:367.

Courtney, p. 101.

Johnson's Contribution: Preface.

Copies: New York Public Library; British Museum (3 copies); Royal Academy; Victoria and Albert (3 copies); Dr. R. W. Chapman; C. R. Grundy; W. S. Lewis; Geoffrey Madan; Lord Rosebery.

All catalogues of the Society of Artists are very rare; those for 1760 and for the second exhibition of 1768 are the most difficult to find.

JOHNSON expressed to Baretti, in an interesting letter which he wrote soon after the second Exhibition of the Society of Artists, his opinion of artists' exhibitions:

The Artists have instituted a yearly Exhibition of pictures and statues, in imitation, as I am told, of foreign academies. This year was the second Exhibition. They please themselves much with the multitude of spectators, and imagine that the English School will rise in reputation. Reynolds is without a rival, and continues to add thousands to thousands, which he deserves, among other excellencies, by retaining his kindness for Baretti. This Exhibition has filled the heads of the Artists and lovers of art. Surely life, if it be not long, is tedious, since we are forced to call in the assistance of so many trifles to rid us of our time, of that time which never can return.[1]

It is not without interest that when, a year later, he furnished the Preface to the Catalogue of the new Exhibition, he undertook to justify the institution against his own doubts of its value.

That Johnson was the author of the Preface to the Catalogue for 1762 has not until recently been seriously doubted; but in 1928 Mr. Whitley asserted, and has since maintained,

1. Letter 138, 10 June 1761; reprinted in Boswell, *Life,* i:363.

that Reynolds was the author of this Preface.[2] One could wish that the proof of Johnson's authorship might be more decisive; yet I have no doubt whatever that the Preface as it stands is chiefly if not wholly the work of Johnson.

2. W. T. Whitley, *Artists and their friends in England 1700–1799* (London 1928), i:178–9. In discussing this Preface, he writes: 'Boswell includes it in the list of Johnson's works printed at the end of the famous biography but admits that his attribution is based only on internal evidence. An entry in the minutes of the Society, made on the 20th of April, just before the opening of the exhibition of 1762, seems to suggest that the preface was written by Reynolds, not Johnson. "Mr. Reynolds having presented a preface it was agreed to and ordered to be printed." Johnson had been asked more than a month before to supply a motto for the catalogue to accompany a design "agreeable thereto" to be drawn by Hayman. The name of Johnson does not appear again in the matter and there is nothing to show whether it was he who chose the quotation from Martial that appears on the frontispiece of the catalogue. But the design on the frontispiece in which a figure of Britannia is the principal object was drawn by Samuel Wale.'

Dr. L. F. Powell joined battle with Mr. Whitley in the columns of *The Times:* 22 Jan. 1934, p. 13e; 5 Feb. 1934, p. 8b; 14 Feb. 1934, p. 8a; 27 Feb. 1934, p. 10c. The correspondents stray at times from the point in question, and the logic is sometimes faulty, but the following facts appear. The minute of the 20th of April proves only that Reynolds brought a suitable preface, not that he had written one; the failure of Reynolds to mention Johnson is not unlike his refusal to admit that Johnson furnished the Dedication to his *Seven Discourses;* the mention of Johnson in connection with the motto has no bearing on the question; the style is unquestionably Johnsonian, and it has been accepted by Dr. Birkbeck Hill, Professor D. Nichol Smith, and Dr. R. W. Chapman. Four facts are adduced by Dr. Powell in confirmation of Johnson's authorship: (1) Volume xiv of the *Works* included the Preface four years before the death of Reynolds; (2) Boswell, a close friend of Reynolds to whom he dedicated the *Life*, admitted it as Johnson's in 1791 (the Chronological Catalogue to which Mr. Whitley refers was first printed in 1793 after the death of Reynolds); (3) Malone, who edited the *Life* and who was the executor of Reynolds and the editor of his Literary Works, did not deny the ascription of the Preface to Johnson; (4) Northcote printed the Preface, but indicated that it was by Dr. Johnson. Each of these facts is important though none of the evidence is conclusive: Boswell indeed very probably included the Preface chiefly because he found it in Volume xiv of the *Works*, a volume that is not without serious errors.

One important bit of evidence was overlooked by Dr. Powell: the Preface was included in the second volume of Davies's *Miscellaneous and Fugitive Pieces* (1773); and, what is more important, it was there inserted among the undoubted Johnsonian works—between the Preface to *Shakespeare* and the Preface to the *London Chronicle*. Davies is not altogether reliable, but he knew Johnson well, and his attribution, ten years after the publication of the *Artists' Catalogue*, is even more impressive when it is confirmed years afterwards by the editor [probably Isaac Reed] of Volume xiv of the *Works* and by Boswell.

It is not improbable that Johnson furnished the motto, 'Aurea si tuleris dona, minora feres,' for Wale's engraving, but no certainty is attainable. Mr. C. Reginald Grundy has suggested to me that the mottoes in the Catalogues of the early years of the Exhibitions of the Royal Academy were very probably selected by Johnson, but again there seems to be no way of proving or of disproving the suggestion.

On the verso of the title-page of the *Catalogue* of the Royal Academy's Exhibition of 1769 is an Advertisement of two sentences to explain the charge that was made for admission. (The Advertisement was repeated in 1780.) The late Algernon Graves wrote under this Advertisement in his own copy, 'Said to have been written by Dr. Johnson.' The style of the Advertisement hardly supports this tradition, and I think that it has been confused with the Preface to the *Catalogue* of the Society of Artists of 1762, which was also written to justify the collection of an admission fee. See also F. W. Hilles, *Literary Career of Sir Joshua Reynolds* (Cambridge 1936), p. 38.

Bibliographical Description

A / Catalogue / of the / pictures, sculptures, models, drawings, prints, &c. / exhibited by the / Society of Artists / of / Great Britain, / at the / great room, in Spring Gardens, Charing Cross. / May the 17th, Anno 1762. / (Being the third year of their exhibition.)

Small quarto in half-sheets. 24 × 18 cm. The handsome engraving by Grignion, from the design of Samuel Wale, on the title-page is reproduced in A. Graves, *The Society of Artists* (London 1907), p. 350.

Signatures: engraved title-page; A–E².

Pagination: [i] title-page; [ii] blank; 3 (in brackets), iv–vi Preface; [1]–16 Catalogue.

The Catalogue of 1762 is the only one with an engraved title-page. It is printed on a separate plate. The lettering is by Joseph Champion.

The Catalogue of 1761 was sold for one shilling. In 1762 the Society decided to institute a charge for admission and make no charge for the Catalogue itself.

The variations in different copies should be of some interest to historians of art: bibliographically, the evidence seems quite clear that each sheet was reprinted as the necessity arose, and that the assembled Catalogue may well have an early state of one sheet and a much later state of another.

Sig. A. In Johnson's Preface I have never seen any variations, and I think that when the Preface was approved enough copies were printed to supply all the demand.

Sig. B. No. 26—Twelfth-night is in the wrong line, and this error is corrected by the Errata on p. 11. In the revised sheet, Twelfth-night is correctly printed, and there are two additional entries, *5 and *23. Soapin has also been corrected to Scapin, p. 3.

Sig. C. I have seen two states, as follows: (1) Myntz (p. 6) and French (p. 7). These errors are corrected by the Errata on p. 11. I have seen two copies in which these errors have been corrected in the text bound with a Sig. D containing Errata. (2) Muntz and Finch corrected.

Sig. D. At least three states, as follows: (1) No. 136 is printed but has no picture listed; Errata of eight lines on p. 11. (2) No. 136 omitted; No. *138 added; Errata retained. (3) No Errata, and has Nos. *138, *129, *170.

Sig. E. Probably only two states. (1) Last line of p. 14 reads 'were not offered on account of the expence.' This is heavily blotted, presumably before the Catalogue was issued. (2) Last line of p. 14 reads 'are not executed.' In addition the description of Nos. 208, 209 is much abbreviated, and p. 16 is entirely reset, with the addition of one name.

Since all these variants, except the changes in Sig. C, are represented in the three copies at the Victoria and Albert Museum, it is possible that a careful collation of other copies would disclose other 'states.' The responsibility of the historian of art is perhaps rendered greater by the knowledge of these changes, for he can never be certain that another edition of the Catalogue may not list a particular picture. It seems clear that the added entries with asterisks represent pictures which were offered for exhibition after the first Catalogue had been printed. In the Royal Academy Catalogues such pictures were usually grouped at the end and listed as 'omitted' pictures. (W. T. Whitley, *Artists and their friends,* i:319.)

In some Catalogues, the asterisk was used to indicate pictures that were for sale. The first time that this was done was, I think, in the Catalogue of the Society of Artists of 1764.

Concerning the Catalogue of 1761, it seems not to be generally known that the engraved headpiece by Wale is not in the first issue, and that the satirical endpiece by Hogarth has the dates 1502, 1600, 1604 usually, but in three copies that I have examined the dates are 1502, 1600, 1606. These are, I should suppose, intended to indicate the dates of certain artists.

The text of Johnson's Preface has been recently reprinted in A. Graves, *The Society of Artists* (London 1907); and, less accurately, in W. Sandby, *History of the Royal Academy,* Volume i (London 1862), as well as by Northcote and in Volume xiv of the *Works* (1788). It was first reprinted by T. Davies, in his *Miscellaneous and Fugitive Pieces* (1773), ii:151, 152.

PREFACE.

The public may justly require to be inform'd of the nature and extent of every design, for which the favour of the public is openly solicited.[3] The Artists, who were themselves the first projectors of an Exhibition in this nation, and who have now contributed to the following catalogue, think it therefore necessary to explain their purpose, and justify their conduct. An Exhibition of the works of art, being a spectacle new in this Kingdom, has rais'd various opinions and conjectures among those, who are unacquainted with the practice in foreign nations; those, who set out their performances to general view, have been too often consider'd as the rivals of each other, as men actuated, if not by avarice, at least by vanity, and contending for superiority of fame, tho' not for a pecuniary prize. It cannot be denied or doubted, that all who offer themselves to criticism are desirous of praise; this desire is not only innocent but virtuous, while it is undebased by artifice and unpolluted by envy; and of envy or artifice these men can never be accused, who, already enjoying all the honours and profits of their profession, are content to stand candidates for public notice, with genius yet unexperienced, and diligence yet unrewarded; who, without any hope of encreasing their own reputation or interest, expose their names and their works only that they may furnish an opportunity of appearance to the young, the diffident, and the neglected. The purpose of this Exhibition is not to enrich the Artists, but to advance the Art; the eminent are not flatter'd with preference, nor the obscure in-

3. In the original, the word is divided at the end of the line, 'sol-licited.'

sulted with contempt; whoever hopes to deserve public favour is here invited to display his merit.

Of the price put upon this Exhibition some account may be demanded. Whoever sets his work to be shewn, naturally desires a multitude of spectators, but his desire defeats its own end, when spectators assemble in such numbers as to obstruct one another. Tho' we are far from wishing to diminish the pleasures, or depreciate the sentiments of any class of the community, we know however, what every one knows, that all cannot be judges or purchasers of works of art; yet we have already found by experience, that all are desirous to see an Exhibition. When the terms of admission were low, our room was throng'd with such multitudes as made access dangerous, and frightened away those, whose approbation was most desired.

Yet because it is seldom believed that money is got but for the love of money, we shall tell the use which we intend to make of our expected profits.

Many Artists of great abilities are unable to sell their works for their due price; to remove this inconvenience, an annual sale will be appointed, to which every man may send his works, and send them if he will without his name. These works will be review'd by the committee that conduct the Exhibition. A price will be secretly set on every piece, and register'd by the secretary. If the piece exposed is sold for more, the whole price shall be the Artist's, but if the purchasers value it at less than the committee, the Artist shall be paid the deficiency from the profits of the Exhibition.

THE UNIVERSAL CHRONICLE

First Number: 8 April 1758.
References: Boswell, *Life,* i:330.
           Courtney, p. 79.
Johnson's Contributions: Two introductory essays; the *Idler.*
Copies: Yale (one volume, containing first thirty-nine numbers);
    Bodleian (without title-pages); British Museum (Burney Collection—uncut, bound three volumes in one with title-page of first volume only, without No. 65).

THE *Universal Chronicle,* or *Payne's Universal Chronicle,* is remembered chiefly because the *Idler* was first published in it. The original parts and the collected editions of the *Idler* are listed briefly by Courtney. I do not know why the original parts should be so much more rare than those of the *Rambler:* they were of course printed in the columns of a weekly paper, and might therefore have been less carefully preserved, yet the first volume of the *London Chronicle* is not at all rare. The suggestion was made by Hill that the frequent changes which occurred in the title and colophon indicate that it did not sell well. This is a possible explanation.[1]

The imprint of the title-page of the first volume has the name of R. Stevens, who seems to have become the publisher at the beginning of 1759, when this title-page was issued with the Index for the volume. The colophon of each of the thirty-nine numbers in 1758 reads, 'Printed for J. Payne'; numbers 40–91 and 102–105 have 'R. Stevens' in the colophon, but numbers 92–101 have the names of R. Stevens and W. Faden.[2] The title was 'Universal Chronicle or Weekly Gazette' (numbers 1–4, 40–91); 'Payne's Universal Chronicle or Weekly Gazette' (numbers 5–39); and 'Universal Chronicle and Westminster Journal' (numbers 92–105). There are, therefore, only two important changes: at the end of 1758, when Payne relinquished control; and after the ninety-first number, when it was combined with the *Westminster Journal,* a periodical which later resumed separate publication.

All writers, from Hawkins down, have asserted that John Newbery was the projector of the *Universal Chronicle.*[3] It is

1. Like the *London Chronicle,* the *Universal Chronicle* carried no advertising at first. In No. 29 was inserted a notice that advertisements would now be accepted, 'but such Advertisements only will be admitted as are perfectly decent, and intended to promote Trade, or that are otherwise serviceable to the Publick.'

In the next number, accordingly, the first advertising appeared: it included an advertisement of Dr. James's Powders and one for John Payne's *New Tables of Interest.*

2. This is the William Faden who printed the *Rambler* and who is said to have been editor of the *Literary Magazine.* He was, I believe, associated for a time with Newbery.

3. J. Hawkins, *Life of Johnson* (1787), p. 363; A. Chalmers, Preface to *Idler* in his *British Essayists* xxxiii(London 1802):vii, viii; A. Chalmers, in *General Biographical Dictionary* xix(London 1815):61, 'Newbery . . . in conjunction with Mr. John Payne'; Forster's *Life of Goldsmith* (6th ed. 1877), i:204; and of

possible that Newbery was associated with Payne in the project, but it seems more likely that Hawkins was misled by the fact that the first collected edition of the *Idler* was published by Newbery in 1761. Newbery was one of the proprietors of *Lloyd's Evening Post and British Chronicle* (1758), so that Hawkins may have confused the two 'Chronicles.'

A full bibliographical description belongs with the *Idler,* and is beyond the scope of the present study. The paper appeared weekly, and was continued for 105 numbers. Each number contains eight pages, one sheet in quarto, with vertical chain-lines. This format is identical with that of the *London Chronicle:* the uncut file of the *Universal Chronicle* in the Burney Collection in the British Museum furnishes additional proof that a special unwatermarked paper of about twice the usual size was utilized, of which a half-sheet was printed as a normal quarto. The title-page to Volume I reads as follows:

The / Universal chronicle, / and / weekly gazette, / for / the year 1758. / Volume I. / From April 8, to December 30. / [*rule*] / [*motto*] / [*rule*] / To be continued. / [*parallel rule*] / London, / Printed for R. Stevens, at Pope's-Head, in Paternoster Row.

Copy at Yale: 28.5 × 20.5 cm. Price: Two pence half-penny.
Uncut copy in British Museum: approximately 30 × 21 cm.
Facsimile of first page of first number in Stanley Morison, *English Newspaper* (Cambridge 1932), p. 136.

Evidence for Johnson's authorship of these introductory essays is slight,[4] but the style is so convincing that it is difficult

course Boswell, *Life,* i:330. All these accounts seem to derive ultimately from Hawkins, who wrote: 'The engagement for the *Idler* was with Newbery. . . . He planned a weekly paper, which he called "The Universal Chronicle," and . . . it was part of his scheme, that it should have an essay or short discourse. . . . A share in the profits of this paper was Johnson's inducement to the furnishing such a discourse.'

4. A correspondent who signed himself 'C. D.' attributed the second essay, *Of the Duty of a Journalist,* to Johnson in the *European Magazine* xiii(February 1788):77; and Mr. D. C. Gallup points out to me that Baretti (in his *Grammar,* 1760) included some sentences from this essay among the extracts 'collected from the works of . . . Mr. Samuel Johnson.'

to believe that they are not by him. It is not surprising that they were not collected with the *Idler*, for these introductory essays have little significance apart from their function as a Preface to a new periodical, while the *Idler* formed a consecutive series which began in the second number of the paper.

Since the series was projected by Johnson in concert with the same people who had been associated with the *Rambler*, people to whom he was well known as a writer of Prefaces (to the *Literary Magazine* and *London Chronicle* among others),[5] it is difficult to believe that an introductory article would not have been planned by Johnson. Secondly, the discussion of the contradictions in the newspapers[6] is too similar to that in the seventh number of the *Idler* to be a mere coincidence. That Johnson was not averse to the repetition of ideas is well known;[7] and that he elaborated the sketch in the *Idler* from his own remarks in the Preface seems highly probable. It seems much less likely that he would have discussed a question which had been proposed a month earlier by some other writer. The repetition of words seems to me not unlike Johnson's usual manner.[8]

In the third place, the bibliographical evidence points to Johnson's authorship. The characteristic feature of each issue is that the *Idler* is printed in leaded type, which occupies usually about two and one-half columns of the first page.[9] In the first number, the first two essays are in the same leaded

5. Less than two months earlier he had written the Preface to John Payne's *Tables of Interest*. This is the same John Payne who published the *Rambler* and the first thirty-nine numbers of the *Universal Chronicle*.

6. See the text below, third paragraph.

7. An instance is cited by Hill, Boswell, *Life*, i:334n.

8. For example, the repetition of 'different' in the second paragraph. In writing to Miss Cotterell in 1755, Johnson did not attempt to avoid an awkward repetition: 'Mr. Baretti being a single being. . . .' (*Letters*, ii:44.) The last paragraph of the first essay may have been added to Johnson's text.

9. This point offers an amusing illustration of the propagation of error. Both Hill and Courtney said that the *Idler* was printed in larger type than the rest of the paper. This was recently amplified by an American scholar who wrote that the *Idler* was set in type one point larger than the news matter. The error has been corrected, silently, by Professor D. Nichol Smith in his discussion of the newspapers in *Johnson's England*, edited by A. S. Turberville (Oxford 1933), ii:349.

type, and they fill all the first page as well as half a column of the second page. The rest of the first number is printed in unleaded type, exactly like the other issues aside from the *Idler* essays. It seems very clear that these first essays were regarded by the editor and compositor as exactly analogous to the *Idlers* of the later numbers, and that they really form the first of the series, although the Idler does not introduce himself until the second number. I have already pointed out that there would have been no point in reprinting these essays with the collected edition of the *Idler,* yet that need not exclude them from a small but honorable position in the canon of Johnson's prose. To me they seem better than the preface to the *Literary Magazine* which Boswell praises so highly.

TEXT

The number of News-Papers already published is so great, that there appears, at the first view, very little need of another; but the Truth is, that this great number makes another necessary.

The different Compilers of the Papers now circulated round the Nation endeavour, according to their various Opportunities of Information, and Tracks of Correspondence, to excel in different kinds of Intelligence: it is therefore proper to unite weekly in some single Paper the different Accounts of different Transactions, which are now so widely scattered, that many useful Hints may pass unregarded for want of Leisure to peruse all the Papers, and for want of Knowledge where to enquire.

It is well known to all those whose curiosity hastens them to the earliest Intelligence, that the same Event is every week affirmed and denied; that the Papers of the same day contradict each other; and that the Mind is confused by opposite Relations, or tortured with Narrations of the same Transactions transmitted, or pretended to be transmitted, from different places. Whoever has felt these inconveniencies will naturally wish for a Writer who shall once a week collect the Evidence, decide upon its probability, reject those Reports which, being raised only to serve the day, are naturally refuted before the end of the week, and enable the Reader to judge of the true State of Foreign and Domestic Affairs.

By such a method of Intelligence, that Knowledge, which, in

times of Commotion, every man's Interest or Curiosity makes necessary or pleasing, will be obtained at less Expence both of money and time; many foolish Triumphs and needless Terrors will be prevented or suppressed, the History of the last week will be clearly known, and the gradual progress of Affairs be distinctly traced in the memory.

This CHRONICLE, besides a judicious Collection of News, will contain a variety of such other matter as may be thought either useful or entertaining. A part whereof will be composed of Letters on interesting Subjects, which we expect to receive, nay, which we are assured will be communicated, by Persons of Eminence in the Literary World, who are friends to this Design; a Design, not hastily conceived, and imperfectly formed, but which has, for near twelve months past, been under the inspection of those who are able to promote the Undertaking.

A Portion of our Paper will be assigned to some of those Productions of Genius or Learning which daily receive their birth from the Press, and occasional Extracts or Specimens of Books and Pamphlets will be exhibited, with such candid remarks, as may contribute either to the Instruction or Entertainment of the Reader; and in this last case if we err at all, we hope it will be on the side of Good-nature: we shall not attempt (as many have basely done) to clip the wings of Genius, but to plume and direct its flight.

This Paper, which will be made as useful as possible to Readers of every denomination, may be sent in a frank to any part of Great Britain or Ireland; and may be had from *the Secretary of States Office,* or *General Post Office,* by those Gentlemen, Ladies, and Others, who will please to leave their orders with the Postmaster in their neighbourhood, or send to the Publisher, Mr. PAYNE, in *Pater-noster-Row.* It may also be had of the News-Carriers in Town and Country. And as it is intended to be bound in volumes, a General Title and complete Index to all the Literary articles will be given *gratis* at the end of the year; so that those who preserve their Papers will have, not only a Political History, but also an useful Body of Literary Compositions, of more value than the original price of the Papers.

Of the Duty of a JOURNALIST.

It is an unpleasing consideration that Virtue cannot be inferred from Knowledge; that many can teach others those Duties which they never practise themselves; yet, tho' there may be speculative

Knowledge without actual Performance, there can be no Performance without Knowledge; and the present state of many of our Papers is such, that it may be doubted not only whether the Compilers know their Duty, but whether they have endeavoured or wished to know it.

A Journalist is an Historian, not indeed of the highest Class, nor of the number of those whose works bestow immortality upon others or themselves; yet, like other Historians, he distributes for a time Reputation or Infamy, regulates the opinion of the week, raises hopes and terrors, inflames or allays the violence of the people. He ought therefore to consider himself as subject at least to the first law of History, the Obligation to tell Truth. The Journalist, indeed, however honest, will frequently deceive, because he will frequently be deceived himself. He is obliged to transmit the earliest intelligence before he knows how far it may be credited; he relates transactions yet fluctuating in uncertainty; he delivers reports of which he knows not the Authors. It cannot be expected that he should know more than he is told, or that he should not sometimes be hurried down the current of a popular clamour. All that he can do is to consider attentively, and determine impartially, to admit no falsehoods by design, and to retract those which he shall have adopted by mistake.

This is not much to be required, and yet this is more than the Writers of News seem to exact from themselves. It must surely sometimes raise indignation to observe with what serenity of confidence they relate on one day, what they know not to be true, because they hope that it will please; and with what shameless tranquillity they contradict it on the next day, when they find that it will please no longer. How readily they receive any report that will disgrace our enemies, and how eagerly they accumulate praises upon a name which caprice or accident has made a Favourite. They know, by experience, however destitute of reason, that what is desired will be credited without nice examination: they do not therefore always limit their narratives by possibility, but slaughter armies without battles, and conquer countries without invasions.

There are other violations of truth admitted only to gratify idle curiosity, which yet are mischievous in their consequences, and hateful in their contrivance. Accounts are sometimes published of robberies and murders which never were committed, mens minds are terrified with fictitious dangers, the publick indignation is raised, and the Government of our country depreciated and contemned. These Scriblers, who give false alarms, ought to be taught, by some public animadversion, that to relate crimes is to teach them, and that as most men are content to follow the herd, and to be like their neighbours, nothing contributes more to the frequency of wickedness, than the representation of it as already frequent.

There is another practice, of which the injuriousness is more apparent, and which, if the law could succour the Poor, is now punishable by law. The Advertisements of Apprentices who have left their Masters, and who are often driven away by cruelty or hunger; the minute descriptions of men whom the law has not considered as criminal, and the insinuations often published in such a manner, that, though obscure to the publick, they are well understood, where they can do most mischief; and many other practices by which particular interests are injured, are to be diligently avoided by an honest Journalist, whose business is only to tell transactions of general importance, or uncontested notoriety, or by Advertisements to promote private convenience without disturbance of private quiet.

Thus far the Journalist is obliged to deviate from the common methods of his Competitors, by the laws of unvariable morality. Other improvements may be expected from him as conducive to delight or information. It is common to find passages, in Papers of Intelligence, which cannot be understood: Obscure places are sometimes mentioned, without any information from Geography or History. Sums of money are reckoned by coins or denominations, of which the value is not known in this country. Terms of war and navigation are inserted, which are utterly unintelligible to all who are not engaged in military or naval business. A Journalist, above most other men, ought to be acquainted with the lower orders of mankind, that he may be able to judge, what will be plain, and what will be obscure; what will require a Comment, and what will be apprehended without Explanation. He is to consider himself not as writing to Students or Statesmen alone, but to Women, Shopkeepers, and Artisans, who have little time to bestow upon mental attainments, but desire, upon easy terms, to know how the world goes; who rises, and who falls; who triumphs, and who is defeated.

If the Writer of this Journal shall be able to execute his own Plan; if he shall carefully enquire after Truth, and diligently impart it; if he shall resolutely refuse to admit into his Paper whatever is injurious to private Reputation; if he shall relate transactions with greater clearness than others, and sell more instruction at a cheaper rate; he hopes that his labours will not be overlooked. This he promises to endeavour; and, if this Promise shall obtain the Favour of an early Attention, he desires that Favour to be continued only as it is deserved.

ANNA WILLIAMS'S *MISCELLANIES*

Published: 1 April 1766 (*London Chronicle*).
References: Boswell, *Life*, ii:25.
           Courtney, p. 111.
Johnson's Contributions: Advertisement, Poems, *The Fountains*, editorial supervision.
Copies: Harvard; Huntington Library; Yale; Birmingham Public Library; Bodleian; British Museum; Glasgow University; Victoria and Albert (Dyce—3 copies); Johnson House, Gough Square; Lichfield Birthplace (2 copies); R. B. Adam; Professor C. B. Tinker.

IN 1750 Johnson had written Proposals for Miss Williams's *Poems*.[1] Perhaps it was the fault of no single person that the publication was delayed for sixteen years. Miss Williams blamed Johnson, and in the Advertisement which he furnished Johnson seems to admit that it was in part his fault. The slightness of the material seems also to have caused some delay while Johnson endeavored to procure contributions sufficient to make the book large enough to be considered worth its price. Mrs. Thrale, in a note in a presentation copy which is now at the Johnson Birthplace in Lichfield,[2] wrote:

> The tale of the Fountains was written by Dr. Johnson for the purpose of *filling up this Book:* and he asked H. L. Thrale for something of hers beside. . . . She contributed the Three Warnings, and a Translation of Boileau's Epistle to his Gardener.

And John Hoole wrote in 1800:

> It may be proper to mention, that the little elegant drama of the *Un-*

1. *Gentleman's Magazine,* September 1750, p. [432]. Printed in *Works* in edition of 1825.
2. It was sold at Sotheby's, 9 December 1909. Another of Mrs. Thrale's presentation copies has recently been acquired by the Bodleian.

inhabited Island, was translated many years ago at the desire of Dr. Johnson, to be inserted in a volume of Miscellanies, in prose and verse, published by Mrs. Anna Williams, in the year 1766.3

Boswell ascribes the Advertisement to Dr. Johnson on internal evidence, but Tyers had written in 1785 that Johnson 'composed the Preface to the Poems of Miss Williams,'4 and this Advertisement was reprinted in Volume xiv of the *Works* (1788).

A portrait of Miss Williams, by Frances Reynolds, is now in the Johnson House, Gough Square.

A copy of the book with Malone's annotations is in the Dyce Collection of the Library of the Victoria and Albert Museum. The copy in the Library at Yale, with some annotations, has the name of James Boswell the Younger pasted on the fly-leaf. These notes are in part the authority for the following attributions. Johnson was the author or reviser of *The Ant, The Happy Life, Epitaph on Claudy Phillips, The Excursion, The Happy Solitude* (four lines), *An Ode on Friendship,* and *To Miss ——, playing the harpsichord.* He revised largely for Miss Williams the *Verses to Mr. Richardson,*5 *Ode on the Death of Stephen Grey,* and *Reflections on a grave digging in Westminster Abbey.* Two poems which Boswell ascribed to Johnson, *To Miss ——, On her giving the Author a net-work Purse* and the *Epitaph on Sir Thomas Hanmer,* are at best of doubtful authenticity. The *Sonnet,* addressed to a lady of indiscreet virtue, was by Thomas Percy. *The Wish,*6 *The Three Warnings,* and *Boileau to his Gardener* were by Mrs. Thrale. Frances Reynolds was probably the author of the two poems signed 'Stella': *Rasselas to Imlac,*

---

3. J. Hoole, *Dramas of Metastasio* (1800), i:xxvi. Mrs. Carter wrote in 1762: 'Poor Mrs. Williams is endeavouring to get a subscription to some Essays which are to be published next spring. . . .' *Letters from Mrs. Carter to Mrs. Montagu,* edited by M. Pennington (London 1817), i:164.

4. *Gentleman's Magazine* lv(1785):87. The hurried Memoir by Tyers was reprinted as a book and in the *New Annual Register.*

5. See also Dr. Powell's Appendix, in Boswell, *Life,* ii:479.

6. Marked as Mrs. Thrale's in Malone's copy.

and *An Ode.*[7] The translation of *The Uninhabited Island*
was made by John Hoole. The other pieces I presume were
chiefly by Miss Williams, save for Johnson's prose fairy tale,
The Fountains. Mrs. Carter seems not to have suspected that
this was by Johnson.[8]

Bibliographical Description

Miscellanies / in / prose and verse. / By Anna Williams. /
[*ornament*] / [*parallel rule*] / London: / Printed for T.
Davies, in Great Russel-Street, Covent-Garden. / M,DCC,
LXVI.

Quarto; 26 × 20.5 cm. Price: 5/–.
Facsimile of title-page in the second volume of the Catalogue of
the R. B. Adam Library.

Signatures: half-sheet; B–Aa⁴.

Pagination: [i] title-page; [ii] blank; [iii–iv] Advertisement by
Johnson, followed by one Erratum; [1]–184 Text.

Occasional mistakes in direction lines (catch-words) seem to indicate some uncertainty about the poems which were to be included in each sheet.
Copies were still for sale in 1770.

ADVERTISEMENT.

To those, by whose favour and encouragement the following
Collection has appeared, the motives of its publication are already known: and it were superfluous to inform the rest of the
world of that about which the world will have no Curiosity.
Complaints however natural are not pleasing; and I therefore

7. See *Miscellanies,* ii:279.
8. See her letter of 28 June 1766, to Miss Talbot: 'Why did not we read
and talk over Mrs. Williams's fairy tale together? . . . It is surely very beautiful, and yet there is something in the conclusion so unsatisfactory and mel-
ancholy, that it left only a gloomy impression on my mind.' *A Series of letters
between Mrs. Elizabeth Carter and Miss Catherine Talbot,* edited by M. Pennington (London 1809), iii:135. See also her letter of 30 June 1775, in *Letters
from Mrs. Carter to Mrs. Montagu,* edited by M. Pennington (London 1817),
ii:316.

would not mention the misfortunes of my life but to return my thanks for the kind endeavours to alleviate them, exerted by those who have subscribed, and procured Subscriptions, and those who by contributing their Compositions, have left my friends less reason to repent their solicitations.

To the few by whom the dilatoriness of my performance has been censured, I shall answer only by reminding them of my utter inability to hasten it by any diligence of my own, and by wishing that they may never learn from experience how slowly that is done, which is done gratuitously.

THE WORLD DISPLAYED

Published: 1 December 1759 to 1 July 1761 (one volume each month).
References: Boswell, *Life,* i:345, 546.
        Courtney, p. 98.
Johnson's Contribution: Introduction.
Copies: Harvard; University of Chicago; Bodleian (some volumes reprinted); Dr. R. W. Chapman; Professor C. B. Tinker.

JOHNSON had no desire to be a navigator, and there are several passages in his Introduction which indicate that he was not at all convinced that the voyages and discoveries of the Portuguese and Spaniards were of value, or that their cruelties towards the natives were justifiable. Despite this lack of sympathy with the aims of the early navigators, the Introduction is a fair summary of the discoveries prior to 1492, and parts of it are still of more than passing interest to the social historian and to the general reader.

The compilation must have been made by some of the writers who were then in the service of John Newbery, and assignment to specific men is difficult. That Johnson knew the general plan is probable, both because his Introduction discusses only the discoveries that were made before the first voyage of Columbus, with which the first volume of the collection begins, and because he furnished one paragraph in the Advertisement which was circulated a month before the publication of the first volume. That Johnson was concerned in the selection and arrangement of the voyages seems un-likely.¹ At this time, however, both Goldsmith and Christo-pher Smart were working for Newbery and both were avail-able for such a task. I therefore find nothing improbable in the suggestion that Goldsmith and Smart prepared the vol-umes, and that Johnson who knew the general plan of the work furnished the Proposals and the Introduction.²

I have never seen any record of a separate publication of the Advertisement (or Proposals) for ·the *World Displayed*, but from the form of the Advertisement in the newspapers I believe that there was a separate printing. It is dated October 30, 1759; it announces that the first volume of the *World Dis-played* will be published on the first of December, and lists the contents of the first volume. The paragraph addressed 'To the Public' must surely be by Johnson:

> Curiosity is seldom so powerfully excited, or so amply gratified, as by faithful Relations of Voyages and Travels. The different Appearances of Nature, and the various Customs of Men, the gradual Discovery of the World, and the Accidents and Hardships of a naval Life, all concur to fill the Mind with expectation and with Wonder; and as Science, when it can be connected with Events, is always more easily learned, and more certainly remembered, the History of a Voyage may be con-sidered as the most useful Treatise on Geography; since the Student fol-lows the Traveller from Country to Country, and retains the Situation of Places by recounting his Adventures. [There is one more sentence which is hardly Johnson's.]³

Johnson in his Introduction gives as his authorities Sousa, whom he also calls the Spanish historian, and Lafitau. These are, in the editions which have been easily available to me,

1. But among his projects was 'Collection of Travels, Voyages, Adventures, and Descriptions of Countries.' Boswell, *Life*, iv:382n.
2. The only direct evidence that is known to me is the title-page of the first American edition, published in eight volumes at Philadelphia in 1795, which reads, 'by Smart, Goldsmith, and Johnson.' What tradition led to this attri-bution I am unable to say.
3. See *London Chronicle*, 13 November 1759. The Advertisement was fre-quently inserted both in the *London Chronicle* and in *Lloyd's Evening Post*. This same paragraph was utilized in the advertisement of the second volume: see Dr. Powell's Appendix, in Boswell, *Life*, i:546. I have found it repeated as late as 1773, in an advertisement of a new edition.

Manuel de Faria y Sousa, *The Portugues Asia* (English translation in three volumes, London 1695), and J. F. Lafitau,
Histoire des découvertes et conquestes des Portugais (Paris
1733). In general, the first pages of the Introduction are translated from Sousa's first chapter, and the last half of the Introduction is translated from the first Book of Lafitau. More interesting to most readers are the occasional passages in which
Johnson added his own reflections concerning the narratives
of Sousa (spelled 'Souza' by Johnson) and Lafitau.[4]

The spelling, punctuation, and capitalization show extensive revision in the later editions, another demonstration of
the authority of the compositor. Six important verbal changes
in the fourth edition I have indicated in footnotes. Since
none of them appear to me to be Johnsonian, I do not consider this an exception to the general rule of non-revision.
These changes seem to have been made by the printer in an
attempt to regularize the diction of Johnson's Introduction,
an attempt which destroyed, it must be admitted, some of
Johnson's vigor.[5]

Editions:

The publication in monthly (in the later editions, weekly) numbers, together with their small size and great popularity, tended
to break up any perfect sets, so that most sets which are now
offered for sale are formed from more than one edition.[6] To increase the confusion, one might think, Newbery issued at least
one new edition of the earlier volumes before the first edition of
the later volumes had been printed.[7] The Second Edition of Volume I is dated 1760, but I have a record of other volumes of the
Second Edition which are dated 1768. Volumes which are marked
'Third Edition' or 'Fourth Edition' may be found with dates
ranging from 1762 to 1778. There were intermediate issues from
time to time, as the stock of particular volumes was exhausted,

4. For example, at the bottom of pp. 227 and 228 of the text.
5. The only cases of revision in the Prefaces and Dedications are the *Preceptor* and, perhaps, Lindsay's *Evangelical History*.
6. The Library of Congress, for example, has a set in which the imprints
range in date from 1762 to 1790. Sets were perhaps made up by the publishers
from more than one edition.
7. *London Chronicle*, 3 January 1761: 'A new edition of those volumes
which were all sold, is now at the press.'

often without any indication of the edition.[8] A revision of the *World Displayed,* edited by William Mavor, under the title *Historical Account of the most celebrated voyages . . .,* was published by the Newbery firm in 1796–7 in the same format, that is, twenty volumes in eighteens.

Two other early editions require separate notice. The set was bound by Newbery, for those who preferred fewer volumes, in ten double volumes. It was in that case bound 'in the vellum manner,' an innovation by Newbery. The books were half-bound, with an open back in green vellum and green paper. This made them open easier, and it was cheaper than a leather binding. The plan did not become permanent because it was soon completely superseded by cloth bindings.[9] A set bound in this manner, dated 1760, with an inscription from Johnson (not in his hand) to Sir Joshua's niece, Mary Palmer, was sold at the Kern Sale[10] for $400. Dr. Chapman's set of the first edition is bound in ten volumes.

In 1761 the work was reprinted with the omission of the first words of the title-page. The title therefore reads: *A Curious Collection of Voyages selected from the writers of all nations.* The rest of the title-page corresponds to that of the first edition, although the type is different.[11] The text seems to be a page-for-page reprint.

Johnson's Introduction was reprinted by T. Davies in his *Miscellaneous and Fugitive Pieces* (1773).

8. In the *London Chronicle,* 23 January 1770, the Third Edition is announced, although many volumes had been marked Third Edition in previous years. Similarly, the Fourth Edition was announced 9 April 1778. Reprinted volumes without any indication of edition have the dates 1761, 1766, 1767, and doubtless others. The numbering of these editions, although it seems capricious, may have been logical to the printer.

The first separate Dublin edition of which I have a record is 1779, the Sixth Edition, but there were perhaps earlier editions there. It was reprinted in octavo in Dublin in 1814–15. The early editions, with the names of Newbery and Hoey in their imprints, were probably sold in both countries.

9. C. Welsh, *Bookseller of the last century* (London 1885), p. 117. See also Newbery's advertisements of this new binding in M. Sadleir, *Evolution of Publishers' Binding Styles* (London 1930), pp. 10, 11.

10. New York, 7 January 1929.

11. Harvard has the first volume of this edition, and there is one orphan (Volume IV) in the library at Yale. Presumably only the first ten volumes were issued as *A Curious Collection of Voyages.*

The last ten volumes were numbered from one to ten in a second series, with the title: *A Curious Collection of Travels.* (The Library of Congress has such a set, and another was offered for sale in 1936 by Messrs. Rimell of London.) Perhaps Newbery decided that the sets would be easier to sell if divided in this way.

Bibliographical Description

The / World displayed; / or, a / curious collection / of / voyages and travels, / selected from / the writers of all nations. / In which the / conjectures and interpolations / of / several vain editors and translators are / expunged, / every relation is made concise and plain, / and / the divisions of countries and kingdoms are / clearly and distinctly noted. / Illustrated and embellished / with variety of maps and prints / by the best hands. / [*rule*] / Vol. I. / [*parallel rule*] / London: / Printed for J. Newbery, at the Bible and Sun, / in St. Paul's Church-Yard. / MDCCLIX.

20 volumes, 18mo in sixes; 13.7 × 8.5 cm. Price: 1/6 each, sewed.[12]

Signatures: A,a,b,B–Q⁶. Sigs. a & b are in brackets.

Pagination: [i] title-page; [ii] blank; [iii]–xxxii Introduction; 4 pp. unnumbered Contents ([xxxiii–xxxvi]); [1]–179 Text; [180] blank.

Folded map facing first page of text; plate opposite title-page, and 8 other plates bound in to face pp. 12, 36, 53, 61, 63, 90 (91 in error), 115, 118. I collate only the first volume.

In Vols. II–XVII the date is MDCCLX; in Vols. XVIII–XX the date is MDCCLXI. Vols. IV–XX have in the imprint, in addition to Newbery, the name of J. Hoey, Jr. of Dublin. His name first appears with Newbery's in the advertisements (in the newspapers) of the sixth volume.

Newbery introduced a large number of engravings into the volumes of the series, and no doubt by this means greatly increased the attractiveness of the volumes to the purchasers. These engravings are unsigned, and the artists (or artist) are not known to me.

The format is an unusual one for English books of this period: Dr. McKerrow wrote that he had not met with it in English printing.[13] Newbery seems to have found it a satisfactory size, however, for the *World Displayed* and its successors were printed in 18mo until the end of the century. The books seem to have

12. The price for the set was two pounds bound, or, if bound two volumes in one, the ten volumes were sold at £1/12/0. (*London Catalogue* 1773, p. 83.)

13. *Introduction to Bibliography* (Oxford 1927), p. 173.

puzzled the cataloguers, for I have seen them listed as 12mo, 16mo, and 24mo; they have been correctly described, I think, only by Courtney in 1915 and by the compiler of the *Catalogue* of the Library of Colonel Isham (4 May 1933). The chain-lines are vertical, and the watermarks, when visible, are centrally placed on the page toward the inner margin.[14] It is a temptation to carry such a small volume in one's pocket, to be read at odd moments: Washington Irving says that he used to take them to school and read them slyly 'to the great neglect of my lessons.' (S. T. Williams, *Irving*, 1935, i:21.)

INTRODUCTION.

Navigation, like other arts, has been perfected by degrees. It is not easy to conceive that any age or nation was without some vessel, in which rivers might be passed by travellers, or lakes frequented by fishermen; but we have no knowledge of any ship that could endure the violence of the ocean, before the ark of *Noah*.

As the tradition of the deluge has been transmitted to almost all the nations of the earth; it must be supposed that the memory of the means by which *Noah* and his family were preserved, would be continued long among their descendants, and that the possibility of passing the seas could never be doubted.

What men know to be practicable, a thousand motives will incite them to try; and there is reason to believe, that from the time that the generations of the postdiluvian race spread to the sea shores, there were always navigators that ventured upon the sea, though, perhaps, not willingly beyond the sight of land.

Of the ancient voyages little certain is known, and it is not necessary to lay before the reader such conjectures as learned men have offered to the world. The *Romans* by conquering *Carthage,* put a stop to a great part of the trade of distant nations with one another, and because they thought only on war and conquest, as their Empire encreased, commerce was discouraged; till under the latter Emperors, ships seem to have been of little other use than to transport soldiers.

Navigation could not be carried to any great degree of cer-

14. The proper imposition and manner of cutting for this format may be studied with the aid of the scheme in John Johnson's *Typographia* (London 1824), ii:*26. The possibilities of error in the bindery would seem to be much increased when each sheet was to be cut into six parts, but I have observed no instances of faulty imposition or binding.

tainty, without the compass; which was unknown to the ancients. The wonderful quality by which a needle, or small bar of steel, touched with a loadstone or magnet, and turning freely by equilibration on a point, always preserves the meridian, and directs its two ends north and south, was discovered according to the common opinion in 1299, by *John Gola* of *Amalphi,* a town in *Italy.*

From this time it is reasonable to suppose that Navigation made continual, though slow, improvements, which the confusion and barbarity of the times, and the want of communication between orders of men so distant as sailors and monks, hindered from being distinctly and successively recorded.

It seems, however, that the sailors still wanted either knowledge or courage, for they continued for two centuries to creep along the coast, and considered every headland as unpassable, which ran far into the sea, and against which the waves broke with uncommon agitation.

The first who is known to have formed the design of new discoveries, or the first who had power to execute his purposes, was Don *Henry* the fifth son of *John* the First, King of *Portugal,* and *Philippina,* sister of *Henry* the Fourth of *England. Don Henry* having attended his father to the conquest of *Ceuta,* obtained by conversation with the inhabitants of the continent, some accounts of the interior kingdoms and southern coast of *Africa;* which, though rude and indistinct, were sufficient to raise his curiosity, and convince him that there were countries yet unknown and worthy of discovery.

He therefore equipped some small vessels, and commanded that they should pass as far as they could along that coast of *Africa,* which looked upon the great Atlantic Ocean, the immensity of which struck the gross and unskilful navigators of these times, with terror and amazement. He was not able to communicate his own ardour to his seamen, who proceeded very slowly in the new attempt, each was afraid to venture much further than he that went before him, and ten years were spent before they had advanced beyond cape *Bajador,* so called from its long progression into the ocean, and the circuit by which it must be doubled. The opposition of this promontory to the course of the sea, produced a violent current and high waves, into which they durst not venture, and which they had not yet knowledge enough to avoid by standing off from the land into the open sea.

The Prince was desirous to know something of the countries that lay beyond this formidable cape, and sent two commanders,

named *John Gonzales Zarco,* and *Tristan Vaz* (1418), to pass beyond *Bajador,* and survey the coast behind it. They were caught
by a tempest, which drove them out into the unknown ocean,
where they expected to perish by the violence of the wind, or perhaps to wander for ever in the boundless deep. At last, in the
midst of their despair, they found a small island, where they shel-
tered themselves, and which the sense of their deliverance dis-
posed them to call *Puerto Santo,* or the *Holy Haven.*

When they returned with an account of this new island, *Henry*
performed a publick act of thanksgiving, and sent them again
with seeds and cattle; and we are told by the *Spanish* historian,
that they set two rabbits on shore, which encreased so much in a
few years, that they drove away the inhabitants, by destroying
their corn and plants, and were suffered to enjoy the island without opposition.

In the second or third voyage to *Puerto Santo,* for authors do
not well agree, a third captain called *Perello,* was joined to the
two former. As they looked round the island upon the ocean,
they saw at a distance something which they took for a cloud, till
they perceived that it did not change its place. They directed
their course towards it, and (1419) discovered another island
covered with trees, which they therefore called *Madera,* or the
isle of *Wood.*

Madera was given to *Vaz* or *Zarco,* who set fire to the woods,
which are reported by *Souza,* to have burnt for seven years together, and to have been wasted, till want of wood was the greatest inconvenience of the place. But green wood is not very apt to
burn, and the heavy rains which fall in these countries must
surely have extinguished the conflagration, were it ever so violent.

There was yet little progress made upon the southern coast,
and *Henry's* project was treated as chimerical, by many of his
countrymen. At last *Gilianes* (1433) passed the dreadful cape, to
which he gave the name of *Bajador,* and came back, to the wonder of the nation.

In two voyages more made in the two following years, they
passed forty-two leagues further, and in the latter, two men with
horses being set on shore, wandered over the country, and found
nineteen men, whom according to the savage manners of that age
they attacked, the natives having javelins, wounded one of the
Portuguese, and received some wounds from them. At the mouth
of a river they found sea-wolves in great numbers, and brought
home many of their skins, which were much esteemed.

Antonio Gonzales, who had been one of the associates of *Gi-lianes,* was sent again (1440) to bring back a cargo of the skins of sea wolves. He was followed in another ship by *Nunno Tristam.* They were now of strength sufficient to venture upon violence, they therefore landed, and without either right or provocation, made all whom they seized their prisoners, and brought them to *Portugal,* with great commendations both from the Prince and the nation.

Henry now began to please himself with the success of his projects, and as one of his purposes was the conversion of infidels, thought it necessary to impart his undertaking to the *Pope,* and to obtain the sanctions of ecclesiastical authority. To this end *Fernando Lopez d'Azevedo* was dispatched to *Rome,* who related to the *Pope* and Cardinals the great designs of *Henry,* and magnified his zeal for the propagation of religion. The *Pope* was pleased with the narrative, and by a formal Bull conferred upon the crown of *Portugal,* all the countries which should be discovered as far as *India,* together with *India* itself, and granted several privileges and indulgences to the churches, which *Henry* had built in his new regions, and to the men engaged in the navigation for discovery. By this Bull all other Princes are forbidden to encroach upon the conquests of the *Portuguese,* on pain of the censures incurred by the crime of usurpation.

The approbation of the *Pope,* the sight of men whose manners and appearance were so different from those of *Europeans,* and the hope of gain from golden regions, which has been always the great incentive of hazard and discovery, now began to operate with full force. The desire of riches and of dominion, which is yet more pleasing to the fancy, filled the courts of the *Portuguese* Prince with innumerable adventurers from very distant parts of *Europe.* Some wanted to be employed in the search after new countries, and some to be settled in those which had been already found.

Communities now began to be seized with the infection of[15] enterprise, and many associations were formed for the equipment of ships, and the acquisition of the riches of distant regions, which perhaps were always supposed to be more wealthy, as more remote. These undertakers agreed to pay the Prince a fifth part of the profit, sometimes a greater share, and sent out the armament at their own expence.

The city of *Lagos* was the first that carried on this design by

15. 4th edition: animated by the spirit of.

contribution. The inhabitants fitted out six vessels, under the command of *Luçarot*, one of the Prince's household, and soon after fourteen more were furnished for the same purpose, under the same commander; to those were added many belonging to private men, so that in a short time, twenty-six ships put to sea in quest of whatever fortune should present.

The ships of *Lagos* were soon separated by foul weather, and the rest, taking each its own course, stopped at different parts of the *African* coast, from Cape *Blanco* to Cape *Verd*. Some of them in 1444, anchored at *Gomera*, one of the *Canaries*, where they were kindly treated by the inhabitants, who took them into their service, against the people of the isle of *Palma*, with whom they were at war; but the *Portugueze* at their return to *Gomera*, not being made so rich as they expected, fell upon their friends, in contempt of all the laws of hospitality and stipulations of alliance, and, making several of them prisoners and slaves, set sail for *Lisbon*.

The *Canaries* are supposed to have been known, however imperfectly, to the antients, but in the confusion of the subsequent ages, they were lost and forgotten, till about the year 1340, the *Biscayneers* found *Luçarot*, and invading it, for to find a new country and invade it has always been the same, brought away seventy captives and some commodities of the place. *Louis de la Cerda*, Count of *Clermont*, of the blood royal both of *France* and *Spain*, nephew of *John de la Cerda*, who called himself the prince of Fortune, had once a mind to settle in those islands, and applying himself first to the king of *Arragon*, and then to *Clement* VI. was by the *Pope* crowned at *Avignon*, king of the *Canaries*, on condition that he should reduce them to the true religion; but the prince altered his mind, and went into *France* to serve against the *English*. The kings both of *Castile* and *Portugal*, though they did not oppose the papal grant, yet complained of it, as made without their knowledge, and in contravention of their rights.

The first settlement in the *Canaries* was made by *John de Betancour*, a *French* gentleman, for whom his kinsman *Robin de Braquement*, admiral of *France*, begged them, with the title of king, from *Henry the Magnificent* of *Castile*, to whom he had done eminent services. *John* made himself master of some of the isles, but could never conquer the *Grand Canary*, and having spent all that he had, went back to *Europe*, leaving his nephew *Massiot de Betancour*, to take care of his new dominion. *Massiot* had a quarrel with the vicar-general, and was likewise disgusted by the long absence of his uncle, whom the *French* king detained in his service, and being able to keep his ground no longer, he transferred his rights to Don *Henry,* in exchange for some districts in the *Madera,* where he settled his family.

Don *Henry,* when he had purchased those islands, sent thither in 1424, two thousand five hundred foot, and an hundred and twenty horse; but the army was too numerous to be maintained by the country. The king of *Castile* afterwards claimed them, as conquered by his subjects under *Betancour,* and held under the crown of *Castile* by fealty and homage; his claim was allowed, and the *Canaries* were resigned.

It was the constant practice of *Henry*'s navigators, when they stopped at a desert island, to land cattle upon it, and leave them to breed, where neither wanting room nor food, they multiplied very fast, and furnished a very commodious supply to those who came afterwards to the same place. This was imitated in some degree by *Anson,* at the isle of *Juan Fernandez.*

The islands of *Madera,* he not only filled with inhabitants, assisted by artificers of every kind, but procured such plants as seemed likely to flourish in that climate, and introduced the sugar canes and vines, which afterwards produced a very large revenue.

The trade of *Africa* now began to be gainful,[16] but a great part of the gain arose from the sale of slaves, who were annually brought into *Portugal,* by hundreds, as *Lafitau* relates, and relates without any appearance of indignation or compassion; they likewise imported gold dust in such quantities, that *Alphonsus* V. coined it into a new species of money called *crusades,* which is still continued in *Portugal.*

In time they made their way along the south coast of *Africa,* eastward to the country of the *Negroes,* whom they found living in tents, without any political institutions, supporting life with very little labour by the milk of their kine, and millet, to which those who inhabited the coast added fish dried in the sun. Having never seen the natives or heard of the arts of *Europe,* they gazed with astonishment on the ships when they approached their coasts, sometimes thinking them birds, and sometimes fishes, according as their sails were spread or lowered; and sometimes conceiving them to be only phantoms, which played too and fro in the ocean. Such is the account given by the historian, perhaps with too much prejudice against a negroe's understanding; who

16. 4th edition: profitable.

though he might well wonder at the bulk and swiftness of the first ship, would scarcely conceive it to be either a bird or a fish; but having seen many bodies floating in this water, would think it what it really is, a large boat; and if he had no knowledge of any means by which separate pieces of timber may be joined together, would form very wild notions concerning its construction, or perhaps suppose it to be a hollow trunk of a tree, from some country where trees grow to a much greater height and thickness than in his own.

When the *Portugueze* came to land, they encreased the astonishment of the poor inhabitants, who saw men clad in iron, with thunder and lightening in their hands. They did not understand each other, and signs are a very imperfect mode of communication even to men of more knowledge than the negroes, so that they could not easily negociate or traffick; at last the *Portugueze* laid hands on some of them to carry them home for a sample; and their dread and amazement was raised, says *Lafitau,* to the highest pitch, when the *Europeans* fired their cannons and muskets among them, and they saw their companions fall dead at their feet without any enemy at hand, or any visible cause of their destruction.

On what occasion, or for what purpose cannons and muskets were discharged among a people harmless and secure, by strangers who without any right visited their coast; it is not thought necessary to inform us. The *Portuguese* could fear nothing from them, and had therefore no adequate provocation; nor is there any reason to believe but that they murdered the negroes in wanton merriment, perhaps only to try how many a volley would destroy, or what would be the consternation of those that should escape. We are openly told, that they had the less scruple concerning their treatment of the savage people, because they scarcely considered them as distinct from beasts; and indeed the practice of all the *European* nations, and among others of the *English* barbarians that cultivate the southern islands of *America* proves, that this opinion, however absurd and foolish, however wicked and injurious, still continues to prevail. Interest and pride harden the heart, and it is vain to dispute against avarice and power.

By these practices the first discoverers alienated the natives from them, and whenever a ship appear'd, every one that could fly betook himself to the mountains and the woods, so that nothing was to be got more than they could steal; they sometimes surprised a few fishers, and made them slaves, and did what they could to offend the negroes and enrich themselves. This practice of robbery continued till some of the negroes who had been enslaved learned the language of *Portugal,* so as to be able to interpret for their countrymen, and one *John Fernandez* applied himself to the negroe tongue.

From this time began something like a regular traffick, such as can subsist between nations where all the power is on one side; and a factory was settled in the isle of *Arguin,* under the protection of a fort. The profit of this new trade was assigned for a certain term to *Ferdinando Gomez,* which seems to be the common method of establishing a trade that is yet too small to engage the care of a nation, and can only be enlarged by that attention which is bestowed by private men upon private advantage. *Gomez* continued the discoveries to Cape *Catherine,* two degrees and a half beyond the line.

In the latter part of the reign of *Alphonso* V. the ardour of discovery was somewhat intermitted, and all commercial enterprises were interrupted by the wars, in which he was engaged with various success. But *John* II. who succeeded, being fully convinced both of the honour and advantage of extending his dominions in countries hitherto unknown, prosecuted the designs of Prince *Henry* with the utmost vigour, and in a short time added to his other titles, that of king of *Guinea* and of the coast of *Africa.*

In 1463, in the third year of the reign of *John* II. died Prince *Henry,* the first encourager of remote navigation, by whose incitement, patronage, and example, distant nations have been made acquainted with each other, unknown countries have been brought into general view, and the power of *Europe* has been extended to the remotest parts of the world. What mankind has lost and gained by the genius and designs of this Prince, it would be long to compare, and very difficult to estimate. Much knowledge has been acquired, and much cruelty been committed, the belief of religion has been very little propagated, and its laws have been outrageously and enormously violated. The *Europeans* have scarcely visited any coast, but to gratify avarice, and extend corruption; to arrogate dominion without right, and practise cruelty without incentive. Happy had it then been for the oppressed, if the designs of *Henry* had slept in his bosom, and surely more happy for the oppressors. But there is reason to hope that out of so much evil good may sometime be produced, and that the light of the gospel will at last illuminate the sands of *Africa,* and the desarts of *America,* though its progress cannot but be slow, when it is so much obstructed by the lives of christians.

The death of *Henry* did not interrupt the progress of king *John,* who was very diligent[17] in his injunctions, not only to make discoveries, but to secure possession of the countries that were found. The practice of the first navigators was only to raise a cross upon the coast, and to carve upon trees the device of Don *Henry,* the name which they thought it proper to give to the new coast, and any other information for those that might happen to follow them; but now they began to erect piles of stone with a cross on the top, and engraved on the stone, the arms of *Portugal,* the name of the king, and of the commander of the ship, with the day and year of the discovery. This was accounted sufficient to prove their claim to the new lands; which might be pleaded with justice enough against any other *Europeans,* and the rights of the original inhabitants were never taken into notice. Of these stone-records nine more were erected in the reign of King *John,* along the coast of *Africa* as far as the Cape of *Good Hope.*

The fortress in the isle of *Arguin* was finished, and it was thought[18] necessary to build another at *S. Georgio de la Mina,* a few degrees north of the line, to secure the trade of gold dust, which was chiefly carried on at that place. For this purpose a fleet was fitted out of ten large and three smaller vessels, freighted with materials for building the fort, and with provisions and ammunition for six hundred men, of whom one hundred were workmen and labourers. Father *Lafitau* relates in very particular terms, that these ships carried hewn stones, bricks, and timber for the fort, so that nothing remained but barely to erect it. He does not seem to consider how small a fort could be made out of the lading of ten ships.

The command of this fleet was given to *Don Diego d'Azambue,* who set sail *Dec.* 11. 1481, and reaching *La Mina, Jan.* 19. 1482, gave immediate notice of his arrival to *Caramansa,* a petty prince of that part of the country, whom he very earnestly invited to an immediate conference.

Having received a message of civility from the negroe chief, he landed and chose a rising ground proper for his intended fortress, on which he planted a banner with the arms of *Portugal,* and took possession in the name of his master. He then raised an altar at the foot of a great tree, on which mass was celebrated, the whole assembly, says *Lafitau,* breaking out into tears of devotion at the prospect of inviting these barbarous nations to the profession of the true faith. Being secure of the goodness of the end they had no scruple about the means, nor ever considered how differ-

17. 4th edition: strict.   18. 4th edition: found.

ently from the primitive martyrs and apostles, they were attempting to make Proselytes. The first propagators of christianity recommended their doctrines by their sufferings and virtues, they entered no defenceless territories with swords in their hands; they built no forts upon ground to which they had no right, nor polluted the purity of religion with the avarice of trade or insolence of power.

What may still raise higher the indignation of a christian mind, this purpose of propagating truth, appears never to have been seriously pursued by any *European* nation; no means whether lawful or unlawful, have been practised with diligence and perseverance for the conversion of savages. When a fort is built and a factory established, there remains no other care than to grow rich. It is soon found that ignorance is most easily kept in subjection, and that by enlightening the mind with truth, fraud and usurpation would be made less practicable and less secure.

In a few days an interview was appointed between *Caramansa* and *Azambue*. The *Portuguese* uttered by his interpreter a pompous speech, in which he made the negroe Prince large offers of his master's friendship, exhorted him to embrace the religion of his new ally, and told him that as they came to form a league of friendship with him, it was necessary that they should build a fort which might serve as a retreat from their common enemies, and in which the *Portuguese* might be always at hand to lend him assistance.

The negroe, who seemed very well to understand what the Admiral intended, after a short pause returned an answer full of respect to the king of *Portugal,* but appeared a little doubtful what to determine with relation to the fort. The commander saw his diffidence, and used all his art of persuasion to overcome it. *Caramansa* either induced by hope or constrained by fear, either desirous to make them friends or not daring to make them enemies, consented with a shew of joy, to that which it was not in his power to refuse, and the new comers began next day to break the ground for the foundation of a fort.

Within the limit of their intended fortification, were some spots appropriated to superstitious practices, which the negroes no sooner perceived in danger of violation by the spade and pickax, than they ran to arms and began to interrupt the work. The *Portuguese* persisted in their purpose, and there had soon been tumult and bloodshed, had not the Admiral who was at a distance, to superintend the unlading the materials for the edifice, been informed of the danger. He was told at the same time that the support of their superstition was only a pretence, and that all their rage might be appeased by the presents which the Prince expected, and of which he had been offended by the delay.[19]

The *Portuguese* Admiral immediately ran to his men, prohibited all violence, and stopped the commotion; he then brought out the presents, and spread them with great pomp before the Prince; if they were of no great value they were rare, for the negroes had never seen such wonders before, they were therefore received with extasy, and perhaps the *Portuguese* derided them for their fondness of trifles, without considering how many things derive their value only from their scarcity, and that gold and rubies would be trifles, if nature had scattered them with less frugality.

The work was now peaceably continued, and such was the diligence with which the strangers hastened to secure the possession of the country, that in twenty days they had sufficiently fortified themselves against the hostility of negroes. They then proceeded to complete their design. A church was built in the place where the first altar had been raised, on which a mass was established to be celebrated for ever once a day for the repose of the soul of *Henry*, the first mover of these discoveries.

In this fort the Admiral remained with sixty soldiers, and sent back the rest in the ships, with gold, slaves, and other commodities. It may be observed that slaves were never forgotten, and that wherever they went they gratified their pride if not their avarice, and brought some of the natives, when it happened that they brought nothing else.

The *Portuguese* endeavoured to extend their dominions still farther. They had gained some knowledge of the *Jaloffs,* a nation inhabiting the coast of *Guinea,* between the *Gambia* and *Senegal.* The King of the *Jaloffs* being vicious and luxurious, remitted[20] the care of the government to *Bemoin* his brother by the mother's side, in preference to two other brothers by his father. *Bemoin* who wanted neither bravery nor prudence, knew that his station was invidious and dangerous, and therefore made an alliance with the *Portuguese,* and retained them in his defence by liberality and kindness. At last the King was killed by the contrivance of his brothers, and *Bemoin* was to lose his power or maintain it by war.

19. 4th edition: the delay of which had greatly offended him. [Hardly a Johnsonian revision.]
20. 4th edition: committed.

He had recourse in this exigence to his great ally the King of *Portugal*, who promised to support him on condition that he should become a christian, and sent an ambassador accompanied with missionaries. *Bemoin* promised all that was required, objecting only that the time of a civil war, was not a proper season for a change of religion which would alienate his adherents, but said, that when he was once peaceably established, he would not only embrace the true religion himself, but would endeavour the conversion of the kingdom.

This excuse was admitted, and *Bemoin* delayed his conversion for a year, renewing his promise from time to time. But the war was unsuccessful, trade was at a stand, and *Bemoin* was not able to pay the money which he had borrowed of the *Portuguese* merchants, who sent intelligence to *Lisbon* of his delays, and received an order from the King, commanding them under severe penalties to return home.

Bemoin here saw his ruin approaching, and hoping that money would pacify all resentment, borrowed of his friends a sum sufficient to discharge his debts, and finding that even this enticement would not delay the departure of the *Portuguese*, he embarked his nephew in their ships with an hundred slaves, whom he presented to the King of *Portugal*, to solicit his assistance. The effect of this embassy he could not stay to know, for being soon after deposed, he sought shelter in the fortress of *Arguin*, whence he took shipping for *Portugal* with twenty-five of his principal followers.

The King of *Portugal* pleased his own vanity and that of his subjects, by receiving him with great state and magnificence, as a mighty monarch who had fled to an ally for succour in misfortune. All the lords and ladies of the court were assembled, and *Bemoin* was conducted with a splendid attendance into the hall of audience, where the King rose from his throne to welcome him. *Bemoin* then made a speech with great ease and dignity, representing his unhappy state, and imploring the favour of this powerful ally. The King was touched with his affliction and struck by his wisdom.

The conversion of *Bemoin* was much desired by the king, and it was therefore immediately proposed to him that he should become a christian. Ecclesiasticks were sent to instruct him, and having now no more obstacles from interest, he was easily persuaded to declare himself whatever would please these on whom he now depended. He was baptized on the third day of *December* 1489, in the palace of the Queen with great magnificence, and named *John* after the King.

Some time was spent in feasts and sports on this great occasion, and the negroes signalized themselves by many feats of agility, far surpassing the power of *Europeans,* who having more helps of art, are less diligent to cultivate the qualities of nature. In the mean time twenty large ships were fitted out, well manned, stored with ammunition, and laden with the materials necessary for the erection of a fort. With this powerful armament were sent a great number of missionaries under the direction of *Alvarez* the King's confessor. The command of this force, which filled the coast of *Africa* with terror, was given to *Pedro Vaz d'Acugna* surnamed *Bisagù;* who soon after they had landed, not being well pleased with his expedition, put an end to its inconveniences by stabbing *Bemoin* suddenly to the heart. The King heard of this outrage with great sorrow, but did not attempt to punish the murderer.

The King's concern for the restoration of *Bemoin* was not the mere effect of amicable kindness, he hoped by his help to facilitate greater designs. He now began to form hopes of finding a way to the *East-Indies,* and of enriching his country by that gainful commerce: This he was encouraged to believe practicable, by a map which the Moore had given to Prince *Henry,* and which subsequent discoveries have shewn to be sufficiently near to exactness, where a passage round the south-east part of *Africa,* was evidently described.

The King had another scheme yet more likely to engage curiosity, and not irreconcileable with his interest. The world had for some time been filled with the report of a powerful christian Prince called *Prester John,* whose country was unknown, and whom some, after *Paulus Venetus,* supposed to reign in the midst of *Asia,* and others in the depth of *Ethiopia,* between the ocean and Red-sea. The account of the *African* christians was confirmed by some *Abissinians* who had travelled into *Spain,* and by some friars that had visited the holy land; and the King was extremely desirous of their correspondence and alliance.

Some obscure intelligence had been obtained, which made it seem probable that a way might be found from the countries lately discovered, to those of this far-famed monarch. In 1486, an ambassador came from the King of *Bemin,* to desire that preachers might be sent to instruct him and his subjects in the true religion. He related that in the inland country three hundred and fifty leagues eastward from *Bemin,* was a mighty monarch called

Ogane, who had jurisdiction both spiritual and temporal over other Kings; that the King of *Bemin* and his neighbours at their accession, sent ambassadors to him with rich presents, and received from him the investiture of their dominions, and the marks of sovereignty, which were a kind of scepter, a helmet, and a latten cross, without which they could not be considered as lawful Kings; that this great Prince was never seen, but on the day of audience, and then held out one of his feet to the ambassador who kissed it with great reverence, and who at his departure had a cross of latten hung on his neck, which ennobled him thence forward, and exempted him from all servile offices.

Bemin had likewise told the King that to the east of the kingdom of *Tombut,* there was among other Princes, one that was neither Mahometan nor Idolater, but who seemed to profess a religion nearly resembling the christian. These informations compared with each other, and with the current accounts of *Prester John,* induced the King to an opinion, which though formed somewhat at hazard, is still believed to be right, that by passing up the river *Senegal* his dominions would be found. It was therefore ordered that when the fortress was finished, an attempt should be made to pass upward to the source of the river. The design failed then, and has never yet succeeded.

Other ways likewise were tried of penetrating to the kingdom of *Prester John,* for the King resolved to leave neither sea nor land unsearched till he should be found. The two messengers who were sent first on this design, went to *Jerusalem* and then returned, being persuaded that for want of understanding the language of the country, it would be vain or impossible to travel farther. Two more were then dispatched, one of whom was *Pedro de Covillan,* the other *Alphonso de Paiva;* they passed from *Naples* to *Alexandria,* and then travelled to *Cairo,* from whence they went to *Aden* a town of Arabia, on the Red sea near its mouth. From *Aden, Paiva* set sail for *Ethiopia,* and *Covillan* for the *Indies. Covillan* visited *Canaver, Calicut,* and *Goa* in the *Indies,* and *Sosula* in the eastern *Africa,* thence he returned to *Aden,* and then to *Cairo,* where he had agreed to meet *Paiva.* At *Cairo* he was informed that *Paiva* was dead, but he met with two *Portuguese Jews,* one of whom had given the King an account of the situation and trade of *Ormus:* They brought orders to *Covillan,* that he should send one of them home with the journal of his travels, and go to *Ormus* with the other.

Covillan obeyed the orders, sending an exact account of his adventures to *Lisbon,* and proceeding with the other messenger to *Ormus;* where having made sufficient enquiry, he sent his companion homewards with the caravans that were going to *Aleppo,* and embarking once more on the Red-sea, arrived in time at *Abissinia,* and found the Prince whom he had sought so long with so much danger.

Two ships were sent out upon the same search, of which *Bartholomew Diaz* had the chief command; they were attended by a smaller vessel laden with provisions, that they might not return upon pretence of want either felt or feared.

Navigation was now brought nearer to perfection. The *Portuguese* claim the honour of many inventions by which the sailor is assisted, and which enable him to leave sight of land, and commit himself to the boundless ocean. *Diaz* had orders to proceed beyond the *River Zaire,* where *Diego Can* had stopped, to build monuments of his discoveries, and to leave upon the coasts negroe men and women well instructed, who might enquire after *Prester John,* and fill the natives with reverence for the *Portuguese.*

Diaz with much opposition from his crew, whose mutinies he repressed partly by softness and partly by steadiness, sailed on till he reached the utmost point of *Africa,* which from the bad weather that he met there, he called *Cabo Tormentoso,* or the *Cape of Storms.* He would have gone forward, but his crew forced him to return. In his way back he met the victualler, from which he had been parted nine months before; of the nine men which were in it at the separation, six had been killed by the negroes, and of the three remaining, one died for joy at the sight of his friends. *Diaz* returned to *Lisbon* in *December* 1487, and gave an account of his voyage to the King, who ordered the *Cape of Storms* to be called thenceforward *Cabo de buena Esperanza,* or *the Cape of Good Hope.*

Some time before the expedition of *Diaz,* the river *Zaire* and the kingdom of *Congo* had been discovered by *Diego Can,* who found a nation of negroes who spoke a language which those that were in his ships could not understand. He landed, and the natives whom he expected to fly like the other inhabitants of the coast, met them with confidence, and treated them with kindness; but *Diego* finding that they could not understand each other, seized some of their chiefs, and carried them to *Portugal,* leaving some of his own people in their room to learn the language of *Congo.*

The negroes were soon pacified, and the *Portuguese* left to their mercy were well treated, and as they by degrees grew able to make themselves understood, recommended themselves, their nation, and their religion. The King of *Portugal* sent *Diego* back in a very short time with the negroes whom he had forced away; and when they were set safe on shore, the King of *Congo* conceived so much esteem for *Diego,* that he sent one of those who had returned, back again in his ship to *Lisbon,* with two young men dispatched as ambassadors, to desire instructors to be sent for the conversion of his kingdom.

The ambassadors were honourably received, and baptized with great pomp, and a fleet was immediately fitted out for *Congo,* under the command of *Gonsalvo Sorza,* who dying in his passage was succeeded in authority by his nephew *Roderigo.*

When they came to land, the King's uncle who commanded the province, immediately requested to be solemnly initiated in the christian religion, which was granted to him and his young son, on *Easter* day 1491. The father was named *Manuel,* and the son *Antonio.* Soon afterward the King, Queen, and eldest Prince received at the font, the names of *John, Elenor* and *Alphonso;* and a war breaking out, the whole army was admitted to the rites of christianity, and then sent against the enemy. They returned victorious, but soon forgot their faith, and formed a conspiracy to restore paganism; a powerful opposition was raised by infidels and apostates, headed by one of the King's younger sons; and the missionaries had been destroyed had not *Alphonso* pleaded for them and for christianity.

The enemies of religion now became the enemies of *Alphonso,* whom they accused to his father of disloyalty. His mother, the Queen *Elenor,* gained time by one artifice after another, till the King was calmed; he then heard the cause again, declared his son innocent, and punished his accusers with death.

The King died soon after, and the throne was disputed by *Alphonso,* supported by the christians, and *Aquitimo* his brother followed by the infidels. A battle was fought, *Aquitimo* was taken and put to death, and christianity was for a time established in *Congo,* but the nation has relapsed into its former follies.

Such was the state of the *Portuguese* navigation, when in 1492, *Columbus* made the daring and prosperous voyage, which gave a new world to *European* curiosity and *European* cruelty. He had offered his proposal, and declared his expectations to King *John* of *Portugal,* who had slighted him as a fanciful and rash projector, that promised what he had no reasonable hopes to perform.

Columbus had solicited other Princes, and had been repulsed with the same indignity; at last *Isabella* of *Arragon,* furnished him with ships, and having found *America,* he entered the mouth of the *Tagus* in his return, and shewed the natives of the new country. When he was admitted to the King's presence, he acted and talked with so much haughtiness, and reflected on the neglect which he had undergone with so much acrimony, that the courtiers who saw their Prince insulted, offered to destroy him; but the King who knew that he deserved the reproaches that had been used, and who now sincerely regretted his incredulity, would suffer no violence to be offered him, but dismissed him with presents and with honours.

The *Portuguese* and *Spaniards* became now jealous of each others claim to countries, which neither had yet seen; and the Pope to whom they appealed, divided the new world between them by a line drawn from north to south, a hundred leagues westward from *Cape Verd* and the *Azores,* giving all that lies west from that line to the *Spaniards,* and all that lies east to the *Portuguese.* This was no very satisfactory division, for the east and west must meet at last, but that time was then at a great distance.

According to this grant, the *Portuguese* continued their discoveries eastward, and became masters of much of the coast both of *Africa* and the *Indies,* but they seized much more than they could occupy, and while they were under the dominion of *Spain,* lost the greater part of their *Indian* territories.

APPENDIX

DOUBTFUL AND REJECTED WORKS

See also William Payne's *Introduction to the Game of Draughts,*
Preface; and William Lauder's *Essay on Milton's Paradise Lost,*
additional paragraphs in the Preface.

JOHN ANGELL'S *STENOGRAPHY*

Published: October, 1758 (*Critical Review*).
References: Boswell, *Life*, ii:224, 504.
        Courtney, p. 85.
Dedication improperly included in Johnson's *Works*.
Copies: Boston Public Library; New York Public Library (3 copies); Library of Congress; Yale; British Museum; Glasgow University; R. B. Adam.

EVERY student of Johnson from the time of Alexander Chalmers has doubted whether this Dedication could be by Johnson, yet there has been an understandable hesitation about dropping it from the Johnsonian canon because of Boswell's statement. I believe that there is no longer any need to include this work, and I shall discuss it only sufficiently to make clear that it can hardly be by Johnson.

In the first place, Boswell's statement is merely that Angell came to Johnson, not that Johnson furnished a dedication.

JOHNSON: I remember one, Angel, who came to me to write for him a Preface or Dedication to a book upon short hand.[1]

Johnson did not say that he wrote it. In fact the implication from the passage that follows is that Johnson disapproved Angell's system. Contrary to his custom, Boswell did not mark either the Dedication or the Preface with an asterisk or dagger, and there is no mention of Angell in Boswell's Chronological List. Unless one is to assume that Boswell was here guilty of another error of omission, after he had complained of the difficulty which he experienced in his endeavor to ascertain the extent of Johnson's miscellaneous writings, it is evident that he did not believe that either the Dedication or the Preface was by Johnson. Later editions of the book were readily available, so that Boswell could easily have seen the book, had he not been satisfied by Johnson's relation of the incident that Angell's request had not been granted.

In the second place, the Dedication is stylistically not John-

1. Boswell, *Life*, ii:224.

sonian. (No one has ever seriously supposed that the historical Preface was by Johnson.) To make the point clear, I quote
the Dedication:

To the Most Noble Charles, Duke of Richmond, Lenox, Aubigny,
&c. &c.

May it please Your Grace.

The Improvement of Arts and Sciences has always been esteemed
laudable; and in Proportion to their Utility and Advantage to Mankind, they have generally gained the Patronage of Persons the most distinguished for Birth, Learning, and Reputation in the World.

To improve the Art of SHORT-HAND, is the Design of the ensuing
Pages. An Art not inferior to many Sciences, as adapted to various important Purposes; notwithstanding it has not yet arrived at the Perfection it is capable of; some Authors having rendered it very difficult by a
Multiplicity of Rules, and others perplexed and confounded it, by arbitrary, intricate, and impracticable Schemes. To rectify those Errors,
adapt it to all Capacities, and fit it for the most useful Purposes, has
been my sole View in the following Plates; which I have endeavoured to
illustrate by a suitable Introduction. To this I have prefixed a concise
and impartial History of the Origin and progressive Improvements of
this Art: And as I have submitted the Whole to the Inspection of accurate Judges, whose Approbation I am honoured with, I most humbly
crave Leave to publish it to the World under your Grace's Patronage;
not merely on account of your great Dignity and high Rank in Life;
though these receive a Lustre from your Grace's Humanity; but also
from a Knowledge of your Grace's Disposition to encourage every useful
Art, and favour all true Promoters of Science. That your Grace may
long live, the Friend of Learning, the Guardian of Liberty, and the Patron of Virtue; and then transmit your Name with the highest Honour
and Esteem to latest Posterity; is the ardent Wish of Your Grace's Ever-
respectful, Most dutiful, and Most humble Servant,

John Angell.

The salutation and the complimentary close are unlike Johnson's acknowledged dedications. The first sentence might be
by Johnson, though it reminds the reader somewhat of Fanny
Burney's attempts to write Johnsonese in her *Memoirs of Dr.
Burney*. The second sentence could well be by Johnson, although the use of 'ensuing' in the sense of 'following' is peculiar. The fourth sentence seems to me not unlike some of
Johnson's statements. For the confused grammar and awkward expression of the third and fifth sentences I know not

how to apologize. That Johnson's grammar is frequently faulty is admitted, but he seldom, perhaps never, stumbles, like this writer, over his own constructions.

The book is a small octavo in half-sheets; the Dedication is printed on a cancel-leaf; the title-page was engraved by Thomas Kitchin. Three states of the first edition have been distinguished.[2] In the list of subscribers, Johnson's is the only well-known name. Perhaps to escape Angell's importunity Johnson subscribed for a copy.

Proposals for the work were advertised in March 1757.

DR. ARNE, *THE MONTHLY MELODY*

Published: 1 April 1760.[1]
References: Boswell, *Life*, ii:2.
          Courtney, p. 98.
Johnson's Contribution: Dedication (?).
Copies: Library of Congress; Yale; British Museum.[2]

BOSWELL, when he was discussing the great number of Johnson's dedications, remarked: 'He once dedicated some Musick for the German Flute to Edward, Duke of York.'[3] That assertion seems fairly definite, yet no one has ever discovered certainly what book Boswell had in mind. Since Boswell failed to name it, he himself was perhaps unable to identify the book. Prince Edward was created Duke of York in 1760 and he died in 1767: these dates therefore limit one's search

2. A brief collation, with one error, is printed in the *Bulletin of the New York Public Library* xxxviii(Jan. 1934):45–6. For further discussion, see Alexander T. Wright, *The Two Angells of Stenography* (1919); also an article in the *Phonetic Journal* xlvi(1887):63–4. The editions are listed in J. Westby-Gibson's *Bibliography of Shorthand* (London 1887), pp. 8, 9.

1. The Dedication is dated March 30, 1760, and the first number (March) was announced in the *London Chronicle* April 1. The numbers were issued monthly. I believe that the last number was that for January, 1761 (No. xi, published 1 February 1761).

2. There was a copy in Sir John Stainer's collection, which was bought by Pickering & Chatto (Hodgson's, 27 May 1932). Imperfect copies are in the Boston Public Library and in the Library of the Royal College of Music.

3. Boswell, *Life*, ii:2. For a number of reasons I am induced to hope that Boswell intended to refer to Dr. Burney's *Six Duets for Two German Flutes*, but I have not yet been able to discover a copy of this work.

for probable books. In that period, however, hundreds of musical works were published, and many of them were intended for the German Flute or were suitable for the German Flute. Whether many were dedicated to the Duke of York it is impossible to determine. Courtney included the *Monthly Melody* in his *Bibliography of Johnson,* and no one has yet suggested any other book.

The *Monthly Melody* is not wholly satisfactory. Prince Edward was created Duke of York on April 1, 1760, and the later numbers of the book were advertised as 'dedicated to the Duke of York,' so that this part of Boswell's sentence is satisfied; but the book contains chiefly vocal music, so that Boswell apparently ought to have written 'He once dedicated some songs to Edward, Duke of York.' It is not impossible, however, to evade this difficulty, for some songs include the score for the German Flute, and the parts were advertised as suitable to the Violin, German Flute, and Guitar.

A further difficulty is the unsatisfactory quality of the Dedication itself. Like the Dedication to Gwynn's *London and Westminster Improved,* it is not noble and it is not even felicitous. It does have certain favorite Johnsonian words, but it lacks the perfection of diction and smoothness of rhythm that distinguish most of Johnson's dedications. If it is by Johnson, it is one of his least successful attempts. Johnson wrote his best Prefaces and Dedications only when he was stirred by emotion or roused by friendship to his best efforts, but it is difficult to believe that he ever allowed his work for booksellers, perfunctory as it was on occasion, to lack felicity of expression; Dr. Chapman insists, indeed, that Johnson always pulled himself together when he was addressing royalty and that under no circumstances would he have laid a book at the patron's feet.[4] Professor Tinker also finds the style unlike that of Johnson.

Until a more satisfactory work is discovered, this must be

4. Before rejecting this work, the reader may want to compare it with the Dedications to Gwynn's *London and Westminster Improved* (certainly by Johnson) and to Hoole's *Cyrus* (probably by Johnson).

accepted with some misgiving as a possible Johnsonian Dedication. I include the text, since the book is not easily available, and invite opinions concerning its author.

Bibliographical Description

The / Monthly melody: / or / polite amusement / for / gentlemen and ladies. / Being a collection of / vocal and instrumental music / composed by Dr. Arne. / [*allegorical design*] / London. / Printed for G. Kearsly at the Golden Lion, in Ludgate Street. / M.DCC.LX.

Folio; 32.2 × 20.5 cm. Price: 1/– each number.

Signatures: engraved title-page; [A],b,B,D–H,H,K,M,N²; 37 leaves; 35 leaves.

Pagination: title-page with verso blank; [i]–ii Dedication; [iii]–vi, 7–48 The Compleat Musician (a dissertation on music, in twelve chapters. Pp. [iii]–vi contain the Introduction; pp. 7–8 contain the plan of the work); 37 leaves of engraved music; 35 leaves of engraved music.

The leaves of music are numbered in two series, 1–37 and 1–35. In the second series, there is no leaf 19, and two different songs are numbered 23. In the copy in the Library of Congress, six leaves have been pasted to stubs.

In the first series nearly every song bears the imprint: 'Printed (by Assignment from Dr. Arne) for G. Kearsly.' The second series contains no songs with this imprint.

The title-page was engraved by J. Ellis, who was apparently an engraver of Copy-Books. (See A. Heal, *English Writing Masters*, p. 205.) I think that he was not Johnson's friend Jack Ellis, but I do not know. No name is attached to the design on the title-page, and Ellis may have drawn it himself.

The publishers seem to have learned that suspense is the secret of success in serial publication, for 'Ah se un Cor' is left incomplete at the bottom of p. 12, with the note: 'To be continued in our next.'

The only composers named with the songs are Arne, Cocchi, Geminiani, and Giardini.

This book appears to have been Kearsly's only venture into the field of musical publication. (See F. Kidson, *British Music Pub-*

lishers, p. 69.) But Dr. Arne also contributed some songs to Kearsly's *Royal Female Magazine.*

DEDICATION

TO HIS ROYAL HIGHNESS PRINCE EDWARD.

SIR,

Your well known readiness to countenance and protect all works of genius, and to encourage, as far as may be, every attempt to facilitate the progress of the polite arts, has emboldened the proprietors, of the present publication, most humbly to lay it at Your Royal Highness's feet.

It would be presumption in them to enter into encomiums on the merit of a performance, of which Your Royal Highness, through Your own great skill in the science of Music, are no doubt a much better judge than they can possibly be: Yet, permit them to say, that, from the extraordinary abilities which Doctor ARNE has manifested in his hitherto so much admired compositions, they would fain hope You will find something in the following miscellanies, not often to be met with in collections of such a nature, nor wholly unworthy of Your attention.

One circumstance they are sure of, that nothing has been wanting on their parts to render them deserving of so great an honour! and if, from that condescension, and goodness, which has rendered Your Royal Highness so justly amiable in the eyes of all his Majesty's subjects, You should think proper to receive this dedication as a well-meant testimony of respect, it will be answering all the purposes of,

SIR, Your Royal Highness's Most obedient, Most devoted, And Most humble Servants,

THE PROPRIETORS.

March 30,
1760.

EDWARD BRODHURST, *SERMONS*

Joseph Hill wrote in 1907 that Johnson's hand 'apparently may be traced in the Preface' to Brodhurst's *Sermons,* and this remark was reprinted by Courtney without comment.[1]

1. Joseph Hill, *Bookmakers of Old Birmingham* (1907), pp. 43, 45. Courtney, p. 2. Mr. A. L. Reade, in his *Johnsonian Gleanings* (v:95), believes that Joseph Hill's suggestion is correct.

The book is a rare octavo, printed by Warren at Birmingham in 1733. One copy was owned by Hill, Cambridge University has a copy (possibly the same), and a third copy is now in the Birmingham Collection of the Birmingham Public Library. The Preface is very long and very florid, filled with Biblical allusions and pious sentiments. It is true that some of the sentences are not unlike Johnson's English, but there seems to be nothing that is unmistakably Johnson's and much that is certainly not Johnson's: the bare fact that Johnson at the time was working for Warren and writing for the *Birmingham Journal* is not sufficient evidence.

This work, I believe, should not be included in the Johnsonian canon.

JAMES HAMPTON'S *POLYBIUS*

Published: 13 March 1756 (*London Evening-Post*).
Copies: Not rare.

DR. PARR considered the Preface to Hampton's *General History of Polybius* to be certainly and unmistakably by Johnson.[1] I am aware of no external evidence that could confirm such a conjecture. The date is suitable enough, to be sure, for it is just after the completion of the *Dictionary,* when Johnson was free for such work as the Preface to Rolt's *Dictionary.* Johnson did review the book,[2] so that he was at least aware of its existence. Furthermore, in at least two other cases[3] he reviewed books to which he had contributed. It seems, therefore, that from the external evidence the Preface may be attributed to him without any particular difficulty, but there is clearly little to support such an attribution.

1. E. H. Barker, *Parriana* (1828), i:488–94.
2. In the *Literary Magazine,* attributed on internal evidence. See Boswell, *Life,* i:309. The Catalogue of Johnson's library (1785) lists Hampton's *Polybius,* 2 vols. quarto, 1772. (The third edition of Part One and the first edition of Part Two appeared in 1772.) If the Catalogue is correct, it seems probable that Johnson, at the time of his death, did not own the first edition: this would tend to make one hesitate in ascribing the Preface to him.
3. Sully's *Memoirs;* Browne's *Christian Morals.*

The decision on grounds of style is a troublesome one. Dr. Parr, who recognized correctly the style of the Dedication for Pearce's *Commentary (ante,* p. 156n.), asserted that this Preface was unquestionably by Johnson because it was so good and so different from the rest of the book. But Dr. Parr seems to have reached this decision many years after the Preface appeared; besides, since the text of the book is a translation, it is hardly proper to compare that prose with the Preface. In the second place, it is difficult to believe that such a long (eighteen pages in quarto) and well-known Preface could have remained unrecognized by the contemporaries of Johnson.

The Preface itself is good, with many felicitous phrases and with much of the balance that is regularly found in Johnsonian prose. The *Critical Review* for May, 1756, quoted extracts from it with approval. Nevertheless, I cannot persuade myself that it is by Johnson; it seems to me to possess certain characteristics of the form, but to lack the clear and exact thinking so characteristic of Johnson. Johnson's prose was esteemed by his contemporaries for its 'nervous' style, by which they meant the energy and forcefulness of his writing: this Preface seems distinctly below Johnson's work in that respect.

MONARCHY ASSERTED

Published: May 1742 (*Gentleman's Magazine*).
Johnson's Contribution: Probably editor of the reprint.
Copies: (folio edition) Yale; National Library of Scotland.

THE Debate on the Proposal of Parliament to Cromwell that he should assume the title of King was originally published in 1660, edited probably by Nathaniel Fiennes, and was reprinted in 1679 and in the Somers Tracts in the eighteenth century. In 1741 an abridged and edited form was printed in the *Gentleman's Magazine;* Boswell assigned this on internal evidence to Johnson, and Dr. Hill emphatically accepted the work as Johnson's.[1]

The note at the end of the article in the *Gentleman's Magazine* reads: 'The whole Debate, as printed in 1660, whence this foregoing is extracted, will soon be publish'd with some Remarks and necessary Illustrations.' Now if the abridgment in 1741 is by Johnson, and I believe that it is, there is presumptive evidence that he also edited the reprint of the original, despite a delay of more than a year in its publication. The editing seems to have been somewhat perfunctory, though I have never collated the editions: a few notes are probably by Johnson. The Advertisement is probably by Johnson, although it lacks distinction.

Bibliographical Description

Monarchy / asserted to be the / best, most antient, and legall / form of government. / In a / conference held at Whitehall, / with / Oliver, Lord Protector, / and a / Committee of Parliament. / . . . London: Printed 1660. / Re-printed for F. Cave, at St John's Gate, 1742.

Folio; approximately 40 × 24 cm. Price: 2/–.
    Of the edition in octavo I have seen no copy: one was offered for three shillings in the *Catalogue* of Thomas Rodd, Part vii (1822), p. 454.

Signatures: [A],B–K².

Pagination: [i] title-page; [ii] blank; [iii] Advertisement; [iv] To the Reader; [1]–35 Monarchy Asserted, &c.; [36] blank.

On the title-page of the copy in the Library at Yale there is added, in a later hand, 'The Editor, Doctor Samuel Johnson.'

---

1. *Gentleman's Magazine* xi(February, March, 1741):93–100, 148–154. Boswell, *Life*, i:150 and note. Professor D. Nichol Smith, in his bibliography in the old *Cambridge History of English Literature* (1913), x:519, seems to doubt the authenticity of this item. It is worth remarking that Johnson once projected a life of Cromwell: Bowles, Memoranda—see Boswell, *Life*, iv:235. See also Croker's edition of Boswell's *Life* (1831), i:121n.

ADVERTISEMENT.

The following important Conference was first published in 1660, and never till now reprinted entire; so that a Copy of it was scarcely to be procured.

A State of the Argument reduced into one Series of Debate, was indeed published in the *Gentleman's Magazine* for the Months of *February* and *March 1741* (*See* VOL. XI, p. 93, 148.) and met with a very favourable Reception. But, as no doubt the particular Speeches at Length will be still acceptable, the whole is reprinted, as promised, from the aforemention'd Edition, except the literal Errors, which in several Places very much obscured the Sense. Some Alterations have also been made with Regard to the Punctuation and Distinction of Paragraphs, which, tho' minute in themselves, serve to remove many Intricacies in the first Edition. There are likewise added some probable Conjectures by Way of Note, for illustrating other Obscurities which may be ascribed to the Causes mentioned in the *Gentleman's Magazine*.

This Conference is also printed in Octavo, for the Conveniency of Gentlemen who desire to bind it up with other Political Tracts of that Size.

CHRONOLOGICAL LIST

	Date of Publication	Page
Brodhurst, *Sermons*	1733	246
James, *Medicinal Dictionary*	4 February 1742	68
Monarchy Asserted	May 1742	248
Harleian Catalogue	12 March 1743	43
Harleian Miscellany	24 March 1744	50
The Publisher	25 December 1744	193
The Preceptor (Dodsley)	7 April 1748	171
Lauder, *Essay on Milton*	14 December 1749	77
Mrs. Lennox, *Female Quixote*	13 March 1752	94
Baretti, *Proposals*	1753-4?	17
Mrs. Lennox, *Shakespear Illustrated*	18 May 1753	104
Baretti, *Introduction to the Italian Language*	19 July 1755	12
Mrs. Lennox, Sully's *Memoirs*	8 November 1755	110
Payne, *Game of Draughts*	January 1756	148
Rolt, *Dictionary of Trade and Commerce*	12 February 1756	198
Hampton, *Polybius*	13 March 1756	247
Literary Magazine	19 May 1756	125
London Chronicle	1 January 1757	131
Baretti, *Italian Library*	14 February 1757	15
Lindsay, *Evangelical History*	16 April 1757	116
Mrs. Lennox, *Philander*	November 1757	102
John Payne, *Tables of Interest*	28 February 1758	142
Universal Chronicle	8 April 1758	205
Angell, *Stenography*	October 1758	241
The World Displayed	1 December 1759	216
Mrs. Lennox, Brumoy's *Greek Theatre*	21 February 1760	91
Dr. Arne, *Monthly Melody*	1 April 1760	243
Baretti, *Dictionary*	24 April 1760	6
Proceedings of the Committee	August 1760	189
Mrs. Lennox, *Henrietta*	19 March 1761	98
Gwynn, *Thoughts on the Coronation*	8 August 1761	41
Bennet, *English Works of Ascham*	7 January 1762	19
Society of Artists, *Catalogue*	17 May 1762	200
Lenglet du Fresnoy, *Chronological Tables*	19 November 1762	84
Kennedy, *Astronomical Chronology*	29 March 1763	74
Hoole, Tasso's *Jerusalem Delivered*	1 June 1763	62
Review of *Sugar-Cane*	5 July 1764	168
Percy, *Reliques*	12 February 1765	158
Mrs. Williams, *Miscellanies*	1 April 1766	213
Fordyce, *Sermons to Young Women*	5 June 1766	33
Adams, *Globes*	10 June 1766	1
Gwynn, *London and Westminster Improved*	14 June 1766	38
Payne, *Geometry*	April 1767	151
Hoole, Metastasio's *Works*	20 June 1767	66
Hoole, *Cyrus*	20 December 1768	60

	Date of Publication	Page
Payne, *Trigonometry*	February 1772	152
Macbean, *Dictionary of Ancient Geography*	19 June 1773	132
Baretti, *Easy Phraseology*	3 October 1775	8
Burney, *History of Music*	31 January 1776	26
Pearce, *Four Evangelists*	18 January 1777	154
Reynolds, *Seven Discourses*	19 May 1778	195
Maurice, *Poems and Miscellaneous Pieces*	May 1780	136
Baretti, *Guide through the Royal Academy*	May 1781	11
Burney, *Commemoration of Handel*	1 February 1785	30

INDEX

ADAM, R. B., 92, 132, 148.
Adams, George, *Treatise on the Globes*, 1–4, 39, 112.
Adams, George, the Younger, 3; *Astronomical and Geographical Essays*, 3.
Allen, Edmund, xvii, 3.
Altieri, *Dictionary*, 6.
Anderson, Robert, 116, 122.
Angell, John, *Stenography*, xiii, 241–243.
Arne, T. A., *Monthly Melody*, xiii, xviii, 243–246.
Ascham, Roger, *The English Works*, see Bennet, James, *Ascham*.
Astle, Thomas, 159.
Author's corrections in proof, xiv.

BARETTI, Joseph, xviii, 4–18, 90–91, 104, 200, 207 n.; *Dictionary of the English and Italian Languages*, xvi, 6–8; *Dictionary of Spanish and English*, 5; *Easy Phraseology*, 8–11; *Guide through the Royal Academy*, xiii, 11–12; *Introduction to the Italian Language*, 12–15; *The Italian Library*, xii, 15–16; *Proposals*, xiii, 17–18.
Beauclerk, Topham, 102.
Beauties of Johnson, ed. by William Cooke, xvi n.
Bennet, James, xx; *Ascham*, xv n., xvi, xvii, xviii, xx, 19–23, 199.
Bibliothèque Britannique, ou Histoire des ouvrages des savans de la Grande Bretagne, 195.
Biographia Britannica, 20–21.
Birch, Thomas, 20, 159.
Boswell, James, xv, xviii, xx, xxii, 1, 6, 19, 33, 35 n., 38–39, 41, 45, 52, 63, 69, 74–75, 84–85, 90, 91–92, 94, 107, 110–112, 116, 126, 128, 138, 146, 147, 154, 155, 161–162, 168–169, 189–190, 198, 201 n., 214, 241, 248, 249; proof-sheets, xiv–xv.
Boswell, James, the Younger, 214.
Brodhurst, Edward, *Sermons*, 246–247.

Browne, Thomas, *Christian Morals*, xvi, 22 n., 199.
Brumoy, Pierre, *The Greek Theatre*, see Lennox, Mrs. Charlotte (Ramsay), Brumoy's *Greek Theatre*.
Burney, Dr. Charles, xvi, xviii, xxii n., 4, 23–33, 126; *Commemoration of Handel*, xix, 30–33, 170 n.; *History of Music*, xiii, 26–30; *Six Duets for Two German Flutes*, 243 n.
Burney, Frances, xx, 8, 23, 95, 133, 242.

CAMPBELL, Dr. Thomas, *Diary*, 9–10.
Cancel title-page, xvi.
Cancels, importance of, xv, xvi.
Carlyle, Thomas, on patronage, xix.
Carter, Elizabeth, 35, 189 n., 215.
Catchword, xiv n.
Cave, Edward, xiii, xvii, xviii.
Chalmers, Alexander, xvii n., 147 n., 241.
Chambers, Robert, 126.
Chapman, R. W., xv, 11, 15–16, 22 n., 74, 79, 107, 134, 156, 193, 201 n., 244.
Charlemont, Viscount, 102.
Churchill, I. L., 159 n., 164, 165; *The Early Literary Career of Thomas Percy*, 158 n.
Collins, William, 184 n.
Committee for Cloathing French Prisoners, Proceedings of, see *Proceedings*.
Corney, Bolton, 148 n.
Court, John, *New Testament of our Lord and Saviour Jesus Christ carefully and diligently compared*, 117.
Courtney, W. P., 79, 92, 142–143, 206, 244, 246.
Crokatt, James, 72, 193–194.
Croker, J. W., 45 n., 113, 127.
Cromwell, Richard, 248.
Crossley, James, 12–13.
Curious Collection of Travels, see *World Displayed*.
Curious Collection of Voyages se-

lected from the writers of all nations, see *World Displayed.*

DALRYMPLE, Sir David, Lord Hailes, 159, 161, 166–167; *Annals of Scotland,* xii.
Davies, Thomas, 19; *Memoirs of Garrick,* xii; *Miscellaneous and Fugitive Pieces,* xviii *n.,* 21 *n.,* 53, 93, 132, 175, 191, 199, 201 *n.,* 204, 219.
Dennis, Leah, 158 *n.*
Derby, Rev. John, 155.
Derrick, Samuel, 85.
Direction line, xiv *n.*
Dodd, Dr. William, xvii.
Dodsley, James, xviii.
Dodsley, Robert, xvii, xviii, xxi, xxiii, 160, 171–172; · ed. *Collection of Poems,* xxiii.
Douglas, John, *Milton Vindicated from the Charge of Plagiarism,* 79.

EDINBURGH University, Library, 2.
Ellis, S. M., 73.
Elphinston, James, 34.
Euripides, *Medea,* 23, 25.
Evangelical History, see Lindsay, Rev. John, *Evangelical History.*

FADEN, William, 126, 206.
Faria y Sousa, Manuel de, *The Portugues Asia,* 217–218.
Farmer, Richard, 159.
Fielding, Henry, 95.
Fiennes, Nathaniel, 248.
Flloyd, Thomas, xviii, 84, 85.
Floyd, Thomas, *see* Flloyd, Thomas.
Flute, Music for the German, 243.
Fordyce, David, *Dialogues on Education,* 172 *n.*
Fordyce, Rev. James, xviii; *Sermons to Young Women,* xiii *n.,* 33–38.

GALLUP, D. C., 207 *n.*
Garrick, David, 38.
Gentleman's Magazine, xiii, xv, xvii *n.,* 248–250.
Goldsmith, Oliver, 217; *Collection of Poems for Young Ladies,* 35.
Goodwin, Gordon, 106, 127 *n.*
Grainger, James, *Sugar-Cane,* 131, 168–171.

Grant, Sir Archibald, 175.
Grant, Edward, *Oratio de vita et obitu Rogeri Aschami,* 20.
Graves, Algernon, 202; *The Society of Artists,* 204.
Greg, W. W., vii *n.,* 2, 165 *n.*
Grignion, Charles, 165.
Grotius, Hugo, *Adamus Exsul, tragoedia,* 78; *see also* William Lauder.
Grundy, C. R., 202.
Gwynn, John, xviii; *London and Westminster Improved,* 2, 38–40, 244; *Thoughts on the Coronation,* 41–42.

HAMPTON, James, *Polybius,* 18 *n.,* 247–248.
Harleian Catalogue, 43–50.
Harleian Library, xvii *n.*.
Harleian Miscellany, 50–59, 137 *n.,* 161 *n.*
Hawkesworth, John, 61.
Hawkins, Sir John, xx, xxi *n.,* 1, 44, 52, 206–207.
Hawkins, L. M., 158 *n.*
Hill, G. B. N., 19, 25 *n.,* 39, 146, 201 *n.,* 206, 246.
Hill, Joseph, 246.
Hilles, F. W., *Literary Career of Reynolds,* 197, 202.
Historical Account of the most celebrated voyages, see *The World Displayed.*
History of the Works of the Learned . . . in Great Britain and foreign parts, 195.
Hogarth, William, 204.
Hollis, Thomas, 53; *Memoirs of,* 190.
Hoole, John, xviii, xxii, 60–68, 213–214, 215; *Cyrus,* xiii, 60–62, 244 *n.;* tr. of *Jerusalem Delivered,* xxii *n.,* 62–66, 67, 169; tr. of *The Works of Metastasio,* xiv, 66–68.
Hornberger, T., 175.
Hume, David, 175.
Hussey, Rev. John, xvii *n.,* 69.

IDLER, *see* Johnson, Samuel, *The Idler.*

JAMES, G. P. R., 73.

James, Dr. Robert, xviii, 206 n.; *A Dissertation on Fevers and Inflammatory Distempers*, 70–71; *Medicinal Dictionary*, xvi, 68–72, 147 n., 194; *Vindication of the Fever Powder*, 71.

Johnson, John, *Typographia*, 221 n.

Johnson, Samuel, *Account of the Harleian Library (Proposals for the Harleian Catalogue)*, xv, 43; Additions to the Canon, xiii; *Beauties of Johnson*, xvi n.; Catalogue of his Library, 7, 10, 21, 26, 39, 60, 64, 67, 76, 86 n., 92, 113, 134, 138, 148, 156, 247 n.; *Dictionary*, xiii, xviii, xix, xxiii, 93, 154; *The Fountains*, 215; *The Hermit of Teneriffe*, 172, 174; translation of the *History of the Council of Trent*, 154; *The Idler*, 205, 207, 208, 209; *Letter to Chesterfield*, xix; *Life of Dryden*, xi; *Life of Milton*, 78; *Life of Sydenham*, 50 n.; *Lives of the Poets*, xv, xviii; *Miscellaneous Observations on the Tragedy of Macbeth*, 106; *Plan of a Dictionary*, xx; ed. of *Plays of Shakespeare*, xiii, xx n., *Proposals for the Harleian Catalogue*, see Johnson, Samuel, *Account of the Harleian Library*; Proposals for Miss Williams's *Poems*, 213; *Proposals for Shakespeare, 1756*, 131; Proposals for the *World Displayed*, 217; *Rambler*, xiii, xxi, xxiii, 142, 173 n., 206, 208; *Rasselas*, 5; *Vanity of Human Wishes*, xxiii, 173 n.; translation of *Voyage to Abyssinia*, xiii; *Works* (vol. xiv), xviii n., 6, 39 n., 41, 80, 92, 94, 107, 127, 147, 150, 201 n., 204, 214; *Works* (vol. xv), 76, 122; *Works, 1806*, 119, 120, 122, 142, 147 n.; *Works, 1825*, 44; *Works*, need for a new edition of, 13.

Jones, Griffith, 127 n., 132 n.

KEARSLEY (Kearsly), George, xviii, 245; *Beauties of Johnson*, xvi n.; publisher of Cooke's *Life of Johnson*, 198.

Kennedy, Rev. John, *Astronomical Chronology*, xvi, xvii, xviii, xx, 74–77, 147 n., 199 n.; *A New Method of . . . Scripture Chronology upon Mosaic Astronomical Principles*, 74.

Kitchin, Thomas, 243.

LA CONDAMINE, C. M. de, 170.

Lafitau, J. F., *Histoire des découvertes et conquestes des Portugais*, 217–218.

Lauder, William, *Essay on Milton*, xiii, 77–84, 154; *Letter to the Reverend Mr. Douglas*, 79.

Lenglet du Fresnoy, Nicholas, *Chronological Tables*, xiii, xv n., xviii, 84–89, 137.

Lennox, Mrs. Charlotte (Ramsay), xiii n., xviii, xx, 18, 89–116; Brumoy's *Greek Theatre*, 91–94, 100, 112; *The Female Quixote*, 94–98; *Henrietta*, 91, 98–102; *Philander*, 102–104; *Shakespear Illustrated*, 104–110; Sully's *Memoirs*, xxii n., 110–116, 147 n.

Leslie, Charles, *Short and Easy Method with the Deists*, 118.

Levett, Robert, 111.

Lindsay, Rev. John, *Evangelical History*, xv, xviii, xxii n., 116–125, 137 n.

Literary Magazine, 125–131, 208, 209.

Lloyd's Evening Post, 85, 207.

Lofft, Capel, *Eudosia*, 3.

London Catalogue, 118.

London Chronicle, xvii, 131–132, 206, 207.

Lounsbury, T. R., 96, 105 n.

Lowndes, William, 106.

Luckombe, Philip, xv; *History of Printing*, xiv n.

Lye, Edward, 159.

MACBEAN, Alexander, *Geography*, xviii, 112, 132–136.

McKerrow, R. B., xiv n., 165 n., 220.

Maittaire, Michael, 43.

Malone, Edmond, 106, 201 n., 214.

Manuscript, revision of, xiv.

Mason, Lowell, 32.

Maurice, Thomas, *Poems*, xviii, 136–142; Verses to Dr. Johnson, 138.

Mavor, William, 219.

Mercer, Frank, 29.

Metastasio, P. A. D. B., *Ciro Riconosciuto*, 61; *Works, see* Hoole, John, *The Works of Metastasio*.
Michelmore, G., and Co., 66.
Millar, Andrew, xvii, xviii, 160.
Milton, John, *Comus*, 78.
Mitford, John, 95.
Monarchy Asserted, xiii, 248–250.
Monthly Melody, see Arne, T. A.
Morison, Stanley, *The English Newspaper*, 132.
Mudge, Zachariah, 131.
Murphy, Arthur, 126.

NEWBERY, Francis, xviii, 20.
Newbery, John, xvii, xviii, 20, 69, 117, 206–207, 216; *Circle of the Sciences*, 171; *The World Displayed, see World Displayed*.
Newcastle, Duchess of, 98–99.
Newcastle, Duke of, 110.
Nichols, J. B., 170 *n*.
Northcote, James, 201 *n*.
Northumberland, Countess of, 160, 166.

OLDYS, William, 44.
Osborne, Thomas, xvii, 43, 72.
Ossian, 9.
Oxford University Press, 194, 195.

PALMER, Mary, 219.
Parr, Dr. Samuel, 136, 156 *n*., 247–248.
Patronage, xix.
Payne, John, xvii, xviii, 146, 190, 206; *New Tables of Interest*, 142–146, 206, 208 *n*.
Payne, Thomas, xviii, 146–147.
Payne, William, xviii, 146–154; *Elements of Trigonometry*, xiii, 18, 152–154; *An Introduction to Geometry*, 147 *n*., 148, 151–152; *Introduction to the Game of Draughts*, xiii, 147, 148–151; reprint of *Introduction to the Game of Draughts*, xvi, 29, 149.
Payne's Universal Chronicle, see The Universal Chronicle.
Pearce, Zachary, *A Commentary, with notes, on the Four Evangelists*, xxii, 154–157, 248.

Percy, Rev. Thomas, xviii, 111, 138, 169, 214; *Reliques*, xii, xv, xx, 59 *n*., 158–168, 196.
Piozzi, Mrs. Hester L., xx, xxi, 9, 69, 74, 133, 162 *n*., 213, 214; *Thraliana*, 147 *n*., 162 *n*.
Polybius, *General History, see* James Hampton.
Powell, L. F., 19, 69, 73, 148, 158 *n*., 164, 165, 165 *n*., 201 *n*.
Preceptor, The, xvii, xxii, xxiii, 93, 171–189.
Princeton University, Library, 86.
Printer, responsibility of, xiv, xv *n*.
Prior, Sir James, 127 *n*.
Proceedings of the Committee for Cloathing French Prisoners, 53, 189–193.
Proof, author's corrections of, xiv.
Publisher, The, 193–195.

RALEIGH, Walter, 52.
Reade, A. L., 246 *n*.
Reed, Isaac, 201 *n*.
Review of Grainger's *Sugar-Cane*, 168–171.
Revision of manuscript and proof, xiv.
Reynolds, Frances, 214.
Reynolds, Sir Joshua, xviii, 24, 161, 162, 201; *Seven Discourses*, xv, xx, 195–197.
Richardson, Samuel, *Verses to*, 214.
Rolt, Richard, *Dictionary of Trade and Commerce*, xvi, xvii, 74–75, 198–200, 247.
Rosenbach, A. S. W., 63, 169.
Royal Academy, xx, 11 *n*., 202.
Rymer, Thomas, 105 *n*.

SANDBY, W., *History of the Royal Academy*, 204.
'Saxon k,' xv, 50, 176 *n*.
Seitz, R. W., 127 *n*.
Shakespear Illustrated, see Mrs. Charlotte (Ramsay) Lennox.
Shaw, William, xii; *Memoirs of Johnson*, 33–34.
Shenstone, William, xxiii, 158 *n*., 159.
Small, Miriam, xiii *n*., 91, 102.
Smart, Christopher, 217.
Smith, D. Nichol, 131 *n*., 147 *n*., 201 *n*., 249 *n*.

Smith, W. H., 165 n.
Society of Artists, *Catalogue*, 165 n., 196, 200–205.
Society of Booksellers for Promoting Learning, 193.
Squire, Sir John, 162 n.
Sterne, Laurence, 191.
Stevens, R., 206.
Strahan, William, xvii, xviii, 90.
Sully, Maximilian de Bethune, Duke of, *Memoirs of, see* Lennox, Mrs. Charlotte (Ramsay), Sully's *Memoirs*.

Talbot, Catherine, 35, 189 n.
Tasso, Torquato, *Jerusalem Delivered, see* Hoole, John, tr. of *Jerusalem Delivered*.
Thrale, Mrs. Hester L., *see* Piozzi, Mrs. Hester L.
Thrale, Hester ('Queeney'), 9.
Tinker, C. B., vi, 50, 244.
Tousey, G. P., *Flights to Helicon*, 35.
Tregaskis, James, & son, 138.
Turberville, A. S., *Johnson's England*, 132.
Tyers, Thomas, xx, xxi n., xxiii, 1, 3, 112–113, 134, 214.

Universal Chronicle, xiii, xvii, 142, 205–213.
Upton, James, 19–20.

Wale, Samuel, 165, 201 n., 202, 204.
Walpole, Horace, 11 n.
Warren, Thomas, 247.
Warton, Thomas, 159, 159 n.
Westminster Journal, 206.
Whatman, James, 18 n.
Wheatley, H. B., 44; *The Dedication of Books*, 148 n.
Whitley, W. T., 200–201.
Williams, Anna, xix, 61; *Miscellanies*, 112, 213–216.
Williams, I. A., 27.
Williams, S. T., 221.
Williams, Zachariah, xix; *Longitude*, 5.
Windham, William, 137; *Plan of Discipline composed for the militia of the County of Norfolk*, 21.
Witherspoon, John, 86.
World Displayed, xvii, xxii n., 121, 172, 216–237.

York, Edward, Duke of, 243.
Young, Karl, 105 n., 106.